COOK
BY THE BOOK

*Every machine needs its special kind of fuel as designed by the manufacturer. Our body machines are no exception. In order to know what are the best foods for our bodies, we must study the owner's manual prepared by the Master Designer. And that is what **Cooking By The Book** is all about.*

by Marcella Lynch

CREDITS

First Published in 1994
Second Printing 1997

Printed in the United States of America
by Consolidated Printers, Inc., Berkeley, CA

Book Design and Typesetting:
Jane Davis, Natalie Wood

Cover Design:
Nancy Singer Graphic Art Service
Mountain View, CA

Cover Photography:
Tony Coluzzi
Mountain View, CA

ISBN No. 0-9639118-0-5
Library of Congress Catalog Card No.: 93-91760

Cover Scripture: Genesis 1:29

COOKING BY THE BOOK

OUR GOAL is to provide recipes that . . .

- Use plant foods in as natural, unrefined a form as possible

- Furnish a good quality and quantity of protein in vegetarian dishes that are tasty, attractive, and healthful

- Use foods low in cholesterol and saturated fat

- Are free of irritating spices, vinegar, raw eggs, soda, baking powder

- Feature low-sugar, low-calorie desserts

- Use readily available ingredients

- Are simple, economical, easy to prepare

Companion cooking videos are also available.

Table of Contents

Foreward 6
Introduction 12
Glossary of Unusual Ingredients 14
Chapter   1   Organizing the Natural Food Kitchen 20

            2   Better Breakfasts I: Getting Acquainted
                 with Whole Grains, Cereals 30

            3   Better Breakfasts II: Pancakes,
                 Waffles, French Toast, and More 45

            4   Pack a Lively Lunch 55

            5   Bread with that Something Extra 64

            6   Meatless Dinner Meals I:
                 Bean Cuisine and Tofu 104

            7   Meatless Dinner Meals II: Grain and
                 Nut Dishes, Pastas, and Gluten 129

            8   Meatless Dinner Meals III:
                 Rice and Potatoes 156

            9   Vegetables All Around 164

          10   Supper Time 178

          11   Favorite Salads and Salad Dressings 186

          12   The Blessing of Fresh Fruit 201

          13   Sugar-Less Desserts 211

          14   Beverages 239

          15   Sprouting 248

          16   Gravies and Sauces 255

          17   Miscellaneous 259

          18   Menu Planning 265

          19   Weight Control 283

          20   Healthful Eating Principles 290

Index 304

Foreward

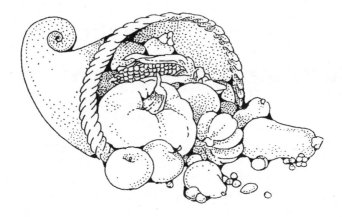

Cooking by the Book

by
Marcella Lynch

Cooking By the Book is a cooking course and cookbook featuring God's eating plan as unfolded through Scripture, and through an understanding of God's other book, the book of nature, which, when studied, includes the laws that govern our bodies: physiology, digestion, etc.

Interestingly enough, the Bible gives a review of many ancient customs and facts, and it tells us a lot about food and food preparation. This is God's book and it has special instruction in the area of nutrition for each one of us. For instance, this book tells us what to eat and *how* to eat it, which is just as important as *what* to eat. It also tells us some-  thing about the attitude we should have when we eat, for it certainly makes a differ- ence doesn't it? Also, this book gives a number of demonstrations and cites a num- ber of interesting examples of the benefits of a simple diet. It also has a lot in it about different ways to prepare food. In these days, when we're facing world famine, this book has a lot of help in conserving food and talks a lot about preserving food. And

7

above all, when our number one disease across the country is coronary artery disease, this book has an answer for that and tells us how to reduce the risk.

Nutritious food is the special fuel for our body machines. Each type of engine runs on its own special fuel. Some of us try to feed our engine unfit fuel—too greasy, too sweet, too fluffy, and too rich—and our machines cough, sputter, break down and wear out too soon.

Having been raised since birth in a vegetarian family, I have grown up cooking and eating without meat, poultry, or fish and with the aroma of freshly baked whole grain breads coming from the oven. What great memories!

For three generations back in my family comes an interest in discovering the Scripture's plan for life and health. In the late 1800's my paternal grandparents became members of the Seventh-day Adventist church, which through the early years of its founding, became world recognized for its health message and sanitariums.

Seventh-day Adventists are listed among the healthiest and long-est-lived people in the United States, and this has not come merely by chance. Almost from its inception in the mid-1800's the Adventist church has placed special emphasis on diet and nutrition. Indeed, the faithful member of this church regards the maintenance of a healthy body, mind and spirit as a privilege and duty not only to God, but to him/herself and to fellow human beings. Consequently, the proclamation of the gospel of health has long gone hand-in-hand with the proclamation of the gospel of Jesus Christ in all their missionary endeavors both here and abroad. They believe first to give attention to the physical needs of men and women and then to provide spiritual aid. They believe that if you feel good physically you will be more mentally acute and will be more receptive to God's leading in your spiritual life.

This course and cookbook present the eating guidelines recommended by Seventh-day Adventists. The position is that God established the ideal diet when He instructed the first man and woman created to eat all kinds of grains, fruits, vegetables, nuts and seeds (Genesis 1:29). There was no death there, no killing and therefore no meat. Through the pages of Scripture you can learn how to eat to prevent disease, prolong life and feel vibrant.

Over a century before the words "cholesterol" and "polyunsaturated" found their way into the dictionary, Adventists were denouncing meat and especially animal fat. This can be attributed almost wholly to the efforts, counsel and guidance of an extraordinary woman named Ellen G. White, one of the leading figures in the formation of the Seventh-day Adventist Church, who shared God's special instructions regarding diet and foods.

When Ellen White in 1864 began to speak and write on proper nutrition and a way of living that took into account nature's laws, average life expectancy in the United States was 32 years; meals, served three, four, or five times a day, were highly spiced, heavy with meats, rich gravies, fried foods, and a vast array of pastries loaded with sugar and fat. Milk was often supplied by cows poorly cared for and sometimes tuberculous. Testing was unknown, and pasteurization was decades away. Except for salting and drying, the science of food preservation was still future.

It was in this climate that Ellen White, with a pen dipped in the wisdom and knowledge of the Designer of the human form and the Author of nature's laws, called for a dietary program that was simple, healthful, nutritious, and appetizing.

Those church members who follow this counsel (about 50% are vegetarians) have reaped many benefits. They are elated to see that science repeatedly confirms the superiority of the non-meat, whole foods diet.

In addition to avoiding meat and eating a nutritious diet, Seventh-day Adventists follow a holistic approach to health and avoid tobacco, drugs, and alcohol as well. They emphasize the importance of daily exercise, proper rest, sunlight, fresh air, water, and trust in Divine Power.

Various studies have long indicated that Adventists are not afflicted as often with the killer diseases of our society: coronary artery diseases; cancer; and diseases of the respiratory system. Such diseases are much lower than the national average in those Adventists who follow the health teachings of Ellen White.

According to scientific studies Seventh-day Adventists have the lowest rate of colo-rectal cancer in the U. S. and the overall cancer rate less than half that of the nation as a whole.

The same is true of heart disease, which Adventists suffer at a rate that is only one-half of the population in general.

To ensure that Adventists and others are supplied with proper nutrition, the church operates 47 health-food factories throughout the world that supply whole-grain breakfast cereals, fruit beverages, soy milk, seasonings, non-meat entrees, and other foods. The church maintains 166 hospitals and sanitariums as well as many clinics and dispensaries around the world. The church operates ten liberal arts colleges and two universities in the United States, including dental and medical schools at Loma Linda, California, and Montemorelos, Mexico. It operates a world-wide humanitarian disaster relief agency (ADRA).

In addition to encouraging people to accept Jesus Christ as their personal Saviour, Adventists are working to meet the challenges of the world today and tomorrow through not only promotion of healthy living habits, but youth activities, education, and communication via radio, television and publishing houses.

Seventh-day Adventists are Christians who share in the joy of:

- Serving God through a daily relationship with Jesus Christ

- Waiting for Christ's glorious return

- Helping people at home and around the world in Christ's name

- Leading an active, healthy Christian life!

The Seventh-day Adventist Church cares about your physical, mental and spiritual well-being.

For information on Adventist services and programs in your area, or availability of their books, periodicals and journals, please check your telephone book yellow pages for the Adventist church in your community. Check your local TV guide for television programs: Christian Lifestyle Magazine, It is Written, and Breath of Life. Voice of Prophecy is the church's official radio program, broadcasting worldwide in dozens of languages.

It does matter what you eat! The best diet doctor found is our all-wise and loving Creator, who provides in nature the very best nourishment for us all. It is my hope that this cookbook and cooking video will play a small part in helping you implement and experience the benefits of eating by God's plan.

Cooking By the Book presents God's ideal eating plan for the human body. Eating right is one of Nature's Eight Laws of Health discovered by studying Scripture and physiology of the human body. Our bodies were created to "move" and be active. By including adequate exercise in the fresh air and sunlight and including natural, whole foods in our diet, our inner cells will operate effectively year after year -- including our heart muscle, stomach muscles, lungs and liver.

The Eight Laws of Health are these:

1. Eat a healthy diet of nutritious food.
2. Exercise adequately. (30 minutes brisk walking or equivalent each day)
3. Rest properly. (7-8 hours daily sleep is ideal)
4. Expose the body to sunlight daily in small doses.
5. Drink at least 6-8 glasses of water a day.
6. Get plenty of fresh air daily.
7. Live a temperate, drug-free life.
8. Trust in a Divine Power. Spiritual health contributes to good physical health.

It has been stated that diet is the single most important environmental factor affecting our health, and I agree. *Cooking By the Book* introduces us to God's ideal diet. Chapters 1-13 follow the sequence of Marcella's Series I Video Cooking Lessons.

You may find it helpful to begin your new adventure in cooking God's way by studying Chapter 18 on menu planning. You will gain an overview of what each meal should include.

I'd like to say, also, that it is not necessary to serve only our recommended breakfast foods for breakfast, dinner foods for dinner, and so forth. If you prefer to begin your day with a main dinner meal of vegetables, rice and entree, do so. Our western culture promotes the typical hot or cold cereal breakfast but other food patterns are certainly adequate as long as daily servings of the five basic food groups are eaten in adequate amounts each day. (See pp. 269-271.)

The healthly eating principles behind the menu planning guidelines can be found in Ch. 20, pp. 291-292.

Eating hearty meals earlier in the day and light at night makes sense when we study the physiology of digestion. We need to start the day with a good fueling up for the day's journey. As we come to the end of the day, our journey is over and additional fuel will be an excess. In fact, our bodies rest more peacefully on an empty stomach instead of churning away to digest food while we are trying to sleep.

The Daily Menu Planner, p. 272, shows a hearty breakfast, followed by the main dinner meal at noon and a light evening meal. For many people, especially middle-aged and older, the two-meal a day plan is ideal -- two meals spaced six hours or so apart (but not late in the day).

Overeating is the worst of all offenses against our bodies. We can prevent disease and live longer by not overeating, by refraining from hurtful foods, and by eating only at meal times.

Whatever meal pattern you follow, be sure to use the Eating Pyramid, pp. 269-271, as a guide to the numbers of servings to include each day of the five basic food groups. Doing so will assure you of getting adequate amounts of the basic nutrients needed to keep your body running smoothly: carbohydrates, proteins, fats, minerals, vitamins, water and fiber. Remember to drink the six to eight glasses of water between meals and not with meals.

AGAR-AGAR: A seaweed-based jelling agent used like gelatin in salads, soups, healthful jams, and desserts in place of animal gelatin or pectin. It jells readily at room temperature and a little goes a long way. Available in health food stores and oriental markets. Use 2 Tbsp. agar flakes (or 1 Tbsp. granules) to 3 1/2 cups liquid. For softer jell use 2 c. liquid and 1 Tbsp. flakes. Proportions vary somewhat with additions of fruits.

ARROWROOT POWDER: A thickening agent similar to cornstarch but considered natural because it is made from the beaten pulp of tuberous rootstocks of a tropical American plant. It is not a refined product but simply a smooth textured dried and powdered root. Use interchangeably with cornstarch. When heated in water it thickens. Basic proportions are 1 cup water and 1 1/2 Tbsp. arrowroot.

BAKON YEAST: A commercial seasoning powder made of Brewer's type nutritional food yeast with a hickory smoked flavor added.

BREWER'S YEAST: A nutritional food yeast available as flakes or powder for seasoning purposes. It is high in B-complex vitamins and yields a desirable flavor to meatless main dishes and non-dairy cheeses. It does not make breads rise. Available in health food stores.

CARDAMOM: A sweet, non-irritating herb used in pastries to replace cinnamon. Native to India, it has a pleasant, pungent aroma and sweet flavor. Cardamom is a popular spice throughout the Arab and Scandinavian countries to flavor sweet pastries, breads, cakes, and cookies. Use 1 tsp. ground cardamom in a batch of sweet rolls or bread. See Cinnamon Substitute recipe on p. 226.

CAROB: Commonly called "St John's Bread" or "Honey Locust," finely ground pods from budded trees are made into carob flour. Rich in natural sugars, Carob is low in starch, low in fat. Delicious in place of chocolate in brownies, hot drinks, cakes and candies. 3 Tbsp. Carob and 2 Tbsp. water equals 1 square of chocolate. Resembling cocoa in appearance, the flavor is delicious too. Chocolate and cocoa contain undesirable caffeine, theobromine, and are high in fat. Available in natural food stores.

CHERVIL: A flavorful herb used to season salad dressings, dips, spreads, and vegetables. A cousin to parsley, Chervil, called the "gourmet's parsley," is sweeter and more fragrant than parsley. Available in select supermarkets.

CHICKEN STYLE SEASONING: A commercially available seasoning powder used to give flavor to main dishes, soups, and vegetables without any chicken. Available in health food stores or can make your own from our recipe on p. 261.

CORIANDER: A non-irritating sweet herb used in pastries in place of cinnamon. It has a delightful sweet, pungent taste similar to a combination of sage and lemon peel. It is used in the Mediterranean region extensively for flavoring cookies, candies, and main dishes.

DATE SUGAR: Dried dates ground up, is used to sweeten foods in place of brown sugar in such recipes as granola, and homemade pancake mix. Not as sweet as brown sugar but entirely unrefined.

DOUGH ENHANCER: A commercially prepared mixture of ingredients added to bread to yield lighter textured products that stay moist longer. Available from Bosch and Magic Mill dealers. For dealer nearest you call 1-801-973-4501. Add 2-3 Tbsp. per 4 loaf batch of bread. Try making your own substitute dough enhancer by adding Vitamin C and soy lecithin to breads. Add 1 Vitamin C tablet (100-250 mg) plus 1 Tbsp soy lecithin granules to 4-5 loaf batch of bread. (See Marcella's Basic Mixer Bread recipe.)

ENER-G-EGG REPLACER: A commercially available product, in powder form, used to replace eggs in many recipes for leavening, and binding. A blend of raising ingredients and stabilizers in a gluten-free base. Sodium free. No preservatives, artificial flavorings, cholesterol, or sugar added. Contains potato starch, tapioca flour, leavening (calcium lactate, calcium carbonate, citric acid), carbohydrate gum. Contains no animal products. Check your local health food store or Ener-G Foods, Inc., P. O. Box 84487, Seattle, Wa 98124-5787. Toll free (800) 331-5222.

EMES GELATIN: A commercially prepared gelatin product made strictly of plant origin. Comes in unflavored and fruit flavors to use in jello type salads, and desserts. See Better Butter and salad dressing recipes in cookbook. Use 1 Tbsp. Emes to jell 1 3/4 c. liquid; 2 (scant) teaspoons Emes jells 1 cup liquid; 3 1/2 tsp. jells 1 pint. Check local health food store for availability or Emes Kosher Products, 4138-42 West Roosevelt Road, Chicago, IL 60624.

FLOUR MILLS: Great addition to the natural foods kitchen for milling fresh flour as needed in baking breads, etc. Mills for home use are available in hand crank style to clamp onto table top or electric models with micronizing disks or stones. These can be ordered through Marcella Lynch, phone (415) 969-9838.

GEORGE WASHINGTON BR0TH POWDER: A seasoning powder available in supermarkets that comes in indivdually wrapped packets inside a colorful little box near bouillon cubes and gravy base products. Used to season main dishes, soups, pilaf and rice dishes.

GRAIN TERMINOLOGY: If many of the new terms in recipes or on bread and cereal labels confuse you, here's a guide to make things easier.

> **Buckwheat:** seeds of the buckwheat plant, hulled or made into groats or flour. A nutritious product, but not a true grain.Used principally in breads, pancake flour, groats, and kasha pilaf dishes.

> **Bulgur:** a product made from whole or cracked grains of wheat with some bran removed, parboiled and dried.

> **Cracked wheat:** kernels of wheat cleaned and milled just enough to crack them open.

> **Gluten**: a protein in wheat that adds elasticity to bread dough, and can be separated out from the wheat flour for making mock meat steaks and meatless entrees. (See Ch. 7)

> **Gluten flour**: a flour extracted from hard red wheat that consists mainly of the protein of the wheat, called gluten. It can

be purchased at health food stores to make homemade bread more elastic or mixed with water to make a stiff dough for mock meat entree dishes. Dough can be cut into chunks and dropped into a seasoned broth to cook. (See p. 149.)

Grits: coarsely ground grain, especially ground hominy (white corn).

Groats: hulled and crushed grain fragments, larger than grits. Generally made from buckwheat, but can be made from other grains too.

Meal: coarsely ground grain unbolted (unsieved). Corn or oat meals are most common.

Micronizing: a newer method of grinding grains into flour in which higher rpms causes the instant exploding of the kernels of grain into flour.

Miller's bran: unprocessed bran as it leaves the mill.

Spring wheat: varieties of wheat grown, in contrast to winter wheat, in a mild climate. Hard spring or winter is used for yeast-leavened breads.

Sprouted wheat (or rye): kernels of grain that have been allowed to germinate before being added to breads.

Stone ground: grains ground by old-fashioned millstones rather than by roller mills.

GRANOLA: A hearty homemade or commercially prepared cold cereal for breakfast. Making you own at home is ideal in order to use less sugars, and fats than commercially available brands use. (See recipe for Golden Grain Granola.) A great way to start your day!

INSTANT GEL: A commercially prepared pre-cooked cornstarch product used by bakeries for a fast, no-cook thickening agent. Used in our cookbook for quick jams, low-fat mayonnaise, etc. Available at bakery wholesale distributors, a few specialty stores, or Ener-G Foods, Inc., toll free (800) 331-5222. It thickens like cornstarch without the cooking process! See our recipes for Instant Gel Jam, Salad Dressings without oil, and Mayonnaise made in the blender. Thickens instantly.

INSTANT YEAST: A new baking yeast product on the market for breadmaking that reacts instantly, requiring no separate dissolving ahead of time in warm water. Just add yeast along with the flour. Instant yeast can stand hotter water without killing yeast action and requires 1/3 less product than other active dry yeast granules on the market. If you forget the yeast until the dough is in the kneading process, just go ahead and throw in the dry instant yeast and keep kneading the dough. The bread will turn out great.

KITCHEN MACHINES: A heavy duty all-purpose kitchen machine is an important tool in the natural food kitchen to save time when cooking "from scratch." The Bosch Universal Mixer is the one used by Marcella in the video cooking shows, and can be ordered from her. For information, call (415) 969-9838.

MAGGI SEASONING AND KITCHEN BOUQUET: Commercially available seasonings available as a dark brown liquid in small bottles for seasoning entrees, grain dishes, gravies, etc. Available in supermarkets.

MEAT ANALOGS: A line of commercially prepared gluten and soy protein products to use in place of meat, poultry, or fish for tasty meals. Many of these products are ready-to-eat from the can or freezer package or with simple heat and serve directions for people in a hurry. They contain no animal products except for occasional egg whites. Available in select supermarkets, natural food stores, and Adventist food stores. Worthington Foods, Inc. in Worthington, Ohio is one of the largest suppliers, distributing products nationwide and internationally. Phone (614) 885-9511. In the gluten section of our cookbook we have a selection of main dish recipes using a few of these products. Examples: Nuteena, Vegetarian Burger, Vegeburger, Wham (for ham), Fri-Chik (for chicken), Big Franks or Veja-Links (for hot dogs), TVP (dry burger-like granules.) Recipes in the gluten section of this cookbook explain directions for making homemade gluten "steak" products at home for a fraction of the cost of commercially prepared products or meat.

SOY MILK POWDER: Commercially available non-dairy milk powder made from soybeans. A brand name, Soyagen, by

Worthington Foods, is available in health food stores. Can use in liquid form to replace dairy milk in the diet or use in cooking.

TAPIOCA: A thickening agent ideal for pies, fruit puddings and other desserts. Prepared from dried cassava starch it is available in granulated form as Minute Tapioca in supermarkets and in small round balls or powder in certain natural food stores.

TAHINI: A commercially available sesame seed butter. Very nutritious. Has a strong flavor used alone. Used in many Middle Eastern recipes. See Tahini French Toast and Tahini Cookie recipes in cookbook. Spread it on bread with a little honey to sweeten. Use it with mashed garbanzo beans to make Hummus, a spread or dip used in Middle Eastern cooking.

TOFU: A soybean curd product available in most supermarkets or Oriental food stores. Made from soybeans by a process similar to the making of cottage cheese, tofu can be used as a good source of protein and calcium in many dishes. See the tofu section of our cookbook for more information.

TOFU NON-DAIRY DRINK MIXES: Commercially available non-dairy milk powder. Reconstitute for a pleasant liquid non-dairy milk. Mix with half the amount of water for use as half & half or thin cream. Some brands supplemented similarly to dairy milk in calcium, riboflavin(B 2) and B 12. Usually lower in protein than dairy milk. Read the labels to compare nutrients to dairy milk. Available in white or natural and carob flavors.

TURMERIC: A yellow-colored herb powder used to give yellowish color along with interesting flavor to tofu dishes, curries, cream soups, sauces, salad dressings, relishes, and main dishes. Used extensively in Middle Eastern cuisine.

VEGEX, OR MARMITE: Commercially available seasoning pastes made from Brewer's yeast or other nutritional food yeast. Dark brown in color, it gives meaty flavor for main dishes. Found in health food stores. Safeway markets carry Marmite. If unavailable, substitute bouillon cubes, Maggi Seasoning, Kitchen Bouquet, Miso or gravy base products in recipes calling for Vegex.

Chapter 1

Organizing the
Natural Food Kitchen

- Tricks to Saving Time (A walk
  through a Natural Food Kitchen)

- Staples for the Natural Food Kitchen

- Check Up on Your Eating Habits

"Beloved, I wish above all things that thou mayest prosper and be in health, even as thy soul prospereth." 3 John 2

"Cooking By the Book" means becoming our own manufacturers...turning wholesome grains, beans, nuts, seeds, fruits and vegetables into tasty, nourishing dishes. It means using foods in their whole, original state. It means bringing whole foods home from the market rather than refined and packaged foods that have had some part removed or something too fatty, salty, or sugary added. It means becoming a label reader, being sure that the fuel we put in our body "tank" contains healthy ingredients.

Becoming a "from scratch" cook may be scarey to many people who are used to eating quick, prepared foods It may sound complicated and time consuming. But take heart! Chapter 1 will get us started. **Just remember that natural food cooking is not difficult, just different!** We will get acquainted with new food staples such as whole grains. We will learn that bugs are smarter than people. They know which foods contain nutrients and good flavor. They may try to help themselves to our whole grains and cereals....but we will learn to outsmart them by storing grains properly.

Keep in mind that if we are too busy to enjoy a little, simple food preparation time in the kitchen we are probably breaking one of God's laws of nature. We can't let life get so lopsidedly stressful and hectic that we neglect daily time to enjoy life, smell the roses, and live sanely. Our bodies will suffer, our families will suffer, and our mental and spiritual life will suffer. Life is too short to be driven by over-work.

Because few of us have time to spend all day in the kitchen like grandmother used to do, it is not practical to return to her technique of creating everything by hand. And after looking at the "fast food" reviews we should not resort to eating them either. What we **can** do is become what I'd like to call a SHORT-CUT cook.

A short-cut cook combines the best of two worlds. Using old fashioned, whole foods such as grains, fruits, vegetables, nuts and seed (God's ideal diet from Genesis 1:29 and 3:18), we can take advantage of electric mixers, blenders, and food processors to make food preparation quick and easy. We can use a pressure cooker or microwave oven to shorten cooking time. We can organize our kitchen, our work, and our food staples according to guidelines from kitchen experts.

By implementing the following tricks to saving time we can cook "from scratch" without taking all day in the kitchen. (See Video L. 1 of Series 1 for more detail.)

TRICKS TO SAVING TIME IN THE NATURAL FOOD KITCHEN

The kitchen is a place where a creative job of management can make life easier, more satisfying and more productive, and where people can enjoy doing things. Smart kitchen storage saves you steps and time. If you organize your kitchen, preparation time will be greatly shortened and there will be time left for yourself...even when cooking from scratch.

Become a SHORT-CUT COOK!

Trick No.1: Organize your kitchen.

Divide your kitchen into work centers, storing food and equipment at the place in the kitchen where it will first be used. This saves time and steps.

The seven kitchen work centers are as follows:

1. **PLANNING CENTER**: Cookbooks, grocery list, phone, paper, pencils

2. **REFRIGERATOR/FREEZER CENTER:** Food items that need to be cool: Perishable fruits, vegetables, beverages, whole grain flours, nuts, seeds, wheat germ, oil, etc. Items that freeze OK: nuts, seeds, breads, flour, dried fruits, carob chips, wheat germ, dried herbs, many vegetarian loaves, casseroles, patties.

3. **SINK CENTER**: Dishwashing supplies, aprons, dishtowels and cloths, garbage container, vegetable brush, colander/strainer, scrub brush, etc.

4. **MIXING CENTER**: Herb and seasoning drawer, grains, beans, flour, mixing bowls and utensils, mixer, mill, blender, food processor.

5. **COOKING CENTER**: Pots and pans, skillets, wooden spoons, spatulas, turn-overs, pot-holders, etc.

6. **BAKING CENTER**: Baking sheets and pans, casserole dishes, bread pans, etc.

7. **SERVING CENTER**: Dishes, flatware, glassware, all items needed to set table.

Mix Center

In locating your work centers the rule is that work should proceed from one step to the next in an orderly manner. Food preparation ideally takes place in a right-to-left or left-to right sequence from beginning to end.

Work proceeds through several work centers and finishes up nearest the eating area. Work should proceed from the point where food is stored to → where it is washed, mixed, or prepared, to → where it is cooked → and finally served. So remember to store foods in the work center in order of planned use. This saves much time, space, and needless repetition of your mental and physical activity.

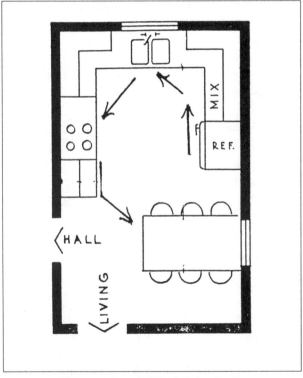

**Example of Right-to-Left
Work Pattern In a Kitchen**

Trick No. 2: Organize your food staples. Store grains, beans, flour, oatmeal, and other baking supplies in airtight, see-through jars for easy access and visibility and to prevent bug problems. Don't toss plastic or cellophane bags of cereals and grains in a cupboard. Bugs can chew through bags and are smarter than people when it comes to going for the nutritious foods. To destroy bug eggs in grain products that might hatch out if temperature warms up, freeze in container for 48 hours before storing in kitchen cupboard. Mount name labels on each jar for easy identification.

Trick No. 3: Organize your work. Spend 20 minutes each week to sketch out the week's menus. Planning in advance will help you stick to a wholesome eating plan. It will help you remember to cook certain foods in advance such as beans or rice. See Chapter 18 for menu planning tips.

Trick No. 4: Keep a grocery list going at all times to save trips to the grocery store for forgotten items.

Trick No. 5: Shop once a week. Don't depend on your memory. Don't shop every day. Shopping once a week with written list in hand saves impulse buying of junk foods as well as saving food budget money.

Trick No. 6: Take advantage of electric mixer, blender, food processor to do quick mixing, chopping, slicing and other food preparation. A natural food cook begins with raw ingredients and creates from-scratch dishes rather than using prepared mixes. Using electric food processors saves time. A pressure cooker and a microwave are time savers also. And don't be without an electric flour mill if you can help it.

STAPLES FOR THE
NATURAL FOOD KITCHEN

LEGUMES (1 lb. each—keep a variety of kinds on hand; store airtight in cupboard.)

Dry

Soybeans	Great Northern (Navy)	Pintos
Lentils	Limas	Kidneys
Garbanzos	Black Beans	Pink or Red
Black-eyed Peas	Split Peas	

Canned Beans for Quick Meals
Kidney Beans
Pintos
Soybeans
Garbanzos
Chili Beans (vegetarian)

GRAINS — whole (Store airtight in cool place. Refrigerator or freezer is ideal. Can crack in blender or cook whole. 1 lb each).

Wheat Berries	Barley
Oats	Rolled Oats
Rye	Quick Oats
Brown Rice	Bulgur wheat (cracked wheat)
Millet	

Flour (Store in refrigerator or freezer)

100% Whole Wheat Flour	1 lb. Rye Flour
1 lb. Soy Flour	1 lb. Gluten Flour (breadmaking)
1/2 lb. Carob Powder	Cornmeal

NUTS AND SEEDS, RAW (Store in refrigerator. Keep several kinds on hand.)

Walnuts	Sesame Seeds
Pecans	Alfalfa Seeds — to sprout
Almonds	Raw or light Peanut Butter and/or other
Cashews	nut butters
Brazils	Sesame Seed Butter (Tahini)
Sunflower Seeds	

MISCELLANEOUS STAPLES

- Lots of fresh fruits and vegetables in refrigerator always!
- Canned or frozen fruits and vegetables.
- Dried fruits.
- Fresh or dried herbs for seasoning.
- Homemade seasoning mixes (recipes in cookbook).
- Vegetable oil such as corn and olive oil.
- Honey, molasses, date sugar, maple syrup.
- Thickening agents such as tapioca, arrowroot powder, or cornstarch.
- Milk powder (soy, tofu or non-fat dairy).
- Hard shortening or non-stick spray for greasing pans.
- Whole grain hot and cold cereals including homemade granola.
- Whole grain crackers.
- Whole grain pancake mix (see recipe in cookbook).
- Whole wheat bread crumbs.
- Tofu.
- Herbal teas and cereal beverages.
- Seasonings/Flavorings: Vegex, Chicken Style Seasoning, George Washington Broth Seasoning, or Vegetable Bouillion cubes.
- Salt, vanilla, homemade curry and chili powder, onion and garlic powder and salt, soy sauce, nutritional food yeast flakes.

According to the American Heart Association and other leading health authorities there is a way to eat that helps prevent disease. If you would like to know where you rate on good eating habits, take the following quiz, add up your score and compare it with the rating guide at the bottom.

1.	If you eat a hearty breakfast give yourself	5———
2.	If you eat 3 meals a day and your evening meal is not the largest or you eat 2 meals a day and they are breakfast and lunch	5———
	if you allow at least 5 hours between meals	2———
3.	If you do not snack between meals or in the evening	5———
4.	If you drink at least 6 glasses of water every day	5———
	if you do not drink more than half a glass with meals	2———
	if you do not use iced beverages with your meals	2———
5.	If you do not use tea, coffee or cola beverages	5———
	if you do not use soft drinks of any kind	2———
6.	If you are careful in your use of salt (Americans use 4-6 gms. daily. Ideal—2 gms or 1 tsp.)	5———
	if you do not use spices	2———
7.	If you limit your desserts that are rich in sugar, fats and/ or refined starches to no more than 2-3 per week	5———
	if you take small servings	2———
	if you do not take seconds	2———
8.	If you eat 6-11 servings of bread, cereal, rice, and pasta foods daily	5———
	if most of these cereal products are whole grain	2———
9.	If you use two or more servings of fruit daily	5———
	if you try to get a vitamin C-rich food daily	2———
10.	If you have 3 or more servings of vegetables daily	5———
	if you cook vegetables carefully in little water, covered	2———
	if you use a green or yellow leafy vegetable 3-4 times per week	2———
11.	If you limit your use of all visible fats	5———
	if you use few fried foods	2———
	if you do not overheat your oil	2———
12.	If you eat a high-protein food each day such as soybeans, other legumes, cottage cheese, eggs, nuts or prepared meat-alternate products	5———
13.	If you use nonfat milk	2———
14.	If you use no more than 2-3 eggs per week	5———
15.	If you take time to chew your food	5———
16.	If you do not eat to the point of discomfort	5———
	if you do not serve a large variety of foods at one meal	2———
	if you neither completely rest nor engage in vigorous exercise immediately following a meal	2———
17.	If mealtime is a happy time at your house	5———
18.	If you set an attractive table	2———
	Total	114———

100 or above— you are really on the right road, leading the pack!
90 - 100— you are headed in the right direction!
70 - 90—you would be wise to change your course.
45 - 70—typical American, headed for trouble.
0 - 45—the laws of health work, you'll see!

Chapter 2

Better Breakfasts I

Featuring:

- Get Acquainted With Whole Grains

- Hot and Cold Cereals

"What? Know ye not that your body is the temple of the Holy Ghost
which is in you, which you have of God, and ye are not your own?
For ye are bought with a price: therefore glorify God in your body,
and in your spirit, which are God's." 1 Cor. 6:19, 20

In this chapter we'll get acquainted with whole grains. Breakfast, our most important meal of the day, centers around grains. Take a look at the vegetarian version of the new U. S. Government sponsored Eating Right Pyramid with Chapter 18 to see that the broad base of our diets should consist of grains in the form of cereals, breads, rice and pasta. (6-11 servings daily).

Emphasis on **whole grain** products made of the entire wheat kernel is recommended. By looking at the Kernel of Wheat chart on p. 302, you will see that the fiber-rich bran layers and the germ carry vital elements for good health.

The nine most commonly available grains are wheat, oats, rye, barley, rice, corn, millet, buckwheat, and triticale. Others such as amaranth, quinoa, spelt, and sorghum (milo) are less common.

In my kitchen's mixing center cupboards are found large jars of grains and beans with tight fitting lids....one jar for each kind of grain or bean I have. These grains and beans are the backbone of our meals. From them we create breads, cereals, pancakes and waffles for breakfast; steamed rice, pilafs, or homemade pasta for dinner; and muffins or crackers to accompany soup and salad suppers.

With a flour mill that sits prominently on our kitchen counter, grains are ground into flour. Our all-purpose kitchen machine then kneads dough, mixes, blends, chops, cracks, or processes most any foods. Meal preparation time is cut in half. The flavor and freshness of homemade dishes is superb...not to mention the nutritional advantage.

For breakfast, I like to select 1/4 cup or so of several grains from the large jars in the cupboard, such as wheat, oats, barley, millet and rye, and crack them in the blender for a few moments for hot cereal. Depending on how finely the grains are cracked, cooking time is from 5-15 minutes, stirred into boiling water and cooked over low heat. See cooking guide and recipes in this chapter.

Don't be afraid to experiment. Have fun and remember to thank God for the blessing of whole grains.

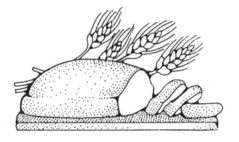

USING WHOLE GRAINS

The benefits of using whole grains are many. Roughage in the diet makes our food digest better and pass through our systems faster. This minimizes cholesterol build-up, a factor related to heart attacks. Fiber also inhibits our bile acids from converting to harmful acids, cancer causing chemicals of the colon. Cancer of the colon is second in deaths to cancer of the lungs.

There are thousands of items on the grocer's shelf. In most cases something has either been added or taken away. By adding preservatives, coloring and flavoring, or by removing the bran and germ from wheat to make white flour, we may make food look better or have a longer shelf life, but the body suffers.

The answer is simple. Nature provides "preventive medicine" when we use food in its natural state. Many illnesses that plague western civilizations are virtually unknown in undeveloped countries. It is because they do not have a chemist between them and the farmer.

WHY A FLOUR MILL AND BREADMAKER/ MIXER?

Whole kernels of grains come with a protective covering that locks the nutrients, flavor and freshness in and protects the oils from rancidity. Each kernel is sealed, we might say, for good keeping quality. Once grains are ground into flour or cracked as for hot cereal, their inside surface areas are exposed to the oxygen in the air and nutrient loss begins to occur through the oxidation process. By milling flour fresh as needed to make breads, cereals, soups, healthful desserts, and main dishes, you have the freshest, most nutritious product possible. At the same time, a heavy-duty mixer, such as the Bosch Universal, makes preparation time much shorter.

BROWN OR WHITE

In light of available evidence, it is clear that *whole wheat bread* is superior to white bread for the following reasons:

1. It contains more of the "B" group of *vitamins.*
2. Some essential *proteins* of high quality are furnished.
3. One of the richest natural resources of *Vitamin E* is found in the wheat germ.
4. Whole wheat bread contains more *minerals*—notably *calcium* and *iron.*
5. It is far easier to build an adequate diet around whole wheat flour than white flour.
6. White flour is deficient in many nutrients whose precise role in human nutrition is not as yet fully understood, such as certain important B vitamins like pyridoxine, pantothenic acid, biotin, and folic acid.
7. Whole wheat bread contains more useful *fiber* for bulk in the diet.
8. It has a distinctive *flavor.*
9. Whole wheat bread avoids bleaches, chemical softeners, and mold retardants.

COOKING WITH WHOLE GRAINS

Of importance in cooking whole grains is the use of longer, slow, low heat cooking after the grain is first brought to a boil. The slow cooking tenderizes the fiber without destroying minerals or other needed values. Whole grains may be cooked on top of the range in a heavy saucepan, in the oven, in a slow cooker pot, in a pressure cooker, or in a wide mouth thermos.

Natural grains are an excellent source of the B-Vitamins and E. These important nutrients are destroyed by high temperatures. Therefore, a paramount rule in whole grain cookery is the maintenance of low temperature.

WHERE TO FIND WHOLE GRAINS

Whole grains are available generally in natural food stores. Certain supermarkets which have a natural food section may have them also.

Whole grains are called by various names. Wheat is sometimes referred to as wheat kernels or wheat berries. Rye is often referred to as rye berries. Oats are often called oat groats. Buckwheat is sold as buckwheat groats. Barley will be called hulled barley or pearl barley. The darker tan the barley the less of the outer covering that has been removed. Hulled millet is the kind to buy. It is whole and round but tough outer covering is removed.

HOW TO STORE WHOLE GRAINS

Grains that are whole, and not cracked or ground into flour, store well in your kitchen cupboard. But bugs are smarter than people! They know a good food when they see one. Bugs don't readily infest white flour products sitting on shelves in your kitchen cupboards,

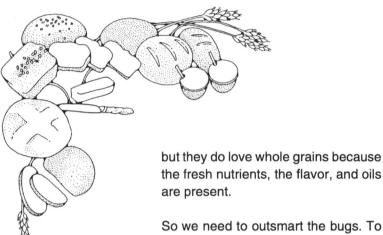

but they do love whole grains because the fresh nutrients, the flavor, and oils are present.

So we need to outsmart the bugs. To avoid a batch of bug eggs from hatching out into first larvae, and then little meal moths, store all grains in airtight containers, such as glass or plastic jars, with tight-fitting lids. If one jar of grain gets infested in your cupboard, it won't spread to everything else.

Store larger amounts of whole grains in 4-5 gallon buckets with tight fitting lids. Try the dry ice method for long term storage. Put grain, such as wheat, immediately over the top of two ounces of crushed dry ice, set the bucket lid on loosely but do not seal down. Allow sufficient time for the dry ice to evaporate (about 30 minutes) then tap the lid tightly onto the bucket. If pressure should develop, cautiously loosen the lid for a few minutes.

With this procedure, the dry ice pushes the oxygen up out of the bucket allowing for storage of grain without the presence of oxygen. Of course, bug eggs, even if they hatch out, will not live without oxygen.

If dry ice is not available, place wheat or other grain not more than 3/4 inches deep in a shallow pan and place in the oven at 150° F for about 20 minutes. Leave the oven door slightly ajar. This will destroy all stages of insect pests and also remove too high a moisture content.

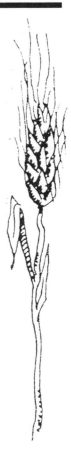

And, there is always the potential of bug eggs on the grains from the field, even though it has been cleaned for human use, especially organic grains that have had no pesticides used. Your kitchen cupboard is warm and acts as an incubator for hatching them. Therefore, always store whole grains in a cool, dry cupboard in airtight containers. The refrigerator or freezer is ideal also, but not always possible.

If you can develop the habit of placing whole grains in the freezer for 48-72 hours as soon as you bring them home from the store this should kill the bug eggs that might be on the grains. Then, transfer them to airtight jars, or plastic containers with tight-fitting lids and store them in your cupboard.

Grains stored properly will keep well for many months. Store airtight to keep the grains from taking on moisture from the air. With moisture content of 10% or less, insects are unable to reproduce. And, grains that are too moist become gummy or sticky when run through a flour mill. Grains also need to be stored airtight to outsmart the bugs, as discussed above. Wheat has been stored up to 100 years and still found to be fresh and quite fine to use. Other grains do not store quite so well. Do try to rotate the use of all your grains so as not to store them any longer than necessary.

A good breakfast includes:

— A Vitamin C-rich fruit*
— One other fruit
— Cereal with milk, nuts, other protein food, or eggs
— Whole grain toast, bread, pancakes or waffles
— Milk

Eat like a KING for breakfast, like a PRINCE at noon time, and like a PAUPER in the evening.

See Chapter 18 for breakfast menu planning ideas.
*Vitamin C-rich fruits include citrus fruits, cantaloupe, strawberries, pineapple, and kiwi.

HURRY-UP BREAKFAST DRINK

Even people in a hurry can whip up this fast, nourishing breakfast drink.

1/4 c. ground raw sunflower seeds
GRIND sunflower seeds in blender.

ADD to seeds, ripe banana, non-fat powder, wheat germ, vanilla, and water.

1 ripe banana
1/4 c. non-fat dry milk powder or Tofu Non-dairy Drink Mix

WHIZ until smooth. Enjoy this creamy, rich, high-fiber drink. It gives just the "pick-me-up" you need to start your day right!

1/4 c. wheat germ
1 tsp. vanilla
1 c. water

SUGGESTIONS TO HELP MAKE
BREAKFAST A HEARTY MEAL

- Natural rice, toasted and steamed with chopped dates and milk.

- Oatmeal cooked with wheat germ and raisins, served with milk.

- Other whole grains well cooked and served with dates, raisins, sliced bananas, or other fruit and milk.

- Wafffles, either whole wheat or reinforced with soy, wheat germ, etc., served with a low-sugar berry or other fruit sauce.

- Crumb griddle cakes with molasses and applesauce and sliced bananas.

- Baked potatoes and boiled eggs, scrambled tofu, or a meat analog.

- Creamed lima beans or peas on toast.

- Potatoes hashed with gluten (homemade or purchased).

- Steamed sweet corn in season.

- Fruit soup over toast.

- Oven-baked fries served with vegetarian Saucettes or other meat analog.

- Breakfast beans over toast.

- Creamed eggs on toast.

- Granola with milk.

- Breakfast wheat cakes with hot applesauce or berry sauce.

- Peanut Butter Special — whole wheat toast spread generously with peanut butter and covered with hot applesauce or hot pureed apricots.

- Cashew French Toast with fruit toppings.

- Corn bread or whole wheat muffins with orange honey butter and served with baked apples.

- Scrambled tofu served with potatoes and whole wheat toast or muffins.

COOKING GUIDE — WHOLE-KERNEL GRAINS

(Amounts of water, salt, cooking time, and yield are approximate but serve as a guide.)

Soaking: Overnight in cold water OR 1 hour with boiling water poured over. Cook in amount of water given in chart. FOR ALL GRAINS: boil 3 minutes; reduce heat to simmer; cover and do not remove lid during cooking time.

AMOUNT OF DRY WHOLE-KERNEL GRAIN	WATER	SALT	COOKING TIME	YIELD
SOAKING UNNECESSARY				
1/2 cup hulled buckwheat (groats)	2 cups	1/4 teaspoon	15 minutes	2-1/2 cups
1/2 cup millet	2 cups	1/4 teaspoon	40 minutes	2 cups
1 cup brown rice	2-1/2 cups	1/4 teaspoon	45 minutes; let stand 10 minutes	2 cups
1 cup quick brown rice	1-1/2 cups	1/2 teaspoon	15 minutes	3 cups
SOAKING NECESSARY				
1 cup hulled barley	4 cups	1/2 teaspoon	1 hour	4-1/2 cups
1 cup oats (groats)	3 cups	1/4 teaspoon	1 hour	2-1/2 cups
1 cup rye	2 cups	1/4 teaspoon	45 minutes -1 hours	3 cups
1 cup triticale	3 cups	1/2 teaspoon	45 minutes to 1 hour	3-1/2 cups
1 cup wheat berries	4 cups	1/4 teaspoon	2-3 hours	2-1/2 cups

GOLDEN GRAIN GRANOLA (delicious cold cereal)

6 c. quick cooking
rolled oats

2 c. whole grain flour
(mix several)

1 c. raw almonds or
other nuts

1/2 c. raw sunflower
seeds or coconut

1/2 c. brown sugar or
date sugar

1-1/2 tsp. salt

1 c. liquid (all fruit
juice or 3/4 c. juice +
1/4 c. oil)

1 tbsp. vanilla

1 tbsp. maple flavoring

CHOP the nuts. Whiz sunflower seeds to a meal in blender.

COMBINE all dry ingredients in large bowl. COMBINE the liquid, and vanilla.

ADD all at once to dry ingredients. Stir with a large spoon or with hands until evenly moistened. If a more moist, chunky granola is desired, add more liquid.

SPREAD OUT on two flat cookie sheet pans with low sides.

BAKE in 250°F oven for 1-1/2 hours, stirring and rotating pans every 1/2 hour.

LET COOL in oven. Store in airtight container.

VARIATIONS: Just as the granola is finished baking, add 1 cup of any of the following: chopped dried apricots, dates, figs, or apples, raisins or currents.

YIELD: 13 cups granola.

FAMILIA

3/4 c. peaches, dried, chopped
3/4 c. apples, dried, chopped
3/4 c. raisins or dates
1 c. shredded wheat (2 large
biscuits) coarsely broken
(optional)
2-1/2 to 3-1/2 c. rolled or
quick oats
1/2 to 3/4 c. powdered milk, dry
1/3 c. wheat germ
1/3 to 1/2 c. date sugar
1/2 c. shredded coconut, unsweetened
1 c. sliced or ground almonds
1/4 c. flax seeds, whizzed to a meal (optional)

TOSS together. Serve with milk and fresh banana slices.

FOUR GRAIN CEREAL

1/4 c. whole millet
1/4 c. whole wheat
  kernels
1/4 c. whole barley
1/4 c. brown rice
3-1/2 c. water
1/2 tsp. salt

COOK all ingredients in electric bean pot (crock pot or slow cooker) all night or steam on lowest heat of burner on range all night or in low oven all night. Breakfast is ready when you get up. Serve with raisins, dates, nuts, etc., stirred in.
For variation: Try adding oats or whole rye in place of two of the other grains. YIELD: 4-6 servings.

HOT CEREAL BLEND

1 c. wheat kernels
1/2 c. hulled millet
1/2 c. brown rice
1/2 tsp. salt
6 c. water
1/2 c. chopped dates

CRACK grains in blender 1/2 cup at a time until all is ground medium-fine. Add to boiling water slowly, stirring quickly so as not to lump. Cook for about 10 minutes. Just before it is done, add chopped dates. YIELD: 6 servings.

COOKED WHOLE KERNEL WHEAT

2-1/2 c. water
1 c. whole kernel
  wheat
1 tsp. salt

METHOD 1: Bring water to boil and add the wheat and salt. Reduce heat to a low boil and cook for 2-1/2 hours.
METHOD 2: Place all ingredients in a crockpot with the temperature set at "low." Let it cook overnight.

MILLET BREAKFAST CEREAL

1 c. whole hulled millet
3 c. water
1/2 tsp. salt
1 c. chopped unpeeled,
  cored apples
1 c. raisins
Honey and milk

PUT the millet, water and salt in saucepan. Bring to boil, cover and let simmer 40 minutes or until soft. Add apples and raisins. Serve with honey and milk. YIELD: 4-6 servings.

THERMOS-COOKED WHOLE WHEAT CEREAL

**1 qt., wide-mouthed
  thermos**
2-2/3 c. water
**1-1/3 c. whole wheat
  kernels**
1/2 tsp. salt

SOAK wheat in the morning in cold water. In the evening drain water into a sauce pan and bring to a boil.
ADD wheat, bring to a boil again, and put in heated thermos. Cover and lay thermos on side overnight. Delicious in the morning.

For variation: Try adding wheat germ, sunflower seeds and raisins or rye flakes. (Beans, lentils, brown rice can be cooked this same way.) YIELD: 4 c. cooked cereal.

MICROWAVE HOT CEREAL
Prepare the evening before needed

PLACE in 2 qt. casserole dish: 1/2 c. whole kernel grains, any combination
ADD: 2 c. water + 1/4 tsp. salt
COVER and microwave on High for 10 minutes.
STIR and microwave another 5 minutes.
Let stand overnight. For breakfast next morning, microwave to heat.
SERVE in cereal bowl with milk.
YIELD: 2 c.

BLUE-RIBBON BUCKWHEAT (Kasha)

2 c. water
**1/2 c. hulled buck-
  wheat groats**
1/3 tsp. salt or to taste

Per Serving: (340)
74 calories
2.6 grams protein
0.5 gram fat

BRING water to boil; stir in buckwheat; let boil for 3 minutes; lower heat; cover; simmer for 15 minutes, stirring a few times; add salt; let stand 15 minutes.
SERVE HOT. Many Americans prefer to eat buckwheat cereal with rich milk and raisins, figs, currants, dates, applesauce, or honey.
YIELD: 2-1/2 cups (4 servings)

NOTE: Buckwheat has an unusual, mellow flavor and is high in nutritional value. It is used in blintzes and other Jewish dishes and is a favorite cereal in Eastern European countries, where olive oil, sesame oil, or sunflower oil is often poured over hot steamed buckwheat. In parts of China and Japan, noodles made from buckwheat flour are a special relish.

ARMENIAN CHRISTMAS PORRIDGE

(Serve this for a company breakfast)
1 c. slivered almonds
1 c. pearl barley
3 qts. water
2 c. chopped dried apricots
1-1/2 c. raisins (or chopped dates)
1/3 c. honey
1 tsp. salt
1/2 tsp. ground coriander

SPREAD slivered almonds in a shallow pan, toast in a 350°F oven for about 8 minutes or until golden. Set aside.

COMBINE barley and 2 qts. of the water in a 4-qt. pan.

PLACE over medium-low heat and cook, uncovered, for 45 minutes, stirring occasionally. ADD chopped apricots, raisins (but not dates), and the remaining 1 qt. water. Continue cooking, uncovered, for 30 minutes until very thick; stir often. Add honey, salt, and coriander and cook, stirring, 5-10 minutes longer.

REMOVE from heat and add dates, if used. SERVE warm with milk. Garnish with whole almonds and apricot halves for a festive breakfast. Can be made the day before and re-warmed. Serves 8.

PRAIRIE "FISH" HOTCAKES

Cornmeal mush
Flour
Oil
Orange Honey Butter

CUT thick, cold cornmeal or millet mush into slices about 1/2" thick. Roll in flour and brown on both sides in hot oiled frying pan. Serve on a plate like pancakes with Orange Honey Butter or other toppings of your choice.

ORANGE HONEY BUTTER

1/2 c. soft margarine
2 tbsp. honey
1/2 tsp. orange rind, finely grated

WHIP margarine and honey. Add rind. Orange juice may be added. Serve on cornbread, toast or muffins.

Chapter 3

Better Breakfasts II

Featuring:

- Pancakes

- Waffles

- French Toast

- Crepes

"How hard it is to find a capable wife! She is worth far more than jewels.....she gets up before daylight to prepare food for her family...she is always busy and looks after her family's needs. Her children show their appreciation, and her husband praises her. He says 'many women are good wives, but you are the best of them all.'"
Prov. 31:10,15,27-29.

MOST IMPORTANT MEAL OF THE DAY

It is not by accident that breakfast is labeled by nutritionists as the most important meal of the day. Numerous studies by leading universities have verified this fact and your own common sense can give you the same answer.

If you knew that you, your spouse or children could have nothing to eat for eighteen hours, you would be mighty concerned, wouldn't you? And rightly so! Yet surveys show that about 40% of the men, women and children in this land of plenty do not eat an adequate breakfast. High school students are notorious for skipping breakfast! If you are a breakfast skipper count up the hours between dinner at six o'clock and lunch at noon the next day and you'll find you've gone eighteen hours wihout food.

When the gas gauge on your car shows "empty" you stop and refuel; otherwise, your car won't run for want of energy.

You can produce inefficiency in yourself by not eating breakfast, eating too little breakfast or too much of the wrong kind of food. Feeling cross and tired, and the familiar "11 o'clock" slump are indications that your body has run out of fuel.

What you need first thing every morning is some stick-to-the ribs food to get you off to a good start and carry you through to lunch. University studies show that breakfast skippers do more poorly in school work, are more accident-prone, are less able to discern between right and wrong, snack more often between meals (which adds calories, usually empty ones). Snacking between meals interrupts the normal process of digestion, overworking the digestive system.

MAKE-AHEAD PANCAKE MIX

8 c. whole grain flour (try combining several kinds)
3 tsp. salt
3 c. dry milk powder
1/2 c. date or brown sugar
3 tbsp. Dough Enhancer (optional)
1/3 c. baking powder OR Ener-G Egg Replacer (or omit and fold in 2 stiffly beaten egg whites to batter just before cooking the pancakes)

COMBINE all ingredients in large mixing bowl.

MIX well and store in airtight container.

USE as directed below for pancakes, waffles, or muffins.

NOTE: For the 8 c. flour one of my favorite combinations is to grind together 1/2 c. soybeans, 1 c. barley, 1 c. oats, 1/2 c. buckwheat, 1/2 c. millet, 1/2 c. corn and 1 c. whole wheat berries.

Dough Enhancer adds lightness and fluffiness to whole grain breads.

TO USE THIS MIX:
FOR PANCAKES:

COMBINE 2 c. Make-Ahead Pancake Mix with enough water to make thick pancake batter (about 1-1/2 c.) but amount varies depending on which grains you have milled into flour for the mix).

ADD 2 tbsp. oil

ADD 1 egg or 2 egg whites if drier interior is desired.

POUR batter onto hot griddle or frying pan to form 6-inch cakes

BROWN on both sides. Flipping pancake up and slapping down hard from a 12-in. height increases the volume and lightness of the pancake.

YIELD: 2 (6 in.) pancakes.

FOR WAFFLES:

SAME as for pancakes; except increase the oil to 4 tbsp. Spray the waffle iron with a non-stick spray and preheat on high heat.

ADD 1 c. to 1-1/2 c. pancake batter (or as needed depending on size of waffle iron). CLOSE lid and bake 4-5 minutes.

YIELD: 2 large waffles.

FOR MUFFINS:

COMBINE 2-1/3 c. Make-Ahead Pancake mix, 1 egg, 2 egg whites or Ener-G Egg Replacer, 1 cup water, 1/4 c. oil, and optional 1/2 c. raisins, shredded apples or chopped nuts.

FILL greased or paper-lined muffin tins 2/3 full of muffin batter.

BAKE at 400° F for 18 minutes.

YIELD: 1 doz. muffins.

BREAKFAST WHEAT CAKES (Pancakes)

3/4 c. wheat kernels (or 1/4 each of wheat, oats, and rye) 3/4 c. milk 2 egg whites 1 tbsp. oil 1/2 tsp. salt 2 dates	SOAK wheat kernels overnight in 3/4 c. cold water. Drain water from wheat and place wheat in a blender with milk and run 3-5 min. Add oil, salt and dates. Mix well. Fold in stiffly beaten egg whites. Cook on hot griddle. Serve topped with plain yogurt and berry sauce. Yield: About 15 pancakes.

DOUBLE CORN FLAPJACKS

1/2 c. cornmeal 1/4 c. whole wheat flour 1/2 tsp. salt 1 tbsp. oil 1 medium ear corn (or 1-1/2 to 2 c. canned or frozen corn) 1 tbsp. dry onion flakes 1 c. buttermilk or sweet milk	CUT AND SCRAPE fresh corn from cob. Combine all ingredients together. Pour batter into 4-6 cakes (about a rounded 1/3 c. each) on oiled skillet and cook about 4 minutes, covered. Turn carefully and brown other side (2-3 minutes). Serve topped with strawberry orange sauce or any sweet sauce. May delete onions if serving with fruit sauce.

OLD FASHIONED STEAM LEAVENED WAFFLES

The following 3 steam-leavened waffle recipes are hearty and heavy but delicious without baking powder, soda or eggs to leaven. They can be made ahead and frozen for quick toaster waffles on busy work days.

TIPS FOR SUCCESS WITH
STEAM-LEAVENED WAFFLE RECIPES

HEAT waffle iron until hot, brush with oil or spray with non-stick product.

CLOSE lid and reheat until just before oil would smoke.

POUR in batter all at once and spread to the edges of the iron. Let it sit for about 15 seconds before closing the lid — this will prevent the batter from running over the side. DON'T raise the lid until the waffle is done — approximately 10 minutes, depending upon your appliance. Some waffle irons take longer than others; you will have to learn how long your iron takes by experience. DO NOT let waffle iron sit unused between waffles. If this should happen, begin the procedure again. RE-SPRAY waffle iron before each waffle.

BASIC OATMEAL WAFFLES (Steam leavened)

REVIEW tips for success on p. 49.
MEASURE into blender and blend smooth:

3 c. water
6 pitted dates (or 1 tbsp. honey)
1/4 tsp. salt

ADD and blend smooth again:
2 c. rolled oats
1/4 c. soy flour or wheat germ

STOP blender.
ADD: **1 c. additional rolled oats** stirring with spoon and not blender.

SPOON one-half the batter into a hot oiled waffle iron and cook until done approximately 10 minutes.

MIX in another 2 to 3 tbsp. water each time you add additional batter into waffle iron. The batter thickens upon sitting.

YIELD: 2 (9-inch) square waffles.

SUNFLOWER SEED-OAT WAFFLES
(Steam leavened)

1/2 c. sunflower seeds	REVIEW tips for success on p. 49.
2-1/4 c. water	COMBINE all ingredients and blend in
2 c. rolled oats	blender until light and foamy; about half a
1/4 c. wheat germ	minute. Let stand while waffle iron is heat-
1 tbsp. oil	ing. The batter thickens on standing. Blend
1/2 tsp. salt	briefly. Grease iron with solid shortening
	for first waffle (not margarine). Bake in hot
	waffle iron 8-10 min. or until nicely browned.
	Do not peek before 8 min.
	YIELD: 2 large waffles.

CASHEW-OAT WAFFLES (Steam leavened)

2-1/4 c. water
1-1/2 c. rolled oats
1/3 c. raw cashews
1 tbsp. corn oil
1/2 tsp. salt

REVIEW tips for success on p. 49.
COMBINE all ingredients and blend until light and foamy — about 1/2 minute. Let stand while waffle iron is heating. The batter thickens on standing. Blend briefly. Grease iron with solid shortening for first waffle (do not use margarine). Bake in hot waffle iron 8-10 min. or until nicely browned. Do not open before 8 minutes. YIELD: 2 large waffles.

CASHEW FRENCH TOAST

3/4 c. water
1/2 c. raw cashews
2 dates, pitted
Pinch of salt

LIQUEFY ingredients together and dip slices of whole grain bread in this mixture. Brown in small amount of oil or bake in quick oven. No oil required on silverstone surface. Turn and brown on other side. Makes enough dip for 6 slices.

TAHINI FRENCH TOAST (Sesame Butter)

1/2 c. Tahini
   (sesame seed
   butter)
3/4 c. water
1/4 tsp. salt

MIX together until smooth. Dip whole grain bread into mixture (Quick in and quick out.) Let excess batter drip off.
BROWN on both sides in medium-hot oiled skilled or griddle. Makes 10 slices.

GARBANZO FRENCH TOAST

1/3 c. dry garbanzos
   (1 c. soaked)
2/3 c. water
1 c. low fat milk
1/2 tsp. salt
6 thin slices dry
   whole wheat
   bread

SOAK garbanzos overnight in 2/3 c. water. Drain and whiz in blender with the milk, and salt. POUR into flat bowl. Dip bread slices into garbanzo batter turning on both sides to absorb as much of the mixture as possible; spread any remaining thick part on slices.
BROWN on both sides.
SERVE with your favorite fruit topping.
YIELD: 6 slices.

BERRY SAUCE

4 c. (1 lb.) frozen
  unsweetened boysen-
  berries (or other berries)
2 tbsp. cornstarch
Juice and water to make
  1-1/2 c.
1/2 c. honey or to taste

PLACE berries in saucepan. Mix cornstarch and juice-water together and pour over berries. ADD honey and cook over medium heat until thickened. Serve hot over pancakes, waffles, or toast.
YIELD: 3-1/2 to 4 c.

ORANGE SYRUP

1/2 c. honey
Juice of one large orange
  (1/2 c.)
1 tbsp. grated orange rind
1 tsp. cornstarch or
  arrowroot powder
  mixed in 2 tbsp of water
  to disolve
2 tbsp. margarine

SIMMER honey and orange juice together until of rich consistency. Add cornstarch and cook until slightly thickened. Take from heat and add margarine and rind. Blend. Serve hot or cold. Good on hot cakes and waffles.
YIELD: 1 c. syrup.

APPLE SYRUP

6-oz can frozen apple
  juice concentrate
6 oz. water
1 tbsp. cornstarch or
  arrowroot powder
1/2 tsp. lemon juice
1/4 tsp. cardamom or
  cinnamon

PLACE all ingredients in small pan and boil until thickened. Serve on waffles, French toast or rice.
YIELD: 1-1/2 c. syrup.

STRAWBERRY ORANGE SAUCE

3 c. frozen strawberries
Juice of 1 orange
2 tbsp. cornstarch or
  arrowroot powder

MIX cornstarch with orange and strawberry juice. Simmer until thickened. Then add fruit and heat through.
YIELD: Approximately 2 c. sauce.

EGGLESS WHOLE WHEAT CREPES

3/4 c. whole wheat
  pastry flour
3/4 c. quick rolled oats
2 c. low fat milk or soy
  milk
1 tbsp. oil
1/4 tsp. salt

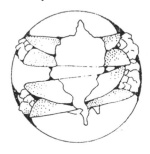

WHIZ all ingredients in blender. Let stand 5 minutes. Batter should be consistency of thin cream.

HEAT a small non-stick skillet or crepe pan; oil lightly for first crepe only.

SPOON in about 3 tbsp. of batter; tilt skillet to spread batter evenly.

BROWN lightly on both sides.

SPREAD immediately with desired filling; roll up like a jelly roll or fold over.

SERVE hot with or without topping, or refrigerate and rewarm in oven at 300°F about 20 minutes or until crepes are heated through.

YIELD: 3 c. batter and 16 (6-inch) crepes. 60 calories per crepe.

FRUIT TOAST

1 qt. fruit (peaches,
  apricots, berries,
  cherries, etc.)
1/4 c. cornstarch or
  arrowroot powder
Pinch of salt
Honey to taste
1/2 c. water or juice
  from fruit

HEAT fruit to boiling. Mix cornstarch and water or juice; add to hot fruit mixture; stir until thickened and clear. Serve hot over toast, waffles or granola.
Serves 4.

HOT PEANUT BUTTER-APPLESAUCE OVER TOAST

On plate: Slice of whole wheat toast, spread with peanut butter and topped with warm applesauce. Sprinkle with shredded coconut or sliced banana to garnish.

To complete the meal: A side dish of fresh fruit and milk to drink.

GRIDDLE HASH BROWNS

PREHEAT griddle or skillet to 350°F. Wash and scrub 6 medium potatoes. Shred on coarse shredder, skins and all, along with a bit of onion. Spread shredded potatoes out on hot, lightly oiled griddle. Sprinkle with salt. Cover with foil. When golden brown, cut into section and turn. Brown second side uncovered. Serve with scrambled tofu, whole wheat toast and fresh fruit for a delicious breakfast. Serves 4.

HURRY-UP HEARTY HASH

2 c. cooked brown rice
1/2 c. sauteed onions
1/2 c. chopped celery
1/2 c. chopped Brazil
  nuts
1/4 c. Brewer's flake
  yeast (with B-12)
2 c. shredded raw
  potatoes (unpeeled)
2 tbsp. oil
1/2 tsp. salt
1/8 tsp. garlic powder
2 tbsp. soy sauce

WASH the potatoes well and remove any spots. Shred on a medium shredder. Combine all ingredients. (The flake yeast adds a savory flavor and enhances the protein value.) Stir enough to mix well. Turn into a lightly oiled skillet at 350°F. Cover and let cook until nicely browned, about 10 min. Scrape from bottom and turn. Cover and let cook 10 min. longer. Stir, reduce the heat, and let cook an additional 5 min. Serves 6.

SCRAMBLED TOFU

1 lb. tofu
1 tsp. onion powder or
  1 bunch green
  onions
2 tsp. soy sauce or
  1/2 tsp. salt
1 tsp. margarine or oil
Dash of turmeric
1-1/2 tsp. chicken style
  seasoning (p. 261)

DRAIN tofu, cube it, and simmer in margarine or oil with other ingredients until liquid is absorbed.
SERVE as you would scrambled eggs.
VARIATIONS: Add 1/4 tsp. sweet basil and 1/4 tsp. dill weed or 1/4 c. baco chips. For Spanish style add 1/4 c. each fresh chopped onion, green bell pepper and tomatoes. Add a few tsps. salsa if desired. YIELD: 4-6 servings.

Chapter 4

Pack a
Lively Lunch

- Lunch Suggestions

- Sandwiches

"And God said, Behold, I have given you every herb bearing seed, which is upon the face of all the earth, and every tree, in which is the fruit of a tree yielding seed; to you it shall be for meat." Gen. 1:29.

PACK-IT-LUNCHES should not be hastily thrown together items. They should be well-balanced meals for growing children for whom optimum nutrition is so important. Since lunch should contain one-third of the day's requirement of protein, calories, minerals, and vitamins, it is suggested that it contain:

> A high-protein food (probably in the sandwich)
> Fruit and/or vegetable (preferably raw)
> Milk (or substitute comparable in nutritive content)
> A simple dessert (dried fruit, cookie, etc.)

Many other foods can be included such as a hearty soup, dried fruits, baked beans, olives, or nuts. The practice of including snacks such as potato chips or corn chips may not be such a desirable one. Many children (or adults) will eat these first, since they are high in calories and are quite satisfying, the child will not be hungry for the other foods in the lunch. For a crunchy, chewy food, use carrot, celery, cucumber, or zucchini sticks, which would be more nourishing than the chips.

Providing variety in the lunch box menu is essential. Do not pack only peanut butter sandwiches or insist that the fruit always be an apple. Learn to like many foods and include a surprise quite often. Why not write a note on the paper napkin to be read as the lunch is enjoyed.

LUNCH SURPRISES FOR THE SCHOOL LUNCH

When packing a lunch for someone else why not include a surprise?

1. A surprise apple—remove core, stuff with raisins, nuts, dates, a rolled up note, even a piece of good candy wrapped in waxed paper.
2. A small box of raisins.
3. A note on the paper napkin.
4. A pretty napkin.
5. A hard-boiled egg made into different things—a dolly face with a crepe-paper bonnet, a bunny, etc.
6. A new pencil or eraser.
7. A greeting card to fit the occasion, i.e., birthday, Valentine's Day, etc.
8. You think of some now.

SIMPLE DESSERTS FOR THE LUNCHBOX

1. Dried fruit
2. Date bar
3. Fruit candy (see Dessert Section of cookbook)
4. Oatmeal cookie
5. Small bag of nuts
6. Fruit Whip
7. Peanut-butter cookie
8. Mixed nuts
9. Pudding
10. Stuffed prunes
11. Molasses Cookie
12. Dates
13. Rice Pudding

TRAIL MIX FOR LUNCHES

Mix together some raisins with two or three kinds of nuts:

1/2 cup raisins
1/2 cup walnuts or pecans
1/2 cup sunflower seeds and/or pumpkin seeds

As you might guess, a sandwich made on whole grain bread is the main course of a pack it lunch. Many meatless patties and burger recipes are found in Chapter 4 as well as in the main dish chapters.

DOING it "naturally" with lunchbox sandwiches can be creative. Try the following tricks for variety:

✓ KEEP several kinds of whole grain breads in the freezer for sandwich variety—rye, cracked wheat, whole wheat, pumpernickel, oatmeal, soy, whole wheat French, English muffins, pocket bread.

✓ MAKE up several basic fillings ahead and store in the freezer for weekly variety. Thaw overnight for morning lunch packing. Then return filling to freezer.

✓ MANY kinds of spreads, patties and meatless burgers can be made ahead for the freezer. Pull out as needed. Cooked whole grains and legumes star in the following high-taste, low-cholesterol sandwich fillings.

✓ KEEP an airtight container of sandwich trimmings in the refrigerator for the speedy finale to your nutritious sandwich—tomato, avocado, radish, and cucumber slices; lettuce leaves; alfalfa sprouts; grated carrots: green pepper strips.

✓ TO avoid a soggy sandwich assemble in the morning and pack individually in plastic wrap or sandwich bags for lunchtime.

✓ TO spur your imagination, a few ways to cut a sandwich:

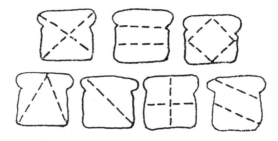

TRY THESE SANDWICH FILLINGS

1. MASHED avocado seasoned with mayonnaise, salt, onion powder, lemon juice. Top with tomato slice and alfalfa sprouts.

2. PEANUT butter topped with: a) sliced cucumber on mayonnaised bread, b) raisins and sliced banana, c) slices of fresh apple on mayonnaised bread.

3. MASHED cooked beans seasoned with mayonnaise and seasonings of your choice.

4. OR See Patties in the Index for more ideas.

GARBANZO SPREAD SPECIAL

1 15-oz. can garbanzos
1 6-oz. can olives, pitted
   (drained)
1/2 small onion
2 tbsp. oil
1/2 tsp. Vegex

GRIND all ingredients with finest blade of meat/food grinder or chop in blender. In skillet place 2 tbsp. oil, 1/2 tsp. Vegex (or 1 tsp. soy sauce and 1 tbsp. Brewer's yeast), and garbanzo mixture. Saute and stir a few minutes. Delicious mixed with mayonnaise for a sandwich spread or on toast.

SOYBEAN FILLING

MASH **2 c. cooked soybeans**. Saute in a **little oil: 1 c. finely chopped onion, 2 cloves finely chopped garlic, 1 c. chopped, fresh parsley**. Add **baco chips** to taste if desired. Mix with **soybeans** along with **1 tsp. dried oregano, 1/3 c. mayonnaise, 1 tbsp. soy sauce. Salt** to taste. Add **toasted wheat germ** to thicken if needed.

TOFU SANDWICH SLICES

PURCHASE one package of firm type tofu. Open and drain off liquid. Blot dry with clean dishtowel. Slice in 1/4 inch slices. Place in oiled skillet. Sprinkle with soy sauce and seasoning salt. Brown on both sides in lightly oiled skillet. Store tofu slices in refrigerator for nourishing sandwiches. Serve with all the trimmings: lettuce, sliced tomato, etc.

SWEET SANDWICH FILLING

GRIND through food grinder or food processor equal amounts of walnuts, pecans, almonds or any favorite raw nuts with dried fruits such as raisins, dates, dried pears, apples, prunes, or apricots. MIX together with a wooden spoon or a hand and moisten with a little fruit juice or mild honey. SPREAD on whole wheat bread. Makes a delicious sweet sandwich with plenty of good protein and staying power for the day...a good alternative to peanut butter and jelly sandwiches.

NUTEENA-OLIVE FILLING

1 19-oz. can Nuteena*
1/2 c. chopped ripe olives
1/2 c. mayonnaise
1 tsp. lemon juice
1 tsp. Vegex (optional)
1/4 tsp. salt
1/4 c. finely chopped
celery

MASH Nuteena and blend all ingredients together.

YIELD: 3 cups.

*(commercially prepared, vegetarian canned product. Use Worthington Numete or Protose also.
See Glossary for Meat Analogs.

TOMATO NUTTOSE

1 c. tomato pulp or puree
6 tbsp. nut butter
2/3 c. hot water less 2
tbsp.
1 c. toasted bread
crumbs (whole grain
preferred)
2 tbsp. soy flour
1/2 tsp. salt
1/4 tsp. sage
1/4 tsp. marjoram
1/8 tsp. onion powder

CREAM nut butter and water.
ADD all other ingredients. Put in greased cans you've saved from other foods.
STEAM , covered with foil, 2-1/2 to 3 hours. Create a steamer by lowering the cans of Nuttose mixture into a pot of boiling water using enough water so water level is 2/3 up on the cans but no more.
USE for sandwich filling or slice and brown on both sides for a dinner entree.
YIELD: 2 cups.

THE VEGETARIAN BURGER

For binding:
Whiz 1/2 c. soaked garbanzo beans in 1/2 c. water OR 2 eggs

1 c. rolled oats, uncooked
1 c. finely chopped walnuts
1 medium onion, minced
4 tbsp. milk
1/2 tsp. salt
1 tsp. sage
1 tbsp. soy sauce

WHIZ garbanzos and water in blender (unless using eggs). Put binder in bowl. Add the remaining ingredients and mix with spoon. Drop from spoon or ice-cream scoop into oiled skillet. Flatten with spoon to form patties. Brown on both sides over medium heat. Cover skillet for first side. Serve in burger buns with all the trimmings or in casserole dish with gravy over top, baking 30 minutes at 350°F. Makes 6 large patties. Protein: 7.2 gm./patty. Calories: 226 gm./patty.

Note: to soak dry garbanzo beans cover with water and let stand overnight. I soak garbanzos ahead, drain, and store in freezer for recipe use.

For additional binders (egg replacers), see p. 260.

TOFU BURGERS

1 c. oatmeal
1 small onion
3 tbsp. wheat germ +
1 tbsp. Brewer's yeast (or 4 tbsp. Brewer's yeast)
1 c. tofu, regular or firm
1/2 tsp. sage
1 tbsp. soy flour
2 tbsp. soy sauce
1/2 tsp. garlic powder
chopped celery, optional

MIX all ingredients together and add just enough moisture to form into patties.

FORM patties between moistened hands and dip in breading meal.

BROWN lightly in small amount of oil.

SERVE in burger buns with all the trimmings. . . or serve hot for dinner with a mushroom or tomato gravy.

BAKE 350° 30 minutes.

Makes 4-6 patties.

THE FUNDAMENTAL BURGER

COOK until well done in just enough water to cover:

> **1/2 c. Azuki beans and 3/4 c. lentils**
> **1/2 tsp. salt**

BRING 3/4 cup water to boil and add:
3/4 cup cracked wheat—remove from heat and let absorb moisture. (To crack wheat: Place 3/4 c. wheat (whole) in blender. Whiz on high speed until wheat is cracked medium to fine. Or you can use bulgar wheat purchased from store.)

SAUTE in oil or a bit of water:

> **1-1/2 c. onions, chopped very fine**
> **1/2 lb. mushrooms, chopped fine**
> **1-1/2 cups chopped zucchini**
> **1 tbsp. sweet basil**
> **1 tbsp. chopped garlic (or 1/2 tbsp. garlic powder)**
> **2 tbsp. (heaping) chicken style seasoning (p. 261)**
> **2 tbsp. Dr. Bronner's Liquid Aminos seasoning**
> **(or 1-1/2 tbsp. soy sauce)**

ADD:

> **1-1/2 c. rolled oats**
> **1/3 c. wheat germ**
> **1/4 c. sesame seeds or sunflower seeds**
> **1/4 c. walnuts or cashews, chopped**

MIX all together well. Make into patties and brown slowly on both sides. Note: This mixture may be frozen. When thawed, mixture may be a little soft. If so, add wheat germ or bread crumbs.
YIELD: 10-12 large burger patties.

SAVORY GARBANZO FILLING (Falafal)

(Serve in Arabian Pocket Bread)

1 c. dry garbanzo beans (not canned)
3 green onions
2 to 3 cloves of garlic
1 tsp. salt
1 tsp. cumin
2 tbsp. sesame seeds
1/3 c. parsley sprigs (packed)
2 tbsp. cream or milk

SOAK beans overnight. Drain and put through fine blade of meat grinder with onions, parsley, and garlic. Mix. Add cream or milk and seasonings. Heat 2-3 tbsp. oil in frying pan. Brown garbanzo mixture about 15 minutes, tossing and turning with spatula. Add a bit of water to moisten if needed. Serve in pocket bread with chopped tomatoes, lettuce, avocados, Ranch Style Dressings, or Sesame Seed Dressing.

MEATLESS RICE BURGERS

Delicious used in place of hamburger in sandwiches with sliced tomato and lettuce.

1 c. cooked brown rice
1/2 c. finely chopped walnuts or other nuts
1 small onion, minced
1 egg or see p. 260 for egg replacers (binders)
1/4 tsp. salt
1/8 tsp. poultry seasoning
1/8 c. bread crumbs

COMBINE all ingredients. Form into patties and fry on medium heat in small amount of oil until firm and brown on both sides. Serves 4.

Chapter 5

Bread with that Something Extra

- The Do's and Don'ts of Dough

- Whole Grain Breads and Rolls (Includes Variations for Basic Bread Dough)

- Whole Grain Crackers

- Bread Spreads

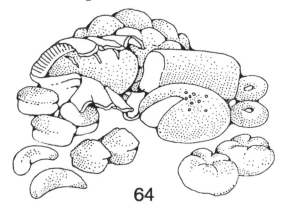

"Take thou also unto thee wheat, and barley, and beans, and lentils, and fitches, and put them in one vessel, and make thee bread thereof." Ezekiel 4:9

EZEKIEL'S BREAD (Pumpernickel texture)

1 c. warm water
2 tbsp. yeast
1-1/2 tbsp salt
3 tbsp oil
1 c. soy flour
1 c. gluten flour
1 c. barley flour
3 tbsp. molasses
1 c. hot water
1 c. sprouted or
soaked lentils
2 c. hot water
1 c. rye flour
1 c. millet flour
4 c. whole wheat flour

1. MIX warm water, 1 tbsp. molasses and yeast; let stand until yeast is growing well (10-15 minutes).
2. LIQUEFY together 1 c. hot water, 2 tbsp. molasses, salt, lentils, and oil until smooth and put in mixer bowl. Add 2 c. hot water and first 5 flours and beat thoroughly (all except whole wheat flour).
3. ADD yeast mixture and beat again and add 1 c. whole wheat flour; allow to stand in warm place 15 minutes.
4. ADD 3 c. whole wheat flour (give or take), enough to make dough stiff enough to pull away from sides of bowl.
5. LET knead on low speed 10 minutes.
6. FORM into loaves and let rise until double.
7. BAKE at 350°F. for 1 hour. (Less for rolls or small loaves)

In Scripture bread is often symbolic of the food we need to nourish our bodies. The Lord's prayer in Matt. 6:11 includes "Give us this day our daily bread." In Old Testament times, God rained bread from heaven in the form of manna to sustain the children of Israel for 40 years in the wilderness. In Deut. 8:3 we are reminded that we cannot live by bread alone but need to live by every word that comes from the mouth of God. Jesus referred to himself as the bread of life which we all need as our spiritual food. Every time we celebrate Communion by the taking of bread and sweet wine we are reminded that Jesus' body, represented by the Communion bread, was broken for us.

Every group of people around the world have a special kind of bread as the backbone of their diet. In the middle east is featured pita bread and in India chapati's. Spanish cultures have their tortillas and the western world has loaves of yeast leavened breads.

And so, today when you walk into a supermarket one entire aisle is generally devoted to bread. Breads are divided into three categories: quick breads, yeast breads, and unleavened breads. Quick breads are generally leavened with baking powder, soda, or steam such as muffins, biscuits, pancakes, and waffles. Yeast breads are leavened with yeast and include all the breads, rolls, hamburger and hotdog buns you see in the supermarket. Unleavened breads include crackers of various types, Communion bread, and tortilla type flat breads.

There's nothing so tasty and special as homemade bread. In this revolutionary, push-button age nutritious bread can be oven-ready in minutes. Almost every kitchen mixer these days comes equipped with a dough hook for mixing bread. Automatic bread makers are popular too and do all the mixing and baking without any human intervention. One loaf of freshly baked bread is ready in approximately 2-1/2 hours.

The secret to making good homemade bread is to develop the elasticity of the dough. It is important to begin with a high protein bread flour such as hard red wheat flour.

In my kitchen I have a Bosch kitchen machine with a heavy duty kneading arm and a flour mill for milling fresh flour. I make 5 large loaves of bread at one time. After they are baked and cooled, I bag the loaves individually in plastic bags and freeze all but one of them. Whole grain breads, being high in natural fiber, dry out rather quickly, so freezing them until needed keeps them moist and fresh longer.

I simply mill the flour, put all the bread ingredients into the mixer bowl and let it knead on low speed for 10 minutes. We skip the by-hand kneading, the rising in the bulk, punching down and rising again.

The dough is ready to go right into the pans after 10 minutes of mixing. In less than 1-1/2 hours, 5 loaves of freshly baked bread are coming out of the oven.

In this chapter you will find a great variety of whole grain bread recipes for dough hook kitchen machines, by-hand methods and automatic bread maker.

Weevils are smarter than people when it comes to knowing whether food is fit to eat. They always turn up their noses at white flour or bread in your cupboard if whole wheat is available. So why not be as smart as they are and eat whole wheat bread instead of white.

> "Back of the loaf is the fluffy flour,
>   And back of the flour the mill
> And back of the mill is the wheat, and the shower,
>   And the sun, and the Father's will."
>   Maltbie D. Babcock

1. **DO USE WHOLE WHEAT FLOUR.**

The milling of wheat into refined white flour *removes*, among other nutrients:

60% of the calcium	57% of the pantothenic acid
71% of the phosphorus	68% of the riboflavin
85% of the magnesium	88% of the niacin
77% of the potassium	97% of the thiamine
78% of the sodium	94% of the pyridoxine
All of the bran	All of the fiber
All of the germ	

PLUS, many trace elements also essential to life and health are removed:

40% of the chromium
86% of the manganese
76% of the iron
89% of the cobalt
68% of the copper
78% of the zinc
48% of the molybdenum

TYPES OF WHEAT

There are two broad classes of wheat: hard and soft. Most of that grown in Oregon and Washington is soft white wheat. Hard red wheat is grown in Montana, the Dakotas and the Great Plain States. Hard white wheat is available on a limited basis now. It yields a lighter colored bread than the hard red wheat flour.

Hard wheats tend to be higher in protein content and are excellent for breadmaking flours. Softer wheats are lower in protein and are chiefly milled into flour for cakes, cookies, pastries, and crackers. Today, all-purpose flour is a blend of approximately 75 percent (75%) hard red wheat and 25 percent (25%) soft white wheat so it is suitable for many baking purposes.

A hard amber colored wheat called durum is grown especially for the macaroni and pasta market. North Dakota is the principal durum wheat growing state.

2. **COMBINING SEVERAL KINDS OF FLOUR IN A BREAD RECIPE** greatly enhances the nutritional quality of the bread, making a good quality protein as well. Wheat is the only grain that has sufficient gluten to give a light, elastic, stable loaf of bread. Therefore, when combining several kinds of grain flours in one recipe, be sure to use at least 65 percent wheat flour. For a 4-loaf bread recipe, replace only 2 cups whole wheat flour with other grain flour.

   The high gluten content of hard wheat flour makes it best for breadmaking. A mixture of flours is more nutritious than only one, as the elements of one will supplement the elements of the other.

3. **FRESHLY GROUND FLOUR** gives superior dough, better flavor and more nutrition. While whole grains are in the kernel form, the nutrients are sealed in, and the kernels will keep for years and years with no nutrient loss. Once grains are ground into flour, thousands of surface areas are exposed, oxidation sets in, and nutrients are lost. It has been estimated that most of the vitamin E of whole wheat flour oxidizes away within 72 hours after grinding.

4. **ADDING SOY FLOUR TO WHOLE WHEAT BREAD** gives a superior finished product. Soy + whole wheat = complete protein. Soy flour is the richest in protein of all known foods, except dried egg whites, and it is one of the richest sources per pound of the entire vitamin B-complex. It is almost starch free and gives an appreciable alkaline reaction. Soy flour prevents staling and helps to keep bread moist. Soy flour gives quicker browning. To prevent overbrowning, turn oven temperature down 25 degrees for last half of the baking or cover tops of loaves with foil. Add 1/2 to 1 cup soy flour for a 4-loaf batch. Too much soy flour gives a strong flavor.

5. **KEEP THE TEMPERATURE OF THE DOUGH RIGHT.** An off-flavor develops in dough that is allowed to get too warm. Too cool a temperature prolongs the rising. Start the dough with 110-degree water. Let the dough rise at 84 degrees room temperature for best results.

6. **SALT AND FAT** both retard the growth of the yeast and should not be added to a yeast mixture until it has grown strong and lively by feeding on sugar and starch.

7. **DEVELOP THE GLUTEN IN THE WHEAT FLOUR** in the batter by beating thoroughly before adding other flours which have no gluten.

8. **ALWAYS PREHEAT THE OVEN** before the bread is ready to go in. It is a good idea to turn it on when you start molding the loaves, as this warms the kitchen and helps the bread to rise quickly.

9. **GLUTEN FLOUR** is an elastic protein wheat flour that gives cohesiveness to the dough. If your bread seems heavy, try adding gluten flour (purchase at a health food store) to the dough for light, elastic bread (1/2 to 1 cup for a 4-loaf batch of bread).

10. **VITAMIN C TRICK**. To achieve whole grain bread that rises higher, add a 100 mg. tablet of vitamin C, crushed, to the dough. It strengthens the cell walls of the dough, allowing for greater expansion.

11. **DOUGH ENHANCER**, a commercially prepared product, combines vitamin C., lecithin and other ingredients to give whole grain breads a lighter, fluffier texture and help the bread stay moist longer. Dough Enhancer is available from Bosch/Magic Mill dealers. A homemade substitute for it is soy lecithin plus Vitamin C. To a 4-loaf batch of bread dough, add 2 tbsp. lecithin and 200-300 mg. Vitamin C. powder. (Crush 1 Vitamin. C tablet with the back of a spoon.)

12. **YEAST**. Buying dry yeast by the pound or in bulk rather than in individual packages saves considerable money and is fresher, giving better results in your bread. One tablespoon dry yeast granules equals 1 individual package or 1 cake compressed yeast. One pound dry yeast granules equals approximately 48 tablespoons. Store dry yeast in freezer or refrigerator to preserve freshness. Water that is too hot kills the yeast. Water that

is too cool will fail to activate it. 110° F. water is ideal for activating dry yeast. (Cooler for compressed yeast.) To test yeast to determine if it is good: add 1 tbsp. yeast plus 1 tsp. sugar to 1/2 c. warm water. It should bubble within 5-10 minutes. If bubbling does not occur, discard the yeast and purchase new yeast. Old, inactive yeast will yield a heavy bread with inadequate leavening action.

INSTANT YEAST is now available and widely used by home bakers. It gives excellent results. Use 1/3 less of instant yeast than active dry yeast. Instant yeast can stand hotter water and does not need to be dissolved separately. Add it directly to the flour during the last half of the recipe. If you forget the yeast and add it at the end, the bread still turns out great.

13. **POTATO WATER** (water in which potatoes have been cooked) works magic in bread—not only helping to keep bread moist, but hastens rising. Use potato water in place of plain water in any bread recipe. Simply cook several chopped potatoes in extra amount of water. Use the water for bread.

14. **RISING OF THE DOUGH**. Don't let the yeast dough rise too high—double in bulk only. Better to punch it down to rise again than to let it over rise. The gluten may be injured if it is allowed to stand too long before being punched down. It will develop an off flavor and texture.

15. **HOW FULL TO FILL BREAD PANS WITH DOUGH**:
1/2 to 2/3 full.

16. **SHAPING THE LOAVES**. To achieve a well-shaped loaf of bread (avoiding finished loaf that is humpy in the middle and skinny on the ends) make a rectangle of dough that is rolled up into a tight roll. The roll should be a little longer than the length of your bread pan. Place the roll of dough into the pan. With your hands open flat, slip hands down, one on each end, between the ends of the loaf and ends of pan. This will push ends of your loaf down nicely and square off the ends.

17. **WHEN TO PUT BREAD INTO OVEN.** When bread dough in pans is doubled in bulk and ready to bake, a slight indentation with the finger into the side of the loaf will partially remain. If indentation completely stays, the bread has over-risen. If indentation pops back out, bread has not sufficiently risen. Bread allowed to over-rise will have an inferior texture and flavor. For a better texture, you can punch down the dough and reshape the loaf, letting it rise again in the pan before baking. Indentation that partially pops out is just right.

18. **OVEN SPRING.** If you put the bread into bake at the right time, not over-raising or under-raising it, the loaves will rise higher in the oven while baking. This is called "oven spring." Over-raised bread may fall in the oven.

19. **WHEN IS THE BREAD BAKED ENOUGH?** When baked properly, bread will be golden brown in color. When tapped, it will sound hollow. When smelled, no taint of yeast should be present. Remove the hot loaf of bread from the pan with potholders and smell the bottom of the loaf for the presence of yeast. If you smell a yeasty smell, return it to the oven to bake a little longer.

20. **"JUST-OUT-OF-THE-OVEN"** is difficult to digest. Bread should be at least 12 hours old before it is eaten.

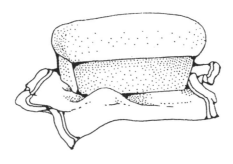

BREAD DISASTERS: SYMPTOMS & DIAGNOSES

FAULT	POSSIBLE CAUSES	POSSIBLE REMEDIES
Excessive Volume	Too much yeast, Too little salt	Reduce yeast to 2 to 3%; check weighing procedures.
	Excess dough	Reduce scaling weights.
	Overproofed	Reduce proofing time.
	Too cool oven	Increase temperature.
Poor Volume	Weak flour, low in protein	Add 1/2 c. gluten flour/4-loaf batch, or use a stronger flour, at
	Flour too old or new	least 12% protein. Use aged flour;
	Lack of leavening	check age of flour. Use good yeast and handle it properly; have dough at proper temperature; reduce quantity of salt.
	Undermixing	Increase mixing times until gluten is properly developed; proper volume of dough to mixer is also a factor to check.
	Overfermented dough	Reduce fermentation time.
	Overmixing	Reduce mixing.
	Improper proofing	Proof between 90°F and 100°F and 80 to 85% relative humidity; watch proofing time and maintain proper ratio between fermentation and proofing procedures.
	Too hot oven	Reduce temperature.
Too Dark Crust	Excess sugar or milk	Reduce.
	Overmixing	Reduce mixing.
	Dough too young	Increase fermentation and proof
	Too hot oven	periods. Correct oven tempera-
	Too long baking	tures. Reduce baking time.
Too Pale or Dull Color on Crust	Wrong proportion or lack of ingredients	Check ratios of sugar, salt, or milk; increase ingredients to
	Soft water	proper ratios. Increase salt or add
	Over-fermentation	conditioner. Reduce temperature
	Excessive dusting flour	or time of fermentation. Use minimum flour when handling
	Too high proof temperature	dough. Reduce temperature.
	Cool oven	Increase temperature.
Spotted Crust	Improper mixing	Follow correct mixing procedures and sequence of adding ingredi-
	Excess dusting flour	ents. Reduce dusting flour.
	Excess humidity in proofing	Reduce relative humidity to between 80 and 85%.

BREAD DISASTERS: SYMPTOMS & DIAGNOSES

FAULT	POSSIBLE CAUSES	POSSIBLE REMEDIES
Hard Crust or Blisters	Lack of sugar	Increase sugars, check weighing of ingredients.
	Slack dough	Reduce liquid; check mixing.
	Improper mixing	Check mixing procedures and sequence of ingredient addition.
	Old or young dough	Correct fermentation time.
	Improper molding	Correct procedures.
	Cool oven or too much top heat	Check damper handling procedures and oven temperatures; check heating elements and heat source to see if functioning properly; check oven circulation.
	Cooling too rapidly	Cool more slowly; keep out of drafts. Reduce brushing of fat after make-up.
	Too much fat on product	
Poor Shape	Improper make-up	Correct procedures.
	Overproofing	Reduce.
Flat Top or Sharp Corners	New flour	Age flour six to eight months under cool, air-tight conditions.
	Low salt	Increase, check weighing procedures. Reduce liquid; check mixing. Increase fermentation time.
	Slack dough	
	Young dough	
Excessive Break on Side ("Oven Shred")	Overmixing	Reduce mixing.
	Improper molding	Check molding, especially seam folds; place seam folds down on bottom of pan.
	Young dough	Correct; check proofing time.
	Hot oven	Reduce temperatures.
Thick Crust	Low shortening, sugar, or milk	Increase; check scaling procedures.
	Mixing improper	Correct mixing procedures.
	Improper proofing	Correct temperature, relative humidity, or time of proofing; check for wet crusts after proofing. Correct fermentation and/or proofing time. Correct temperatures and times.
	Old dough	
	Improper baking	

BREAD DISASTERS: SYMPTOMS & DIAGNOSES

FAULT	POSSIBLE CAUSES	POSSIBLE REMEDIES
Tough Crust	Old or young dough	Check fermentation times.
	Improper mixing	Correct.
	Excess proof or wrong proof conditions	Correct.
	Oven cold	Correct.
Lack of Break or Shred	Soft water	Increase salt or use conditioner.
	Slack dough	Reduce water substantially; check mixing.
	Improper fermentation or proof time	Correct.
	Too hot an oven	Correct temperatures.
Too Close	Low yeast	Increase, check weighing procedures.
	Underproofing	Correct.
	Excess dough in pan	Check scaling procedures.
Too Coarse or Open Grain	Hard or alkaline water	Add lemon or conditioner.
	Old dough	Reduce fermentation time.
	Slack dough	Reduce liquid, check mixing times.
	Improper molding	Correct.
	Overproofing	Reduce time or check temperatures.
	Improper pan size	Check.
	Cold oven	Increase oven temperature.
	Excess greasing	Check oiling or greasing of dough.
	Low protein flour	Use flour with at least 12% protein.
Gray Crumb	High dough temperature or over fermentation.	Check mixing fermentation and proof temperatures and times.
	Cold oven	Check temperatures and
	Pans greasy	conditions of baking. Check
	Yeast water temperature too low	greasing. Active dry yeast requires 105°-115°F water.

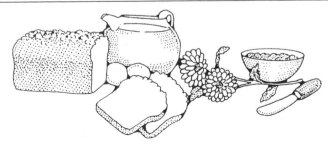

BREAD DISASTERS: SYMPTOMS & DIAGNOSES

FAULT	POSSIBLE CAUSES	POSSIBLE REMEDIES
Streaked Crumb	Improper mixing Too slack or stiff dough	Check ingredient sequence of adding in mixing. Check liquid or flour quantities; check to see if proper mixing times given.
	Excessive oil or grease, or dusting flour used	Correct.
	Crusting of dough in fermentation	Brush with fat; cover to prevent moisture loss.
Poor Texture	Alkaline or very hard water	Use conditioner or lemon.
	Too slack or too stiff dough	Reduce or increase ingredients to correct ratios; check mixing.
	High sugar or excess yeast	Check ingredient ratios.
	Lack of shortening	Increase.
	High dough temperature	Reduce liquid temperature or temperatures during fermentation or proofing.
	Overfermentation or overproofing	Reduce.
	Poor gluten quality flour	Use flour with at least 12% protein.

Adapted from *Quantity Food Production,* L.H. Kotschevar, McCutchan Publishing Corp.

MARCELLA'S BASIC MIXER BREAD

The following bread recipes are designed for a large capacity electric mixer such as a Bosch Universal mixer. Recipes may be easily adapted for smaller mixers by cutting in half or converted to a by-hand method by adding a kneading step and a rising-in-the-bulk step to the recipe.

10 c. hard red wheat (or purchase 16 cups freshly ground whole wheat bread flour from your local health food store).

6 c. very warm water (115°F.) (Try 1/2 water and 1/2 buttermilk for light rolls and bread)

1/3 c. oil (to omit oil use 1/3 c. applesauce and potato water for the liquid see p. 84)

1/3 c. honey or molasses (or dates blended smooth with water)

1-1/2 tbsp. salt

3 tbsp. active dry yeast (or 2 tbsp. Saf Instant yeast)

Optional tricks of the trade:

3 tbsp. commercially prepared dough enhancer or 1 (100 mg) vit. C tablet crushed, and 1 tbsp. soy lecithin to yield a lighter loaf, higher volume and fine grain.

1/3 - 1/2 c. gluten flour (buy from health food store; gives elastic, noncrumbly texture)

1. Grind the 10 cups of wheat in home flour mill on the fine setting. This will yield 16 cups flour. For variety use 2 cups other freshly milled flours in the recipe as part of the 16 c.—such as soy, barley, oats, millet, rye, etc.

2. Measure into mixer bowl equipped with a dough hook: water, oil, honey, salt, vitamin C, lecithin and gluten flour.

3. Add 9 cups of the freshly milled flour. Mix just enough to blend in all flour to smooth consistency.

4. Add the 3 tbsp. dry yeast and mix again just enough to blend.

5. Add 3 cups more flour; mix to absorb all flour. From here on continue to add flour gradually with mixer running (1/4 to 1/2 cup at a time) until dough forms a ball and begins to clean sides of bowl. You may add 1 to 3 cups to achieve this consistency. The amount

MARCELLA'S BASIC MIXER BREAD (Cont.)

of flour varies according to protein and fiber content of the grain. You may not need all the flour, or perhaps you may need a bit more than called for.

6. Let dough knead on LOW SPEED for 10 minutes. Bread kneaded by machine eliminates kneading by hand or rising in bulk. One rising (in the bread pans) is all that is required because the machine develops the elasticity of the gluten in the whole wheat dough very efficiently.

7. Optional: Prepare oven for rising of the bread. Letting the bread rise in the oven shortens the rising time. Preheat oven to 150°F. Turn off. Prepare pans by wiping them with solid shortening or with homemade "Pam" (two parts oil to one part liquid lecithin).

8. Transfer dough to lightly floured or oiled board and form into 5 loaves (for pans measuring 8-1/2 x 2-1/2) or fill pans 2/3 full of dough. Sprinkle tops with sesame seeds after wetting tops lightly with water. Place loaves in warmed oven to rise or on counter.

9. Cover loaves with dry towel allowing bread to rise in oven until doubled in size (just rounding over tops of pans). When you poke bread with fingertip, a slight indentation should remain in the bread to indicate readiness—about 30 minutes.

10. When the dough has risen, remove towel, turn oven to 350°F. Without removing the bread from oven, bake for 45 minutes or until done. Baked bread will be golden brown, sound hollow when tapped, and will not smell yeasty.

11. Remove bread from oven, turn out of pans immediately and cool on cooking rack. YIELD: 5 large loaves

WHOLE WHEAT BAGELS

(Split bagels and serve warm with light cream cheese or homemade almond cheese.) Bagels with soup make a delightful supper.

1. Preheat oven to 450°F.
2. In large kettle bring 2 quarts water to a boil. Add 2 tbsp. brown sugar.
3. Using bread dough from the basic recipe, shape bagels like doughnuts by pinching off pieces of dough, roll into round balls and poke hole in center with thumb, as for doughnuts. Or roll dough flat and cut with donut cutter.
4. Drop bagels into the boiling water one at a time and when they come to the surface turn them over. Boil one minute longer.
5. Place bagels on oiled cookie sheet and bake 10-15 minutes or until golden brown and crisp.

Variations: Dip the tops of wet bagels into sesame seeds, poppy seeds, dry onion flakes, or caraway seeds. Delicious.

POCKET BREAD

1. Using bread dough from the basic recipe, divide dough into balls about the size of a golf ball.
2. Roll each ball into a circle 5 inches in diameter using rolling pin.
3. Place rolled-out circles of dough on a clean dish towel. Cover with other half of towel or another dish towel. Let rest 30 minutes to 1 hour.
4. Preheat oven to 450°F.
5. Lift pocket bread up from the towel and turn *upside down* onto ungreased cookie sheet.
6. Bake at 450°F for 6 minutes in preheated oven. During baking a pocket is magically created.
7. Cool in covered kettle or plastic bag to keep crust soft. When cool, flatten pocket breads and store in plastic bread bag.
8. To serve, cut in half and fill with falafal filling (p. 63), chopped tomatoes, lettuce and dressing. Or stuff with any yummy filling of your choice.

WHOLE WHEAT PIZZA

1. Preheat oven to 450° to 500° F.
2. Roll out approximately 1/2 lb. basic bread dough with rolling pin (or stretch out with fist) a little larger than size of your pizza pans, cookie sheets, or pie plates to 1/8-inch thickness.
3. Place dough on lightly greased pizza pan (or sprinkle pan with cornmeal).
4. Prebake the crust for about 5 minutes before adding pizza sauce and toppings. (Pizza Sauce recipe below or Quick Pizza Sauce p. 262.)
5. Coat with sauce and sprinkle generously with sliced vegetables, such as sliced olives, green pepper, onion, mushrooms, bean sprouts.
6. Drizzle cashew pimento cheese over top.
7. Bake in 350°F oven for 20 to 25 minutes or 425° for 15 minutes.

HOMEMADE PIZZA SAUCE

2 tbsp. olive oil	COMBINE ingredients in skillet. Cover and cook over low heat for 1-1/2 hours.
3/4 cup chopped onion	
1 clove garlic, minced	
1 quart tomatoes	
1 6-oz. can tomato paste	YIELDS: 5 c. pizza sauce. Freeze the extra for next time.
2 tbsp. chopped parsley	
2 bay leaves	
1 tsp. basil	
1-1/2 tsp. salt	
1 tsp. oregano	

Optional: 3 cups homemade ground gluten
   (beef flavored) OR 1 can vegetarian burger

CASHEW PIMENTO CHEESE

1/2 c. water	WHIZ all ingredients together in blender until smooth. Drizzle over pizza before baking.
1/2 c. cashews	
1/2 tsp. salt	
2 tbsp. oil	
2-1/2 tbsp. lemon juice	
1 4-oz. jar pimentos	
1/2 tsp. onion salt	
1/2 tsp. garlic salt	
1-1/2 tbsp. nutritional food yeast flakes	

BURGER BUNS

1. Using bread dough from the basic recipe, divide dough into balls about the size of a small apple (little smaller than a tennis ball).

2. Place on greased cookie sheet 2 inches apart. Cover with towel and let rise until double in size (about 45 minutes). Gently flatten the buns with a second cookie sheet or flat pan.

3. Bake at 350° for 20-25 minutes or until nicely browned.

4. Cover to cool so crust will stay soft.

Note: For softer crust, brush dough with oil before it rises or after baking.

FRUIT-NUT BREAKFAST ROLLS
(cinnamon-type rolls)

1. Make a filling in blender by whizzing until smooth: **1/2 c. pineapple juice, 40 dates and 1 banana.**

2. Grease baking pan and spread a little of the filling mixture on bottom of pan. Sprinkle with chopped nuts.

3. Roll out about **2 to 2-1/2 pounds of the basic bread dough** to a 1/4-inch thick rectangle on a lightly floured board.

4. Spread filling mixture over dough.

5. Sprinkle with raisins, chopped nuts, and cinnamon substitute (p. 226). Roll up as for a jelly roll.

6. Slice into 1-inch thick rolls and turn cut side down onto fruit mixture in baking pan.

7. Cover and let rise 45 minutes or until pan is full of rolls run together.

8. Bake at 350°F 20-30 minutes until done. Leave rolls in pan to cool.

9. Frost while warm with the following glaze.

VARIATIONS FOR BASIC BREAD DOUGH

GLAZE FOR SWEET ROLLS

1 c. dry milk powder (tofu powder or soy milk powder works well)
1/4 c. honey
1 tbsp. lemon juice
1 tsp. vanilla
2 tbsp. water or as needed to make drizzle (pourable) consistency

BEAT together until smooth. Drizzle over warm rolls. Do not make until ready to use as it thickens upon standing.

SEVEN GRAIN — FOUR SEED BREAD

Use the basic bread recipe except replace whole wheat flour with seven grain flour (recipe below) and add the following ingredients:

1/4 c. poppy seeds
1 c. sesame seeds
1 c. sunflower seeds
1 c. pumpkin seeds or soaked millet
1/2 c. gluten flour

SEVEN GRAIN FLOUR

For 5 lbs. flour blend together the following grains and grind in a flour mill. Use in Seven-Grain Bread above.

7 c. hard red wheat berries
1-3/4 c. soft white wheat berries
2/3 c. whole oats
1/2 c. whole barley
1/2 c. millet
1/2 c. brown rice
1/2 c. whole rye

Make 4 kinds of bread from one batch of dough!

FRENCH ONION BREAD

1/4 tsp. onion salt
1 tbsp. onion soup mix (dry)
2 tbsp. nutritional food
  yeast flakes
1/8 tsp. oregano
1/4 tsp. celery seed
1 tsp. Italian herbs or dill
  weed
2 tbsp. lightly toasted
  sesame seeds, ground
  (optional)

TAKE 1/4 of a batch of Marcella's basic bread dough and add all ingredients by kneading them into the dough.

ROLL out into rectangle. Roll up like French bread. Place on greased cookie sheet or French bread pan. Let rise until doubled.
BAKE at 375° F for 35 minutes.

RYE BREAD

TAKE 1/4 of the basic bread dough and add **1/2 tsp. anise seed** and **2 tbsp. caraway seeds**. Shape into rectangular loaf and place in greased bread pan or shape into circles as for peasant bread and place on greased cookie sheet. Slash top 3 times with sharp knife. Let rise and bake at 375°F for 35 minutes.

GARLIC BREAD

TAKE 1/4 of the basic bread dough. Make Garlic Bread by rolling a rectangle at least 14" wide, then roll up like a jelly roll. Place on greased cookie sheet and slash diagonally at 1-1/2" interval with sharp knife. Stretch loaf slightly, sprinkle with garlic salt and let rise. Bake like regular bread at 375° for 35 minutes.

RAISIN — NUT BREAD

TAKE 1-1/2 lbs. of the Basic Bread dough (enough for one standard loaf). Make Raisin-Nut Bread by adding **1 tsp. vanilla, 1/2 c. nuts, 1/2 c. raisins, 1 tsp. lemon or orange rind, 1/4 c. brown sugar, and 1 tsp. cinnamon substitute** (see p. 226). Shape into regular loaf and bake like regular bread at 350° for 35 to 40 minutes.

RYE BREAD (Electric mixer method)

3 c. hot potato water
1 c. buttermilk (or 1 c. warm water + 1/4 c. buttermilk powder)
1/3 c. honey
1/3 c. molasses
1 tbsp. salt
6 tbsp. caraway seeds
1/2 c. to 1 c. gluten flour
4 c. rye flour
5 c. whole wheat flour
2 tbsp. yeast

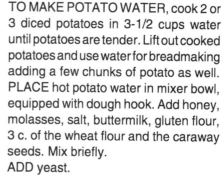

TO MAKE POTATO WATER, cook 2 or 3 diced potatoes in 3-1/2 cups water until potatoes are tender. Lift out cooked potatoes and use water for breadmaking adding a few chunks of potato as well.

PLACE hot potato water in mixer bowl, equipped with dough hook. Add honey, molasses, salt, buttermilk, gluten flour, 3 c. of the wheat flour and the caraway seeds. Mix briefly.

ADD yeast.

WITH MIXER RUNNING on low speed, add the rye flour gradually, then as much more whole wheat flour as needed to bring dough to a consistency where it is pulling away from the sides of the bowl.

LET KNEAD on low speed for 10 minutes.

REMOVE dough to floured board. Divide and shape into rectangular, round, French style loaves or into dinner rolls. Place in greased pans.

COVER with dish towel and let rise until double in warm place.

BAKE at 350°F. Regular loaves 40-45 minutes; dinner rolls 20-25 minutes.

REMOVE from pans immediately and place on cooling rack to cool.

YIELD: 4 loaves.

SWEDISH RYE BREAD VARIATION

Follow Rye Bread recipe above except omit caraway seeds. Add: **3 tbsp. orange rind, 4-1/2 tsp. fennel seed, ground,** and **3 tbsp. anise seed, ground.**

MARCELLA'S ORANGE-RAISIN-NUT BREAD

2 c. walnuts, chopped
2 c. raisins
2 c. boiling water
4 tsp. active dry yeast
1 c. warm water
1/2 c. honey
2 c. orange juice (lukewarm)
1/4 c. oil
11 c. finely ground whole wheat flour
1 tbsp. salt
4 tbsp. grated orange peel
2 tsp. cinnamon substitute (p. 226)

PREPARE walnuts by toasting slightly in 300°F oven.

RINSE raisins in cold water and pour the 2 c. boiling water over them in a pan. Simmer for 5 minutes. Drain immediately. Save liquid.

SETTING raisins aside, pour raisin water (adding more water as needed to make 2 c.) into a blender. Using a sharp paring knife cut stripes of orange peel from 2-3 oranges and add to blender. Whiz to pulverize orange peel.

PLACE raisin water with peel in electric mixer bowl equipped with dough hook, along with the honey, orange juice, and oil.

ADD 8 c. of the whole wheat flour and the salt and mix on speed 1 (low) just until combined nicely with liquids. Add yeast. With motor running on speed 1 gradually add more flour until dough is stiff enough to pull clean away from the sides of the bowl (2-4 c. more). Let knead on speed 1 for 8 minutes.

STOP mixer and add the raisins and nuts all at once. Resume mixing on Speed 1 two more minutes.

REMOVE dough to lightly floured board. Knead a few moments to coat with flour and create a nice round ball of dough.

DIVIDE in four. Roll into rounds and place on greased cookie sheets (2 per sheet) or into greased bread pans.

LET rise until double in size.

BAKE at 350°F oven for about 55 minutes or until done. Remove immediately from bread pans.

YIELD: 4 loaves.

HERBED SEED BREAD

4 c. water
1/2 c. oil
1 tbsp. poppy seeds
1 tbsp. caraway seeds
1 tbsp dill seeds
1 Tbsp. celery seeds
1/4 c. raw onion, grated
1/4 c. fresh parsley, minced
1 tsp. oregano, minced
1 tbsp. salt
2 tbsp. yeast
1/4 c. honey
1 c. tofu or yogurt
1/3 c. sesame seeds
1/3 c. sunflower seeds
8-9 c. whole wheat flour
2 c. unbleached flour

PLACE 2 c. of the water in blender with a few chunks onion and big handful parsley sprigs. Jog 20-30 times. Pour mixture into saucepan and add oil, first four kinds of seeds, oregano and salt. Bring to a boil, remove from heat, and add other 2 c. water. Add honey and 5 cups of the flour. Mix to blend. Add the yeast, tofu (crumbled), sesame and sunflower seeds. Gradually add more flour until dough pulls clean from sides of bowl. Knead on speed 1 (low) for 10 minutes. Remove to floured board. Shape loaves. Round cans are fun. Fill cans 1/2 full. Let rise until double. Bake 350°F 40 min.

YIELD: 4 loaves.

MILLET BREAD

4 c. lukewarm water
2 pkg. yeast
1 tbsp. honey
1 tbsp. salt
1 tbsp. oil
2 c. unbleached white flour
3 c. whole wheat flour
4 c. whole grain millet flour

MAKE and bake as any bread recipe, adding more flour as needed for correct consistency.

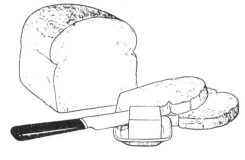

FRENCH BREAD

4-1/2 c. very warm water, 115°F
1 tbsp. sugar or honey
1-1/2 to 2 tbsp. salt
2 tbsp. yeast
9-10 cups hard wheat flour (try 3 c. unbleached white, 1 c. gluten flour and 5 to 6 c. whole wheat flour)

PLACE the very warm tap water, sugar, salt and about half of the flour in electric mixer bowl. Using the dough hook, mix until smooth.

ADD the 2 tbsp. yeast and mix. With mixer running on speed 1 (low) continue adding remainder of flour until a stiff dough is formed. Knead on low speed until smooth and elastic, about 10 minutes.

WITH mixer lids on, let the dough rise until light.

PUNCH DOUGH DOWN by turning on to speed 1 for a few seconds. Remove dough from bowl and separate into 4 portions. Let rest 15 minutes.

SHAPE into long, oval loaves, and place on greased baking sheets. Score loaves diagonally with long, shallow cuts using a sharp knife. Brush with a glaze made of 1/2 cup water with 1 tsp. cornstarch. Sprinkle with sesame seeds if desired.

BAKE in a 400°F oven until golden brown and done, about 35-45 minutes.

YIELD: 4 large loaves French bread. Store in paper bags to keep crusts crisp.

BUTTERMILK BURGER BUNS

This is a tender, featherlight dough. The buttermilk conditions the dough to give the bread its special tenderness. For the lightest, most delicate version, use very finely ground soft wheat flour or half soft and half hard wheat flour.

1-1/4 c. hot water (Potato water, p. 84, is excellent for lightness)

4 tbsp. margarine, melted

1/4 c. honey

2 tsp. salt

2 tbsp. Dough Enhancer

3 tbsp. active dry yeast

1-1/4 c. buttermilk, warm

5-1/2 to 7-1/2 c. whole wheat flour (half hard and half soft wheat or all soft)

MILL 3 cups wheat (part soft and part hard wheat or all soft wheat.) in flour mill on fine setting to yield 5-1/2-7 c. flour.

IN electric mixer bowl (with doughhook in place) add in order: water, butter, honey, salt, Dough Enhancer (optional), and 2 cups of the flour. Put splash ring on. Mix the ingredients on speed 1 (low).

ADD THE YEAST and mix again on speed 1. Add the buttermilk. Add more flour gradually until dough begins to pull away from the sides of the mixing bowl. Knead until the gluten in your wheat is properly developed (about 10 minutes).

WET HANDS and remove dough from mixing bowl to oiled board or counter. Divide the dough into balls about the size of a golf ball, egg, or small apple. Let balls of dough rest 10 minutes to relax the dough.

REROLL each ball of dough into a tight round ball of dough and place on greased cookie sheet two inches apart. Flatten each ball of dough with rolling pin (or your hand) so that they are as big around as you want the finished bun to be: they

BUTTERMILK BURGER BUNS (Cont.)

will rise up, but not out. If you want seeds on the buns, dampen the surface of the rolls by brushing on milk or water and sprinkling with sesame seeds.

COVER and put buns in a warm humid place to rise. (In a slightly warmed oven with a pan of boiling water on the rack below them, for example). Give them plenty of time to become light. A gentle finger indentation doesn't disappear. The dough will feel very spongy.

BAKE at 350°F for 15-20 min. or until light, golden brown. Bake in top half of oven so bottoms of rolls will not get too crusty. Put a pan of boiling water in the bottom of the oven for the first 10 minutes.

REMOVE BUNS to cooling rack. Cool 10 minutes and then finish cooling in plastic bread bags to keep the crust soft. Store in freezer and use as needed with your favorite burger patties with all the trimmings. YIELD: 2 dozen.

WHOLE GRAIN, NO-SUGAR BEAR CLAWS

Dough:
1 c. unsweetened pineapple
  juice
2 oz. skim milk powder
1/4 c. milk

1/2 c. oil
2 tsp. salt
2 tbsp. dry baking yeast
2 eggs (or 1/2 c. egg beater)
1 tsp. vanilla
1 lemon rind, grated
1 orange rind, grated
4 c. whole wheat flour

Date Butter Filling:
2 lbs. pitted dates, blended with
water over low heat for smooth
consistency.

Glaze:
Unsweetened pineapple juice.

Topping:
Slivered almonds or chopped
peanuts.

DISSOLVE yeast in warm pineapple juice. Add oil, other ingredients and knead 10 minutes on speed 1 in kitchen machine using dough hook. Add more or less flour until dough pulls clean from sides of bowl. Chill dough for at least 2 hours.

ROLL dough into rectangular shape wide enough for three 5" strips of dough. Spread with date butter down middle of dough lengthwise. Fold one side over the date butter. Brush other side with water and fold on top of side folded first. Flatten a little. Cut claws. Shrink it down so that dough is in a relaxed (rather than drawn) position. Brush top with juice. Sprinkle sliced almonds or peanuts on top.

COVER bear claws with tea towel. Let rise until double in size in a warm place. Bake at 350°F until golden brown—about 12-15 minutes. Watch closely. YIELD: Approximately 4 dozen bear claws.

BASIC SWEET DOUGH

1. Heat to 125° F:
   2 c. milk (or water + 1/2 c. powder milk)
   1 cube margarine
   1 c. water or fruit juice

*2. Mill in flour mill on fine setting:
   3 c. hard wheat
   3 c. soft white wheat
   Then combine in large bowl:
   8 c. freshly milled flour mixture
   4 c. unbleached white flour (hi-protein bread flour)

3. Place in electric mixer bowl equipped with dough hook:
   heated milk mixture
   3/4 cup honey
   2 tsp. salt
   4 tbsp. natural Magic Dough Enhancer (or 1 250-mg. Vit. C + 2 tbsp. lecithin)
   2 eggs (or egg whites or Ener-G Replacer, see p. 260 for additional egg replacers)

4. Add and mix briefly:
   6 c. of the mixed flours

5. Add:
   4 tbsp. granulated dry yeast

6. Add:
   4 to 6 c. more flour.
   Add just until flour begins to clean sides of bowl - a bit stickier than normal, because of the milk and eggs the dough gets much tighter as it kneads than a regular bread recipe.

7. Let knead on speed 1 (low) for 10 minutes. Remove from bowl and shape into sweet rolls as desired.

*Variation:
   for 100% whole wheat sweet dough, mill on fine setting:
   2 c. hard wheat
   5 c. soft white wheat
Stir to mix evenly:
   12 c. of the freshly milled flour mixture.
Proceed as outlined above in steps 3 through 7.

LINDA'S WHEAT-FREE BREAD

Mill each grain individually:
> **3 c. rye**
> **2 c. quick oats**
> **3 c. rice (short grain if available)**
> **1/4 to 1/2 c. soy**

In electric mixer bowl place:
> **5-1/2 c. water (125°) or: (1-1/2 c. apple juice + 4 c. water)**
> **1 c. applesauce (if using apple juice omit applesauce)**

Add to above:
> **1/2 c. oil (optional)**
> **1-1/2 tbsp. salt**
> **3 tbsp. dough enhancer**
> **3 tbsp. yeast**
> **6 c. rye flour**
> **6 c. rice flour (use short grain brown rice)**
> **4 c. oatmeal flour**
> **1/2 to 1 c. soy flour (to taste, as this is a strong flavored flour)**

This will make a dough the consistency of cookie dough and will not clean the sides of the bowl. Add exactly the amounts of flour given above.

Knead for 15 minutes on speed 1. Divide into fourths and bake in 4x8" pans that have been well greased. Allow to rise for 45 minutes in a warm oven and then bake at 350°F, for 1 hour.

You will not be able to handle this dough and shape loaves as usual. Scrape dough into pans to fill.

The short grain brown rice that is called for is used for it's finer flour and nicer texture. For the same reason the recipe calls for quick oatmeal rather than whole oats, according to Linda, who came up with this recipe and developed it for her son who has a wheat allergy.

After trying the recipe a couple of times, feel free to vary the ingredients.

BASIC BY-HAND BREAD RECIPE

One basic dough can be turned into eight different bread variations by changing a few ingredients.

6 c. flour (3 unbleached, 3 whole wheat, or any combination)
1-1/2 tsp. salt
2 tbsp. soft margarine
1/4 c. brown sugar or molasses (black strap makes dark bread)
1 c. rolled oats
2 c. boiling water
2 tbsp. yeast (or two packages dry yeast)
1/3 c. lukewarm water

PUT oats into large bowl and pour on boiling water. Let sit for about one-half hour. (Mixture will still be warm and this is important.) In cup dissolve yeast in 110˚F water with 1 tsp. brown sugar and let stand 5 minutes. Add salt, sugar, margarine, and special ingredients of your choice (Variation recipes follow) to the soaked oats. Stir yeast and add to oat mixture. Then stir in flour two cups at a time, beginning and ending with wheat flour when using a combination of grains.

KNEAD by leaving dough in bowl, scatter 1/2 cup flour on top of dough and with heel of hand press into the dough with one quick firm press. With the fingers get hold of the dough and shift it around, sometimes turning it over. Repeat this process over and over with rest of flour for about 10 minutes. If dough is sticky, work in a little more flour. Shape dough into mound in center of bowl and cover with damp towel. Let rise until double. Punch down. Divide dough into two equal portions. Shape into loaves and place in two well-greased bread pans, shaping dough out to ends to cover pans. Cover and let rise again until top is well-rounded. Bake 40 minutes at 350˚ F on rack about 4 inches from bottom of oven. YIELD: 2 loaves

Variation 1: RAISIN AND CITRON BREAD

To the Basic By-Hand Bread recipe, add **1 c. seedless raisins** and **3/4 c. citron, dried fruits and peels.**

Variation 2: HERB BREAD

To the Basic By-Hand Bread recipe, add **2 tsp. crumbled leaf sage, 1 tsp. leaf marjoram, 1/2 tsp. caraway seeds, 1/2 tsp. dried parsley, 1 tsp. dried basil, 1/2 tsp. anise seed, 2 tsp. dried summer savory and 1/2 tsp. powdered thyme.**

Variation 3: POPPY SEED BUBBLE LOAF

INSTEAD of making loaf, pinch off pieces of dough to make tiny balls about 1 inch in diameter. Melt **5 tbsp. margarine.** Measure **1/4 c. poppy seed.** Dip top of each ball in margarine, then seeds and pile into lightly greased 10-inch tube pan, seed side up; let rise. Bake at 375° for about 55 minutes.

Variation 4: ORANGE RAISIN NUT BREAD

Use **2 c. near-boiling orange juice instead of water.** Add **1 tsp. grated orange rind, 1 c. seedless raisins and 1/2 c. chopped walnuts.**

Variation 5: RYE BREAD

Use the following flour mixtures:
   Light: **1 c. rye and 5 c. whole wheat** (standard pan)
   Medium: **2 c. rye and 4 c. whole wheat** (smaller size bread pan)
   Dark: **3 c. rye and 3 c. whole wheat** (smaller size bread pan)

Variation 6: DARK MIXED-GRAIN BREAD

Use flour mixture of **1/2 c. wheat germ, 1/2 c. buckwheat , 1 c. rye,** and **4 c. whole wheat.**

Variation 7: PUMPERNICKEL BREAD

Add **1 tbsp. caraway seed (add to oatmeal mixture), 1 c. bran flakes, 1 c. rye flour,** and **3 c. whole wheat flour.**

Variation 8: SOY GRAHAM BREAD

Use a flour mixture of **1 c. soy flour, 2 c. graham flour,** and **3 c. whole wheat flour.**

WAYFARER'S BREAD (no wheat or yeast)

WAYFARER'S Bread is a great recipe to fill the bill for the person who is allergic to wheat or yeast or where there is no electricity available to mill the grains into flour. This bread is heavy and dense, but delicious. SPROUT grains of your choice until white sprouts appear according to directions in sprouting section of our cookbook.

PUT 2 cups sprouted grains (other than wheat) through a meat and food grinder along with 1/2 c. raisins or dates and 1/2 c. nuts. Mix all three ingredients together and add salt to taste.

MOLD with hands to form a loaf shape. Place in bread pan or on cookie sheet. Bake at 300°F. for about 1 to 1-1/2 hours, or bake in the sun on a flat rock. YIELD: 1 loaf.

AUTO BAKERY BREAD MIX
(for the machine that does it all)

Here's an innovative idea to make automatic breadmaking even quicker. Mix up a big batch of bread mix on the week-end for use during the week. Just add yeast and water to the mix and push start. The breadmaker does the rest!

5 lbs. whole wheat flour or Seven-Grain blend flour*
1/2 c. oil
1 c. brown sugar
1-1/2 c. gluten flour or 4 c. white flour
1/2 c. dough enhancer
2 tbsp. salt

COMBINE all ingredients. (Use the wire whips of your electric kitchen machine to evenly mix the oil with part of the flour before adding remainder of flour and other ingredients.) Store in airtight cannister in refrigerator or freezer.

YIELD: 6 to 7 lbs. of bread mix.

*To mill your own Seven-Grain blend flour see recipe on p. 82.

FOR ONE LOAF OF AUTO BAKERY BREAD:
Add to auto bakery in order given and push start:

2 tsp. yeast
3 c. bread mix
1 c. warm water

OLD-FASHIONED HOECAKES

1-1/2 c. cornmeal
1/2 tsp. salt
1 tbsp. brown sugar
1 tbsp. oil
1 c. boiling water

MIX first 4 ingredients well (electric mixer with wire whip works nicely). POUR boiling water over the mixture and stir well.

DROP spoonfuls of the mixture onto an oiled baking sheet in oblong shapes or mounds.

BAKE at 400°F about 30 minutes.

YIELD: 12 hoecakes.

OLD-FASHIONED CORN PONES

2 c. low fat milk (dairy or
    soy) or water
1/2 tsp. salt
2 tbsp. vegetable oil
2 tbsp. sesame seeds,
    ground in blender or seed
    grinder
1/2 c. soy flour
1/4 c. fine shredded coco-
    nut
1-1/2 to 2 c. cornmeal (use
    1-1/2 to begin and add if
    necessary)

PREHEAT cast iron corn pone or muffin pan. Combine all ingredients and beat well with electric mixer. Adjust the cornmeal to make a soft batter. Sprinkle a little corn meal in bottom of pan for each muffin and spoon batter into the hot pan. Bake immediately at 400°F for 35 minutes. This bread will actually rise about 1/4 inch. Flavor is especially good if you use freshly ground corn. YIELD: 1 dozen.

QUICK CORNBREAD

2 c. water
1 tsp. salt
2 tsp. nut butter or
  equivalent
2 tbsp. sesame seeds,
  ground in nut grinder
1/2 c. soy flour
1/4 c. fine coconut
1-1/2 to 2 c. cornmeal
  (use 1-1/2 c. to begin
  and add if necessary)

COMBINE all ingredients and using an electric mixer, beat well. Adjust the cornmeal to make a soft batter. Heat heavy muffin pan — (I use a heavy iron pan); — sprinkle a little corn meal in bottom of pan for each muffin and spoon batter into the hot pan. Bake immediately 400°F for 35 minutes. This bread will actually rise about 1/4 inch. Flavor is especially good if you use freshly ground corn. YIELD: 12 corn muffins.

YEAST CORNBREAD

2 c. flour
2 c. cornmeal
2 tsp. salt
1/2 c. sugar
6 tbsp. oil
1 pkg. (or 1 tbsp.) active
  dry yeast
2 c. warm water

SPRINKLE yeast on warm water, set aside. Mix flour, cornmeal, salt, sugar, and oil until crumbly. Pour water-yeast mixture over the flour mixture all at once. Stir gently just long enough to mix, then pour into 8x8 square pan. Set in warm place to rise. When it has doubled in bulk, bake at 350°F for 35-40 minutes. If using glass pan, reduce heat to 325°F after 5 minutes and continue baking normal amount of time. YIELD: 12 squares.

BOSTON BROWN BREAD

2/3 c. warm water
2 tbsp. yeast
1 tbsp. brown sugar
1/4 c. whole wheat
  flour
2/3 c. boiling water
1/3 c. molasses (or
  honey)
1/3 c. cold water
2 tbsp. oil
1 c. fine bread crumbs
1/4 tsp. salt
1/4 c. brown sugar
1-1/2 c. seedless
  raisins
1/2 c. rye flour
1/2 c. cornmeal
2/3 c. unbleached
  white flour or whole
  wheat pastry flour

DISSOLVE yeast in the warm water. Add sugar and whole wheat flour. Mix and let rise in warm place 15 minutes. Mix boiling water and molasses; stir well. Add cold water, oil, and bread crumbs to molasses mixture; let stand to soak mixture.

ADD yeast mixture and stir well. Add remaining ingredients. Let rise 15 minutes in warm place; stir down. Fill oiled cans about half full with dough and let rise again for 15-20 minutes. Place in steamer (or on rack in large kettle containing water up to 1/4 the height of the cans). Steam 1-1/2 hours or until done.

NOTE: If steamed in kettle over boiling water, cans may be placed in kettle immediately after filling, rather than waiting for dough to rise the final time. YIELD: 6 small loaves (or 3 large).

YEAST BISCUITS

1 c. very warm water,
  115°F
1 tbsp. brown sugar
5 tbsp. oil
1 tsp. salt
1 c. flour, whole wheat
  or white
1 tbsp. dry baking
  yeast
1-1/2 c. more flour (as
  needed)

STIR TOGETHER first 5 ingredients in mixer bowl. STIR IN: baking yeast. GRADUALLY ADD: more flour until dough is just stiff enough to knead and roll out with rolling pin. KNEAD by machine or by hand 2 minutes. ROLL out to 3/4" thick. Cut with biscuit cutter. Place on greased cookie sheet or over Garbanzo Pot Pie Bake at 400°F. for 25-30 minutes.

PIGS IN A BLANKET: Roll dough about 1/4" thick and cut into 3" x 3" pieces. Wrap diagonally around vegetarian hot dogs or Vegelinks. Let rise 20 minutes. Bake until browned at 400°F. YIELD: 12 biscuits.

BRAN MUFFINS (revised for better nutrition)

ORIGINAL RECIPE

1-1/2 c. white flour
3 tsp. baking powder
1 tsp. salt
1/2 c. sugar
1-1/2 c. all-bran cereal
1-1/4 c. milk
1 egg
1/3 c. shortening
1/2 c. chopped nuts
  (optional)

ADJUSTED RECIPE FOR BETTER NUTRITION

3 tsp. baking yeast
1/3 c. warm water
1/2 tsp. sugar or honey
1-1/4 c. skim milk or soy milk,
  warm
3 tbsp. oil or applesauce
3/4 tsp. salt
1-1/2 c. minus 3 tbsp. whole
  wheat pastry flour
1 tbsp. soy flour
1-1/2 c. bran
1/2 c. raisins
1/2 c. nuts (optional)

Directions for revised, better nutrition recipe:
IN A CUP, DISSOLVE baking yeast in the warm water, sweetened with sugar or honey. Let sit until fluffy (5 minutes).
IN LARGE BOWL, COMBINE warm milk, oil or applesauce, and salt.
ADD yeast mixture to the large bowl. Mix gently.
ADD the whole wheat (and soy) flour 1/2 c. at a time, stirring gently after each addition.
ADD and gently stir in the bran.
FOLD IN raisins and nuts. (Soak raisins to soften if desired.)
PLACE BATTER in greased muffin tins, filling each tin 2/3 full.
LET RISE in warm place until rounding over tops of tins, about 1/2 hour.
BAKE in preheated oven at 350°F for 20-25 minutes.
REMOVE from pans.
YIELD: Approximately one dozen.

NOTE: Yeast-raised muffins are best, healthwise, made a day ahead and reheated to serve. They freeze nicely also.

DATE MUFFINS (raised with yeast)

1 pkg. dry yeast
1/4 c. warm water
2 tbsp. warm fruit juice
2 tbsp. oil
1 c. quick oats
1/2 tsp. salt
1 c. warm water
1-3/4 c. whole wheat flour
3/4 c. chopped dates
3/4 c. chopped walnuts

DISSOLVE yeast in warm water combined with warm juice and let stand about 10 minutes. Add rest of ingredients. Drop rounded tablespoons of mixture into oiled muffin tins. Fill muffin tins 2/3 full of batter. Let rise until double. Bake at 350°F for about 20 minutes.
YIELD: 12 muffins.

LECITHIN-OIL MIXTURE (for greasing pans)

1/2 c. corn oil
1/2 c. liquid
    lecithin

SHAKE together. Keep on hand in squeeze bottle for greasing casserole pans, cookie sheets, bread pans, skillets. Oil alone does not create a non-stick surface.
YIELD: 1 c.

CRACKERS

COMMUNION BREAD

1 c. whole wheat
    pastry flour
1/4 tsp. salt
2 tbsp. cold
    water
1/4 c. vegetable
    oil

COMBINE flour and salt in mixing bowl or electric mixer. Combine water and oil in measuring cup but do not stir. Add wet ingredients to dry flour and mix with fork (or electric mixer wire whips) until all the flour is dampened. Roll out between two sheets of waxed paper to the thickness of thick pastry. Place on ungreased, floured baking sheet and mark off with sharp knife into bite-sized squares (cutting only part way through). Prick squares with fork. Bake 425°F 8-12 minutes or until done.
Do not overbrown. Watch carefully during last 5 minutes. Store in cookie tins or foil-lined box with waxed paper between layers.
Serves 50.

WHOLE WHEAT STICKS

1-1/4 c. whole wheat flour	COMBINE all ingredients to make a stiff dough.
3 tbsp. brown sugar or date sugar	KNEAD on lightly floured board 2-3 minutes.
1/2 tsp. salt	
1/2 c. chopped nuts or coconut	
3-1/2 tbsp. vegetable oil	ROLL out on lightly floured board to uniform thickness of 1/4" (an 8" x 12" rectangle will do it).
5 tbsp. milk or water	

CUT into 1" x 3" strips. Bake on ungreased cookie sheet at 300°F. for 35-40 minutes.

YIELD: 20-25 sticks.

SESAME SOUP THINS

1/2 c. + 3 tbsp. water
3 tbsp. oil
1/2 tsp. salt
2 c. whole wheat flour
1/2 c. sesame seeds

PUT first 3 ingredients into blender. Whiz at medium speed till well blended. Remove from blender and add whole wheat flour and sesame seeds.

MIX well and knead a little. Let rest 10 minutes. Divide into 2 parts and roll between waxed paper or on oiled cookie sheets. (If using waxed paper, moisten countertop to prevent paper from slipping.)

SPRINKLE with salt and a generous amount of sesame seeds. Continue rolling to thickness of thin wafers. (Sesame seed rolled in this way will not fall off.) Prick and mark squares. BAKE at 350°F for about 15 minutes.

BREAD SPREADS

BETTER BUTTER

1 tbsp. agar agar flakes
  or Emes unflavored
  gelatin
1-1/2 c. cold water
1 c. cooked millet,
  packed
1/4 c. raw cashews
1 tsp. salt
1 tbsp. cooked, peeled
  carrots

STIR agar flakes into water in small sauce-pan. Let stand 5 minutes. Cook over high heat until gelatin is dissolved and liquid is clear. Blend half of the gelatin with remaining ingredients at low speed, increasing to high speed until super smooth. Blend in remaining gelatin at low speed. Pour into containers and chill. Keeps one week. Do not freeze.
Use as a spread for bread.
YIELD: 2-1/2 cups.

MILLET SPREAD

3/4 tsp. salt
1/3 c. cooked carrots
1/3 c. warm water
1 c. hot, well-cooked
  millet
1/3 c. coconut (fine,
  unsweetened)

WHIZ in blender until creamy smooth.
YIELD: 2 cups.

SESAME SEED SPREAD

1/2 c. sesame seeds
1/2 c. water
1/8 tsp. salt
1/4 c. dates

USING electric blender or moulinex type grinder, whiz sesame seeds to a meal. Add remaining ingredients and blend together until smooth.

Sesame seeds contain 22 percent protein and are rich sources of calcium, phosphorus and magnesium. They contain significant amounts of the B vitamins as well as vitamin E.
YIELD: About 1 cup.

SWEETENED NUT SPREAD

1 c. finely ground nuts
1 c. finely ground dried fruit
(dates, raisins, pears, pineapple, etc.)
1 to 2 tsp. honey or fruit juice to
give spreading consistency

COMBINE all ingredients. Use as delicious spread for bread in place of butter or peanut butter and jam.

NUT OR SEED BUTTERS

LIGHTLY ROAST the desired amount of raw nuts in flat pan in oven at 350°F. Try almonds, cashews, walnuts, peanuts, hazelnuts, sesame seeds, sunflower seeds, etc. Put 1/2 cup water in blender. Add nuts or seeds of any kind until the desired consistency of butter is reached. Add a pinch of salt and flavorings if desired. (A date or two or a few raisins are also good.)

OLIVE-NUT SPREAD

1 c. ripe olives
1/2 c. walnuts
1/4 c. almonds
1/4 c. sunflower seeds
1/4 c. celery, finely chopped
(optional)

GRIND all ingredients together through food grinder, or chop very fine. Mix with sufficient mayonnaise to achieve desired spreading consistency.

ALMOND-DATE SPREAD

In an electric blender, blend a few ounces of almonds and dates together with an equal amount of water. (Or grind them finely with a food mill and mix with water until a satisfactory spreading consistency is reached.)

FILBERT SPREAD

1-1/2 c. filberts
1-1/4 c. water
1 banana
Pinch of salt

PUT FILBERTS and water in blender and blend until smooth. Add banana and salt and blend. Use as spread on bread instead of butter.

Chapter 6

Meatless Dinner Meals I

Featuring:

- Bean Cuisine

- Tofu

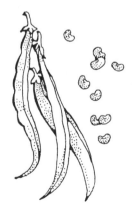

"So Daniel said...test us for ten days. Give us vegetables to eat and water to drink. Then compare us with young men who are eating the food of the royal court, and base your decision on how we look. When the time was up, they looked healthier and stronger than all those who had been eating the royal food. So from then on the guard let them continue to eat vegetables instead of what the king provided." Daniel 1:12-14.

"Beans are worth their weight in protein," says a recent release from the U. S. Department of Agriculture. A cup of cooked beans supplies about 12-15 grams of vegetable protein, depending on variety. A guarantee of complete protein is assured with the addition of bread, tortillas, rice or any grain product.

Legumes, the family name for beans, comprise a group of foods that includes lentils, peas, and beans in their many varieties. They can be made into delicious patties, loaves, and soups. They can be merely cooked and seasoned and served over rice, a baked potato, or toast or eaten in a bowl.

Beans are my favorite main dish. I keep jars of beans in my kitchen cupboard along with the grains, to create tasty, economical dishes.

No refrigeration is needed for long storage of any of the dried beans. They are almost non-perishable. Store beans in cupboard in airtight containers.

Beans contain no cholesterol unless animal fats are added in cooking or seasoning. They are low in sodium. Beans supply bulk and gentle roughage, so important in regulating the digestion of our foods.

All types of dry beans are important sources of thiamine and riboflavin. These members of the B-vitamin complex family are reasonably stable under long cooking or pressure cooking.

Thiamine helps to turn food into energy, to keep nerves healthy and dispositions good, and to promote good appetite and digestion.

Riboflavin works with thiamine not only in keeping the digestive and nervous system healthy, but also the eyes and skin.

Most beans need to be soaked before cooking. This softens the beans and makes cooking time shorter. Another benefit of soaking beans is the removal of some of their gas-forming properties. If you discard the soaking water, and add fresh water for cooking, you will eliminate some of the gas-forming tri-saccharides.

Some cooks go a second step in reducing the gas-forming properties, discarding the cooking water after the first one-half hour of cooking and add new water a second time.

Beans are a versatile food. They can be used in soups, sandwiches, main dishes and salads. They can be ground into flour for breads. What better way to beat the summer heat than to serve a cold bean and vegetable salad for dinner.

I keep a supply of canned garbanzos and kidney beans on my pantry shelf for quick and easy meals in a hurry.

You will find a variety of bean recipes in this chapter as well as in the Lunch and Supper chapters.

STEPS FOR PREPARING DRY BEANS
1. Sort to remove small rocks and dirt clods.
2. Wash in tap water and drain water through strainer.
3. Soak covered in water to 2-3 inches over top of beans by one of the following methods.
   A. Soak overnight (8 hours) in cold water OR
   B. For a fast, shorter method: bring beans and water to boil on high heat. Immediately turn off heat. Let stand 1 hour.
4. Drain off soaking water. Add fresh water to cover beans by 1 to 2 inches.
   Bring to boil, reduce heat, and simmer on low heat until nearly done.

See *How to Cook Dry Beans And Peas* for cooking times for various beans. Beans can be divided into three groups according to the cooking procedure needed.

    A. Beans that take a very long time to cook tender: soybeans and garbanzos

    B. Beans that cook so quickly no soaking needed: lentils, split peas

    C. All other beans such as pintos, reds, pinks, navy, limas, kidneys, blacks, black-eye peas, small whites, etc.

Simmer beans slowly. Cooking too fast can break skins. A teaspoon of oil prevents foaming. At high altitudes beans take longer to cook. A pressure cooker helps, but follow manufacturer's directions.

HOW TO COOK DRY BEANS AND PEAS

Divide beans into 3 groups for cooking procedures.

1 c. beans, most varieties **4 c. water** **1 onion** **Oil, tomato puree** **sweet basil, oregano** **baco chips**	ADD beans to boiling water. As soon as beans boil again, turn off heat. Let stand 1 hour. Simmer until nearly done adding more water as needed; add salt. Saute onion in a little oil. Season as desired with pinch of sweet basil, tomato puree, baco chips, oregano. Cook 1 to 2 hours depending on variety. YIELD: 2 to 2-1/2 cups.
1 c. soybeans or garbanzos **4 c. water**	Same as for beans above, seasoning as desired. Cook 2 to 4 hours until tender. YIELD: 2 to 2-1/2 cups.
1 c. lentils or split peas **3 c. water**	ADD lentils or peas to boiling water. Simmer until done, about 30-45 minutes. Season as desired. YIELD: 2-1/2 cups.

REDUCING GAS FORMING PROPERTIES IN BEANS

After soaking beans, discard the soaking water. Use fresh water to cook the beans as at least part of the gas-forming trisaccharides in the beans go out into the soaking water and can be eliminated. If you continue to have problems with gas when eating beans discard the cooking water after the first 20 minutes and again after a second 20 minutes, adding fresh water each time. Continue to cook beans until done. Eat slowly and chew thoroughly because digestion of carbohydrates begins in the mouth. Time is needed for the digestive juices in the mouth to thoroughly mix with the food.

COOKING SOYBEANS AND GARBANZOS

Soybeans and garbanzos take a long time to cook. Look beans over for small rocks or dirt clods and wash thoroughly. Soak covered in water overnight (or drop into boiling water and soak one hour). Change to fresh water and then boil gently until tender, about 3 to 4 hours. Use 3 times as much water as beans.

FREEZER TRICK: After soaking the soybeans or garbanzos, drain and put in the freezer overnight. This will cut down the cooking time and render the cooked beans completely tender.

USE AS EGG SUBSTITUTE: I keep a supply of soaked soybeans and garbanzos in the freezer at all times to use in recipes calling for eggs as a binder. Whizzing soaked garbanzos or soybeans to a paste with equal amounts of water replaces eggs in recipes for binding mixtures together.   (1/4 c. soaked beans + 1/4 c. water whizzed smooth to a paste = 1 egg as a binder.) Cooked beans lose this binding capability. Garbanzo flour and water can be mixed to a paste for binding use also. You can even make Egg Foo Young without eggs. See our recipe for Garbanzo Foo Young, p. 117. For other egg replacements, see p. 260.

PRESSURE COOKER METHOD

1-1/2 c. soybeans or
  garbanzos
3 c. water
2 tbsp. oil
1 tsp. salt

BOIL soybeans and water in a pressure cooker about 1 minute without pressure. Turn off heat. After 2 hours add the oil, salt, and more water if needed and pressure cook the beans at 15 pounds for 45 min.

BAKED SOYBEANS

6 c. cooked soybeans
2 tbsp. molasses or drop or
  two of maple flavoring
2 tbsp. brown sugar
Juice of one lemon
Salt to taste
1 can tomato soup or 6 oz.
  tomato paste, 1/4 c. water,
  1 tbsp. flour
1 medium onion, whole
2 tbsp. oil
Pinch sage, 1 bay leaf

MIX all ingredients except the onion. Place in bean pot or baking dish. Put the whole onion in the center. Bake in a moderate oven, adding a little bean broth or tomato juice as needed to keep moist. BAKE 1 hour or longer.

SAVORY SOY PATTIES

3 c. water
2 c. soaked soybeans
  (2/3 c. dry)
1-1/4 c. water
1-1/3 c. rolled oats
1 small chopped
  onion or 1 tsp.
  onion powder
1 tsp. Italian season-
  ing
2 tbsp. soy sauce
1/2 tsp. salt
2 tbsp. oil
1 tbsp brewer's type
  yeast (optional)

SOAK 2/3 c. dry soybeans overnight in 3 c. water. Then drain. Blend soybeans in blender in 1-1/4 c. water until quite fine. Remove to mixing bowl. Add seasonings and rolled oats. Allow to stand 10 min. for rolled oats to absorb moisture. Stir again and drop by rounded tablespoons onto lightly oiled skillet on moderate heat (350°F), on electric skillet or range. Cover and cook until lightly browned. Turn, cover and cook other side. Reduce heat and allow to cook 10 minutes longer. Serve with tomato gravy recipe in gravy section (p. 258).
Serves 8. Protein: 11 gm./serving.

YUMMY SOYBEAN LOAF

2 c. cooked soybeans,
   mashed
3 tbsp. flour
2/3 c. soy milk powder
3/4 c. cooking liquid from
   soybeans (containing soy
   sauce and bouillon)
1 c. toast crumbs
1 tbsp. oil
1/2 c. chopped onion
1/2 tsp. thyme
1-1/2 tsp. Vegex or Balanced
   Mineral Bouillon

MIX all ingredients together. Place in loaf pan. Bake at 350°F for 35 to 45 minutes. Serves 4.

ISLAND SOYBEANS (a quickie)

1 onion
1 bell pepper
1 c. crushed pineapple,
   undrained
2 16-oz. cans Soybeans
1/4 c. to 1/2 c. tomato sauce

SAUTE one chopped onion and one chopped bell pepper in oil until limp. Add tomato sauce and soybeans and simmer 15 minutes. Add pineapple and heat through. Serves 4.

FAMILY FAVORITE LIMA BEANS

2 c. large lima beans, dry
4 c. water
1 tsp. salt, or to taste
2 tbsp. honey
1 8-oz. can tomato paste or
   puree
2 tbsp. margarine, melted

SOAK limas overnight. Drain. Add fresh water and salt. Simmer until tender (1-1/2 hour). Add sugar, tomato paste and margarine. Bake in shallow baking dish at 350°F for 2 hours. Serves 6.

BEAN CASSEROLE

3 c. beans (cooked) any kind
1 small onion (chopped)
1 c. diced celery
1/2 c. diced green pepper
2 c. tomato puree
1/2 t. salt
1 c. water from beans
1/2 c. dry bread crumbs
3 tbsp. margarine or vegetable oil

SEASON to taste. Try 1/4 tsp. each Basil, Sage, Italian Herbs. Place beans and seasoning alternately in a baking dish. Cover with buttered crumbs and bake slowly at 350°F for 1 to 1-1/2 hours. Serves 6.

BLACK BEANS ON RICE

1 lb. black beans
1 large onion, chopped
2 green peppers, chopped
1 clove garlic, minced
1/4 c. olive oil
1 bay leaf, 2 tsp. salt
1 lb. brown rice, cooked
Green onions, chopped

COVER beans with 6 c. boiling water and cook 1 hour. Braise onions, green pepper, and garlic in oil. Combine with beans, add other seasonings, and cook until beans are tender and liquid is thick. Serve over brown rice and sprinkle green onions on top of beans. Serves 10.

CHILI BEANS

2-1/2 c. water
1-1/4 c. Red Beans or Pintos, dry
1-2 tsp. salt
1/4 c. chopped celery
1/4 c. chopped green peppers
1/4 c. chopped onions
3/4 c. Vegeburger or 1 c. wheat berries
2 tbsp. oil
1 tsp. honey
1 c. chopped tomatoes or 1/2 c. tomato paste
1/2 tsp. oregano, 1/4 tsp. garlic powder
1/2 tsp. sweet basil, 1 tsp. cumin

SOAK washed beans overnight. Drain water off. Cook in fresh water for 1-1/2 hours. Chop onions, celery and peppers. Saute in the oil with the burger. Add all ingredients to beans and simmer for 30 minutes.
Serves 6 to 8.
Protein: 14 grams
Calories: 212

DELICIOUS BLACKEYE PEAS

2 c. Blackeye Peas, dried
5 c. hot water

SOAK blackeye peas in the water overnight. Place in saucepan and add remaining ingredients.

1 large onion, chopped
1 garlic clove, minced
1/4 c. chopped parsley
1 stalk celery with leaves, chopped
1/4 c. molasses
2 tsp. salt, or to taste
2 tbsp. oil
1/4 tsp. oregano
1 8-oz. can tomato sauce or 1 small can tomato puree

SIMMER on low heat, covered, until peas are tender.
Serves 6.

FRIJOLES VAQUERO (good in tacos)

2 c. Red Kidney beans or
  Pintos, dry
Water

SOAK beans overnight. Next day simmer beans until tender in enough water to cover.

2 large, chopped Spanish
  onions
2 tbsp. olive oil
1 large can solid pack tomatoes
2 cloves garlic, minced
1/2 to 1 tsp. salt
1 tsp. cumin
1/2 tsp. oregano
1 c. low fat cottage cheese
1 can pitted ripe olives, drained
  and chopped

SAUTE onions in small amount of olive oil and tomatoes, garlic, cumin, oregano and salt and simmer. When beans are done, add sauce to beans and bring to boil. Remove from heat and stir in cottage cheese until melted (optional). Mash if desired. Add olives. This reheats nicely, but stir often. Serve with shredded lettuce and warm tortillas.

BOSTON BAKED BEANS

1 lb. Great Northern
  Beans (small whites)

SIMMER beans in enough water to cover until tender. Drain most of the liquid off, but save it to add back later if you prefer soupy consistency.

1 to 2 tsp. salt
2 tbsp. oil
1 c. tomato sauce
3 tbsp. dark molasses
1 onion or more, leave
  whole
3 tbsp. light brown
  sugar or honey

MIX all ingredients together, placing whole onion in center. Push it down under beans. Bake 4-6 hours covered in 350°F oven or for as long as possible, at least 2 hours. Remove onion before serving. Serves 6.

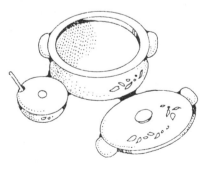

GARBANZO-WHEAT PILAF

1/2 c. garbanzos or lentils, cooked
1 c. Fisher's Ala or cracked wheat
2 tsp. oil
1/2 c. chopped green onions
1/2 c. diced green peppers
2-1/2 c. canned tomatoes + 1 c. water
1 clove garlic, diced
1/2 to 1 tsp. salt, or to taste
1 tsp. paprika
1/4 c. Vegeburger or Baco Chips (optional)

PLACE oil and Ala in skillet. Cook and stir until golden. Add remaining ingredients. Cover, bring to boil, reduce heat and simmer 15 minutes. Serve topped with yogurt and green onions, chopped.

Variations:
Stuffed Peppers: Stuff Garbanzo-wheat Pilaf into pre-cooked green peppers.

BAKE at 350°F for 30 minutes.

SAVORY ZUCCHINI GARBANZOS

2 medium onions, sliced
2 tbsp. oil
1 lb. zucchini, sliced
1 can (1 lb.) garbanzos, drained
1/2 tsp. oregano
1/4 tsp. basil
1 tsp. garlic powder or salt
3 medium tomatoes or 1 c. stewed tomatoes
Salt to taste

BRAISE onions for a few minutes in oil. Add garbanzos, seasonings, and tomatoes. Simmer 10 minutes. Add zucchini and simmer only until crisp-done. Serve immediately.
Serves 6-8.

BAKED GARBANZO CASSEROLE (a quickie)

1 14-oz. can garbanzos
1/2 can celery, mushroom, or tomato soup
1/2 tsp. summer savory
1/2 tsp. sweet basil
1/4 tsp. cumin (optional)

MIX ingredients together, place in a greased casserole and bake in a 325°F oven for 1 hour or until well seasoned. Serve with tossed vegetable salad and sesame seed rolls. Serves 4.

GARBANZO LOAF (quick, 10-min. mixing time)

1 chopped onion

1/2 green pepper, chopped

2 c. cooked garbanzos, mashed or pureed

1/2 c. peanut butter

1 c. cooked tomatoes or a mixture of canned tomatoes, onion, green pepper and celery

3 tbsp. flour

1 tsp. sage

1/2 tsp. garlic salt

1/2 to 1 tsp. salt, or to taste

2 c. crushed cornflakes or dry bread crumbs

SAUTE onion and pepper in small amount of oil. Combine remaining ingredients. Peanut butter should be mixed to a medium paste with water first. Mix well. Pour into oiled loaf pan. Place loaf pan in shallow pan of water and bake. Serve with tomato gravy, mushroom gravy, or cranberry sauce. Bake at 350°F for 1-1/2 hours. Serves 4 to 6.

GARBANZO-SOY-OAT PATTIES

2 c. soaked garbanzos

1 c. soaked soybeans

1-1/2 c. water

1 c. rolled oats

1/3 c. chopped Brazil nuts or other nuts

1 tbsp. oil

1 tsp. salt, or to taste

1/2 tbsp. onion powder

1 tsp. Italian Seasoning

1 tsp. chicken style seasoning (p. 261)

1 tbsp. nutritional yeast flakes

COMBINE all ingredients except rolled oats and nuts in blender and chop fine; or grind beans in food grinder and combine with other ingredients. Place in bowl. Add rolled oats and nuts and let stand 10 minutes to absorb moisture. Drop from tablespoon or half-cup scoop on oiled baking pan or electric skillet. Cover. Bake at 350°F for 10 minutes or until nicely browned. Turn. Cover. Bake an additional 10 minutes. Reduce heat and cook 10 minutes more. Serve with tomato gravy. Serves 10.

EASY GARBANZO NOODLE DISH (quick)

1 pkg. lasagne noodles or regular whole wheat noodles, cooked

2 15-oz. cans garbanzos, drained

1 small can mushrooms

1 can mushroom soup or homemade mushroom soup to moisten (more if needed)

Chicken style seasoning (p. 261) to taste.

MIX and bake at 350°F until heated. Serves 6-8.

QUICK GARBANZO POT PIE

1 medium onion
1 small green pepper
1 stalk celery
2 potatoes
1 10-oz. pkg. frozen peas
1 15-oz. can garbanzos
2 cans cream of mushroom soup
1 soup can of milk
1 tsp. chicken style seasoning (p. 261)
Whole wheat biscuits or pie crust

CHOP coarsely first 4 ingredients; combine with remaining ingredients except the biscuits. Place in greased 9" x 13" casserole dish. Cover with whole wheat biscuits or pie crust. Bake until casserole bubbles, and biscuits brown, about 30-45 minutes at 400°F. Serves 8. Protein: 9.8 gm./serving; calories 333; carbohydrates: 35.4 gm./serving.

GARBANZO-RICE PATTIES

1-1/2 c. soaked garbanzos
3/4 c. water
1-1/2 c. cooked rice
1/3 c. chopped Brazil nuts
1/8 tsp. garlic powder
1/2 tsp. onion powder
2 tsp. chicken style seasoning (p. 261)
1/2 tsp. salt, or to taste
3 tbsp. Brewer's yeast flakes

PUT the soaked garbanzos into blender. Add the cold water. Blend until very fine. Put the cooked rice into a bowl large enough to mix. Add the other ingredients, seasoning, chopped nuts, and the Brewer's yeast and mix together. Turn in the blended garbanzos. Drop from a scoop on a lightly oiled hot skillet, 350°F. Cover and bake for 10 minutes. Turn the patties. They should be a beautiful luggage tan. If they have a tendency to brown more in 10 minutes, lower the heat enough to get the desired results. Cover and bake for 10 minutes. Reduce heat and allow the patties to bake an additional 5 minutes. Serve plain or with a sauce of your choice. Serves 6-8. Two patties provide protein of quality and quantity that approximates a 2-oz. serving of beef.

GARBANZO FOO YOUNG

1 c. garbanzo flour
1 c. water
1/2 tsp. salt
1/2 c. finely chopped onion
1 c. chopped frozen Wham,
    beef or chicken
    Soyameat (optional)
1-1/2 c. bean sprouts
	BLEND together with wire whip: flour, water and salt.
	
	ADD onion, Wham, sprouts.
	
	MIX all lightly and fry in 6 or 8 portions, turning to cook both sides well. Serve with soy sauce gravy and steamed brown rice.

GRAVY
1 tbsp. soy sauce
2 tbsp. cornstarch
2 c. water
1 tbsp. McKay's chicken
    seasoning or chicken
    style seasoning (p. 261)
1 tbsp. Grandma's
    Molasses
	POUR gravy over patties and garnish with chopped chives or parsley.
	
	NOTE: The garbanzo batter has a very good binding value and will form around the pattie much the same as an egg batter and provides a high quality protein.

BEAN-OAT PATTIES

1-1/2 c. soupy
    pinto beans,
    cooked
1/4 c. bean
    liquid or
    broth
1 c. rolled oats,
    old fashioned
1/4 c. nutri-
    tional food
    yeast flakes
1/4 c. chopped
    nuts
1/2 c. sauted
    onions
1/2 tsp. sage
1/2 tsp. salt
	PUT beans in bowl and mash with fork. Some pieces may be left unmashed for texture. Add remaining ingredients. Drop from a tablespoon or a scoop into an oiled baking dish or lightly oiled skillet. Bake covered for 10 minutes at 350°F. Turn. Cover and reduce heat to 300°F. Bake 15 minutes longer.
	
	Variation:
	PRESS a double recipe of same mixture into a well-greased and crumbed medium-sized ring mold. Tap mixture down carefully to fill evenly. Bake at 350°F 45 minutes or until firm and well done. To unmold, loosen by inserting a flat limber knife and ream around the edges both center and outside. Let stand a few minutes to aid in easier removal. Fill center with white parsley sauce or tomato gravy and garnish with slices of tomato and parsley. Serves 4-6.

THANKSGIVING LENTIL-NUT RING

2 c. cooked lentils
1/2 c. milk or tomato puree
2 tbsp. oil
1-1/2 c. dry whole wheat bread
crumbs
2 tbsp. soy flour and/or 1 egg
1 c. chopped walnuts
1 medium onion, finely chopped
1 c. grated carrots
1 c. finely chopped celery
1 tsp. salt, or to taste
1 tsp. sage
1 tsp. thyme, rosemary or
marjoram
1/2 tsp. oregano
1 tsp. poultry seasoning

COMBINE all ingredients and mix thoroughly. Oil ring mold (or loaf pan) well; sprinkle bottom and sides with fine bread crumbs. Add lentil mixture. Bake in preheated 350°F oven 1 to 1-1/4 hours.
LET SIT 5-10 minutes before unmold-ing. Unmold onto serving platter. Fill center with cooked peas if desired. Garnish with parsley and cherry tomatoes or carrot curls.
SERVE in slices with tomato or brown gravy and cranberry sauce.
Serves 8.

LENTIL LOAF

2 c. cooked lentils
2/3 c. milk (evaporated, soy,
nonfat)
2 tbsp. corn oil
1-1/2 c. fine dry bread crumbs
1 egg, beaten, or egg replacer
(see p. 260)
1 c. chopped walnuts
1 tsp. salt or to taste
1 tsp. sage or thyme
1/2 tsp. marjoram
1/2 tsp. oregano
1 tsp. poultry seasoning
1 tsp. Bakon Yeast
1 onion, chopped
1 c. grated carrots
1 c. chopped celery

COMBINE all ingredients and mix thoroughly. Spoon into a greased 1-1/2 quart casserole and bake 1 hour at 350°F. Serve with gravy. Serves 8 to 10.

POT O' LENTILS

2 c. uncooked lentils
1 chopped onion
1 chopped carrot
1/2 c. chopped celery
1/4 c. chopped green bell pepper
1 can tomato soup or paste
1 tbsp. molasses
1/2 tsp. oregano
1/2 tsp. margarine
1/2 tsp. Bakon Yeast
1 tsp. salt
1 tsp. cumin

COOK lentils, onion, carrot, celery and pepper together in 4 c. water. Add a little more water as needed. Add other ingredients and simmer.

NOTE: A good and filling pot for supper. Served with whole grain bread, muffins or cornbread and a salad, it makes a complete meal. Serves 6.

ESAU'S POTTAGE

2 c. cooked lentils, drained
1 c. cooked brown rice
1 small onion, finely chopped
2 tbsp. oil
Salt and fine herbs to taste

BRAISE onion in oil. Mix together cooked lentils, rice, onion and herbs. Heat in skillet until thoroughly heated. Add margarine to flavor and moisten if desired. Serves 4.

LENTIL PATTIES

1 c. cooked lentils
1/4 c. chopped nuts
2 tbsp. oil
2 to 4 tbsp. milk (evaporated, soy, nonfat)
1/2 tsp. salt
1/4 tsp. paprika
1/2 c. dry bread crumbs
1/4 c. chopped onions
1/2 c. water whizzed in blender with 1/2 c. soaked garbanzos (OR 2 eggs)*
1/4 tsp. sage
1/8 tsp. garlic powder

BROWN onion; combine all ingredients, mashing lentils slightly. Form into patties and fry in oil on both sides. Serve with Dill Sauce (p. 120). Serves 4.

*NOTE: For other binders/ egg replacers, see p. 260.

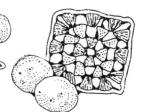

DILL SAUCE

1 tbsp. finely chopped
  onion
1 tbsp. margarine
2 tbsp. flour
1/2 tsp. paprika
1/2 tsp. dried dill weed
Dash of salt
1 c. milk

SAUTE 1 tbsp. finely chopped onion in 1 tbsp. margarine. Blend in 2 tbsp. flour, 1/2 tsp. paprika, 1/2 tsp. dried dill weed, dash of salt. Add 1 c. milk all at once. Cook and stir until thick and bubbly.

LENTIL POT PIE

6 c. water
1 tbsp. Vegex or Marmite
1 medium onion, diced
2 to 3 fresh carrots, cut
  French style
2 stalks celery, diced
3 to 4 uncooked potatoes,
  cut French style
3 tbsp. flour
3 tbsp. margarine
2 c. cooked lentils
1/2 tsp. sage, 1 tsp. salt
1/4 tsp. parsley
Pie crust topping

COOK onion, carrots, and celery in water with Vegex until about half done. Add potatoes. Brown flour in frying pan and blend with margarine. Add 1 cup of hot liquid from vegetables. Cook until thickened and combine with rest of vegetables (drained). Add lentils, sage, parsley, and salt. Mix. Add more of the hot vegetable juice if a thinner consistency is desired. Place in large casserole or baking pan and cover with pie crust. Bake in a 350°F oven until brown. Serves 8-10.

ITALIAN LENTILS

Compares favorably with steak. More protein, less fat, more calcium, phosphorus, iron, thiamine and riboflavin plus Vitamins A and C.

2 c. dry lentils, soaked
  overnight
Water to cover
1 onion, chopped
2 garlic cloves, minced
1 c. tomato puree
3/4 tsp. salt
1/4 tsp. cumin
1/4 tbsp. oregano

PLACE lentils in saucepan and add water to cover. Add remaining ingredients and simmer until done. When done, add 1 tbsp. olive oil (enhances flavors). Serve over brown rice. Delicous made with fresh tomatoes pureed in blender instead of canned.

LENTIL TOSTADOS

**2-1/2 c. lentils, un-
  cooked**
1 tsp. salt or to taste
**Chicken style seasoning
  (p. 261) and onion
  powder to taste**
**Ranch Style Dressing
  (p. 198)**
4 c. chopped lettuce
2 c. chopped tomatoes
1 c. chopped cucumber
**Several green onions,
  chopped**
**6 slices whole wheat
  bread or English
  muffins**

EARLY IN THE DAY: Cook 2-1/2 c. dry lentils in enough water to cover until tender (about 45 min.). Simmer; don't boil out all nutrients. Add 1 tbsp. Chicken Style Seasoning, 1 tsp. salt, and 1 tsp. onion powder to the cooking water for added flavor. Add more water as needed so lentils won't get dry. Finished product should be almost dry, not soupy. Stir occasionally to give lentils a partially mashed consistency. Make the Ranch Style Dressing; refrigerate.

JUST BEFORE MEALTIME: Prepare the tostado trimmings: chopped lettuce, tomatoes, cucumbers, onions. Heat up the lentils. Toast 6 slices of whole wheat bread or English muffins.

TO SERVE: Arrange trimmings on a tray and place in center of table. Pass the toasted bread or muffins and the bowl of hot lentil mixture and let each person assemble their own tostados. Assemble tostado in this order from bottom to top: Toasted bread, Ranch Style Dressing, lentils, vegetable trimmings, more Ranch Style Dressing on top, and a sprinkle of green onions over all. Serves 6.

Calories per serving: 213
Protein per serving: 11.7 gm.

WHAT TO DO WITH TOFU —

Tofu, or "soybean cheese," is a nutritious food with a pleasant mild flavor and a texture similar to soft cheese. It has been widely used in the Orient for centuries and is a most versatile food; here are some ways to use it.

TOFU

Tofu is a versatile, high protein food made from soybeans. It can be used in a variety of dishes by the vegetarian cook. Developed thousands of years ago in the Orient, tofu is available in most supermarkets or can be made at home from soybeans or soy flour.

Tofu comes in several textures: soft, regular, and firm. The soft textured variety is ideal for smoothies, whipped toppings, custard type desserts, and mayonnaise. Regular and firm tofu can be scrambled to resemble scrambled eggs, cubed for soups and wok cooked vegetables, sliced and browned in an oiled skillet, or mashed with a fork to resemble cottage cheese. It can be made into patties and meat-like loaves.

Tofu needs seasoning to make it palatable. If frozen and then thawed out the texture changes and becomes more meat-like. Tofu can be used cold or hot. Slices of tofu fried in a little oil and sprinkled with soy sauce make a delicious sandwich.

Tofu comes commonly packaged in 1-lb. sealed cartons covered with water. Look for an expiration date. Once opened, drain liquid off the tofu to use. Cover unused portion with fresh water and refrigerate for future use, changing the water daily.

PAN-FRIED TOFU is delicious by itself with a sprinkle of soy sauce and lemon juice; or, tofu can be stir-fried along with vegetables, in omelets, in fried rice or fried noodles.

TOFU COMPLIMENTS VEGETABLES SUPERBLY. It can be steamed with greens; boiled briefly in clear soups; used pan fried in sandwiches; cooked in stews; or mashed up and mixed with your favorite salad dressing for added flavor and texture.

SCRAMBLED TOFU

1 lb. tofu
1 tsp. onion powder or
  1 bunch green
  onions
2 tsp. soy sauce or
  1/2 tsp. salt
1 tsp. margarine or oil
Dash of turmeric
1-1/2 tsp. chicken style
  seasoning (p. 261)

DRAIN tofu, cube it, and simmer in margarine or oil with other ingredients until liquid is absorbed.
SERVE as you would scrambled eggs.
VARIATIONS: Add 1/4 tsp. sweet basil and 1/4 tsp. dill weed or 1/4 c. baco chips. For Spanish style add 1/4 c. each fresh chopped onion, green bell pepper and tomatoes. Add a few tsps. salsa if desired.
YIELD: 4-6 servings.

TOFU LOAF

1 lb. tofu, cubed small
1 can mushroom soup
1/3 c. grated carrots,
  fine
1 lg. onion, braised in
  oil
1 c. bread crumbs,
  fresh
1 tbsp. soy sauce
1 tbsp. chicken style
  seasoning (p. 261)

MIX ingredients together and bake in greased loaf pan for 1 hour at 325°F.
Water chestnuts and chopped green onions can be added for variety along with one beaten egg.

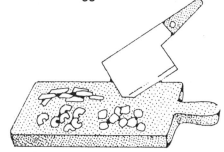

TOFU AND RICE BAKE

3 c. cooked brown rice
1-1/2 c. tofu, cubed
2/3 c. chopped green onions
2/3 c. chopped celery
2 tsp. chopped parsley
1/2 c. sliced water chestnuts
2 tbsp. olive oil
1 tbsp. Vegex or Savorex
1/2 tsp. salt
1 c. sliced mushrooms
1 c. soy milk

COOK onion and celery and mushrooms in skillet with the oil until half done. Add Vegex. Stir until dissolved. Then add soy milk, salt, parsley, water chestnuts, and rice. Blend. Lastly, add tofu, mixing carefully.

BAKE in oiled baking dish for 30 min. at 350°F.

Serves 6.

TOFU OATMEAL PATTIES

2 c. firm tofu
1/2 c. finely chopped celery
1/2 c. finely chopped onion
1 tsp. chicken style seasoning
   (p. 261)
2 c. cooked oatmeal
1 tbsp. soy flour
3 tbsp. arrowroot or cornstarch

FORM into patties. Fry in oil or bake on cookie sheet at 350°F 20-30 min turning once.

YIELD: 15 to 20 patties.

TOFU PANCAKES (Good for breakfast or dinner.)

8 medium potatoes, grated
1/2 lb. tofu, whizzed in
   blender
1 large onion, grated
1/4 c. fresh parsley,
   chopped fine
1 tsp. salt
1/2 tsp. garlic powder
3 tbsp. unbleached
   white flour

MIX together. For each pancake, brush a 6" skillet with oil and heat to medium heat. Spoon about 3/4 c. of the potato mixture into the pan and flatten to 3/8" -1/2" thick. Fry about 5-7 minutes on each side or until golden brown. Serve like pancakes. Top with applesauce.

Serves 6 to 8.

TOFU COTTAGE CHEESE

1 c. tofu, crushed
1/2 tsp. celery salt
1 tsp. soy sauce
1/4 tsp. garlic powder
1/2 tsp. onion powder

MIX ingredients together. Serve in lettuce cup with carrot and celery sticks and other raw vegetable relishes. Mix the tofu cottage cheese with mayonnaise and other seasonings as desired. Serves 4.

BROWNED TOFU

Drain 1 package firm or regular tofu. Cut into 1/2" slices. Place on griddle or in fry pan. Sprinkle with soy sauce or seasoning salt. Brown on both sides. Serve as the main dish at a meal or in sandwiches. Serves 4.

BREADING MIX FOR TOFU

1 c. Brewer's Yeast
1/2 c. wheat germ
1 tbsp. garlic powder
1/2 tsp. sweet basil
1 tbsp. chicken style seasoning (p. 261)
1/2 tsp. onion powder
Salt as needed

MIX and store in covered container. This keeps very well, refrigerated. Use to bread both sides of tofu slices. Then brown in small amount of oil on both sides.
YIELD: 1-1/2 c.

TOFU – GREEN BEAN SAUTE

6 mushrooms, sliced
1 tbsp. sesame oil
1 lb. green beans, sliced
    diagonally or lengthwise
3 tbsp. water
1 tsp. soy sauce
Garlic powder or minced
    fresh garlic
1 to 2 c. fresh or frozen
    peas
8 oz. tofu, cubed

SAUTE mushrooms in oil over low heat. ADD green beans, water, the soy sauce and garlic, and simmer, covered, 4 minutes. ADD peas and tofu, recover, and simmer another 3 minutes. This is a light and easy dish! Serves 4 to 6.

CHINESE WOK DELIGHT

1 lb. fresh tofu, firm
7 dried Chinese black mushrooms or 1 can any kind
   mushrooms
1/4 lb. bok choy or Chinese
   cabbage
1/2 lb. winter melon, zucchini
   or cucumber
1/4 lb. snow peas
2 oz. dried bean curd (optional)
3 tbsp. peanut oil
1 tbsp. soy sauce, or to taste
1 c. water
Optional:
1 onion
1/2 c. bamboo shoots
1/2 c. carrots
2 c. bean sprouts
1 can mock abalone (braised
   gluten)

SOAK dried bean curd and dried mushrooms in water to rehy-drate.

SHRED bok choy or cabbage. Wash and slice other vegetables. Stir fry bean curd, tofu and mush-rooms for 2 minutes. Then add remaining vegetables and stir fry 2 more minutes.

ADD liquid. When it boils, re-duce heat, cover and simmer 10 minutes.

SPRINKLE with toasted sesame seeds. Serve with steamed brown rice.
Serves 8.

SWEET AND SOUR TOFU

1 lb. tofu
Soy sauce
1 lg. onion, sliced
2 celery stalks, sliced diagonally
1 lg. bell pepper, large slices
1 tsp. salt
1/4 c. tomato sauce
1 tbsp. brown sugar
1 20-oz. can pineapple chunks
   (undrained)
2 tbsp. cornstarch added to
   1/2 c. water
2 tbsp. lemon juice
1 lg. tomato

DRAIN 1 lb. tofu. Cut in 1" cubes. Place on greased cookie sheet. Sprinkle with soy sauce. Bake at 450°F for 30 minutes.
CUT the vegetables into bite-size pieces and saute until crisp tender in large skillet.
ADD salt, tomato sauce, brown sugar, pineapple chunks, corn-starch/water mixture and lemon juice and stir until thickened.
LASTLY, stir in cubed tofu and 1 lg. tomato sliced into wedges. Serve over steamed brown rice.
Serves 6-8.

WOK VEGETABLES AND TOFU
over Steamed Brown Rice or Noodles

4 c. water
3/4 tsp. salt
2 c. long grain brown rice
1 lb. tofu cut into cubes
Soy sauce
large package frozen mixed vegetables
1 onion sliced
1 clove garlic
Oil

STEAM BROWN RICE: put 4 c. water and 3/4 tsp. salt in saucepan. Bring to boil. Add 2 cups long grain brown rice. Cover. Reduce heat to low and cook without peeking for 45 minutes. Let sit 10 minutes before serving if time permits.

TOFU CHUNKS: Drain 1 pkg. tofu. Cut into cubes. Place on oiled cookie sheet, sprinkle with soy sauce, and bake at 450°F for 30 minutes or as long as you have time to. This crisps the tofu so it won't crumble when added to the vegetables.

QUICK WOK VEGETABLES - open up a large package of frozen mixed vegetables, any combination. In large skillet or wok, saute 1 sliced onion, 1 clove garlic in small amount oil. Add thawed vegetables. (thaw in microwave). Add tofu chunks just before serving.

TOFU BURGERS

1 lb tofu, mashed or
  crumbled
1/2 c. oatmeal
1/2 c. wheat germ
2 tbsp. onion powder
1-1/2 tbsp. parsley,
  chopped
1 tsp. salt
1 tsp. poultry seasoning
  (or 1/2 tsp. each basil
  and oregano)
1/2 tsp. garlic powder

MIX all ingredients together in bowl. Shape into 8 burgers and brown in 2 tbsp. oil. Serve on buns with all the trimmings.

TOFU SPAGHETTI BALLS

Mix tofu burgers (above). Shape the mix into 20 balls and carefully brown in 1/2 c. oil.

TOFU LOAF

Mix tofu burgers (above). Press the mix into an oiled loaf pan, top with 1/4 c. ketchup and bake at 350°F for about 30 minutes. Cool 10 minutes before slicing.

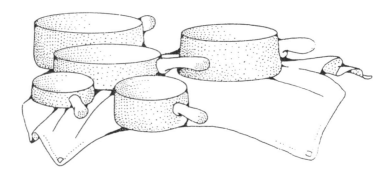

Chapter 7

Meatless Dinner Meals II

Featuring:

- Grain and Nut Dishes

- Pastas

- Gluten

"If thou wilt diligently hearken to the voice of the Lord thy God, and wilt do that which is right in his sight, and wilt give ear to his commandments, and keep all his statues, I will put none of these diseases upon thee, which I have brought upon the Egyptians; for I am the Lord that healeth thee." Exodus 15:26

Grains, Nuts, Pastas, Gluten

With grains, vegetables, and fruits as the base of the Eating Right Pyramid, we change the popular thinking regarding dinner meals. It has been traditionally the expected procedure to base a dinner meal around a meat dish.

Now, we know that building the dinner meal around a carbohydrate (starch) dish such as rice, pasta, or potatoes is more healthy.

What can we serve over pasta to make a delicious dinner? What shall we put over rice or a baked potato for a good dinner? A typical vegetarian dinner includes a hearty grain or potato dish accompanied by legumes, nuts, seeds, or tofu with vegetables. A crisp vegetable salad, whole grain bread and glass of milk round out the meal.

You would be surprised to see how delicious a casserole made with nuts or seeds can be or how simple it is to prepare a dinner of steamed brown rice and wok cooked vegetables with a few nuts or cubes of browned tofu added.

The brown rice, together with the nuts, seeds, or tofu yield plenty of good quality protein. The cholesterol content is zero and the fiber, mineral and vitamin content is high!

GLUTEN

We have included several pages of gluten recipes in our book but I am wondering if you know what gluten is?

Gluten is the protein from wheat that when kneaded sufficiently, makes bread elastic. Many years ago it was discovered that a dough of flour and water, mixed and kneaded well, and left it to sit for awhile covered with water — could then be squeezed and washed to remove the starch and bran.

The small, spongy portion of dough remaining in your hands after washing was the protein part of the wheat called gluten. The gluten can be cooked, and flavored to resemble beef or chicken, pork, fish or hamburger.

My mother made homemade gluten "steaks" for dinner when I was a child at home. It was an inexpensive source of protein for our family of seven.

Through the years, gluten products have been produced on a commercial basis and are available in many natural food stores and some supermarkets. These meatless canned and frozen products come ready to heat and eat in a variety of flavors and are cholesterol free.

Making homemade gluten is a creative three-step project. Exact recipe is found in the gluten section of this Chapter.

1.   Make a flour and water dough.
2.   Wash/squeeze the dough to remove bran and starch.
3.   Cook the cut gluten pieces in a seasoned broth to incorporate flavor.

The flavored gluten pieces can be dipped in breading meal and fried in oil. It can be ground into a hamburger consistency to use in patties, spaghetti sauce, chili, and meat-type loaves. It can be cut into chunks for soups, stews, or wok cooked vegetable dishes.

Grain main dishes have been a middle eastern tradition for centuries. Bulgur wheat, a pre-cooked, cracked wheat, can be purchased in natural food stores and some supermarkets and easily made into casseroles for dinner meals. Whole kernel grains can be cracked in your blender to use as you would bulgur wheat too. By adding cooked garbanzos or lentils or slivered almonds or cashew pieces, pilaf dishes served with steamed vegetables and a fresh salad make a delightful vegetarian dinner.

FOUR-GRAIN PILAF

1/4 to 1/2 c. margarine
2 c. cracked grains
  (wheat, rye, brown rice,
  barley, etc.)
1 c. chopped celery
8 green onions, sliced fine
2 c. broth or bouillon
2 c. boiling water
1 c. slivered almonds
1-1/2 tsp. salt
1/4 tsp. marjoram
1/2 tsp. oregano

SLIVER the almonds using fine blade of slicer/shredder attachment. Add sliced celery and green onions to margarine in skillet and saute. Crack a combination of 4 grains together in flour mill or blender or use 2 c. Ala bulgur wheat or cracked wheat. Measure out 2 c. of cracked grain and add to the skillet and toss to lightly brown. Place sauted mixture in a 2-quart casserole and pour bouillon and boiling water over top. Blend in almonds, salt, marjoram, and oregano. Cover and bake in a 325°F oven for 1-1/2 hours. Serves 8.

BROWN RICE PILAF

Sliced mushrooms
Little margarine
1/2 cup fresh peas
2 cups cooked brown rice
Juice of one lemon
1 tbsp. toasted ground
  sesame seeds
1 tbsp. currants or raisins
1/4 c. coarsely chopped
  almonds (toasted,
  perhaps)

SAUTE mushroom slices in margarine and add half a cup of fresh peas. Cook a few minutes and then add brown rice juice of one lemon, sesame seeds, currants or raisins, and almonds. Toss butter, and add any herb or chopped parsley as desired. Serves 4.

BULGUR VEGETABLE PILAF

1 onion, chopped
1 tbsp. vegetable oil such as olive or sesame oil
2 c. bulgur wheat (cracked pre-cooked wheat)
2 cloves garlic, minced
3 c. hot vegetable broth (can make from bouillon cubes)
1/2 tsp. paprika
1/2 to 1 tsp. salt
1/2 tsp. ground oregano
Various vegetables like broccoli, summer squash, celery, green beans, kale, other leafy greens, cut into bite size pieces.

SAUTE onion in oil until tender, and add cracked wheat until both become golden, then the garlic, stirring for another 2 minutes. Add vegetable broth and seasonings, stir, and cover. Let cook on low about 7 minutes, to allow most of the liquid to absorb. Place the prepared vegetables on top of the grain. Cover again and let the vegetables steam for about 10 minutes. Serve Bulgur Vegetable Pilaf plain or with a low-fat yogurt sauce seasoned with dill weed, and lemon juice. Add marinated tomatoes with fresh parsley and basil.
Serves 8.

SEVEN GRAIN LOAF

2 c. boiling water
1 tsp. salt
1 c. seven grain cereal (or nine grain)
3 tbsp. soy sauce or liquid aminos
2 tsp. onion powder
2 tbsp. margarine
1 tsp. thyme
1/2 tsp. sage or poultry seasoning
1/2 c. finely ground cashews, almonds, etc.
1/2 c. ground sunflower seeds

STIR all ingredients into boiling water and simmer few minutes. Pour into a buttered baking dish and bake at 350°F for 1-1/4 hours. Serve with tomato sauce or almond gravy.
Serves 6.

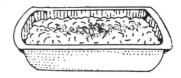

SESAME SEED PILAF

Serve with a leafy green salad and you have an easy dinner meal!

1/4 c. sesame seeds
4 tbsp. margarine or
olive oil
1 large onion (chopped)
1 clove garlic (minced)
1 c. long grain brown
rice or bulgar wheat
2 c. water
2 tsp. chicken style
seasoning (p. 261)
1 10-oz. pkg. thawed,
frozen, petite size
peas

Variation:
1 can diced Worthington
FriChik or 1 can
garbanzos

TOAST sesame seeds in a skillet over low heat, shaking pan frequently until golden, about 5 minutes. Turn out of pan; set aside. In the same pan, melt margarine over medium heat. Add chopped onion, minced garlic. Cook, stirring until onion is limp. Add rice or bulgar wheat. Cook stirring, until lightly toasted. Add 2 c. water and 2 tsp. chicken style seasoning. Bring to a boil, then cover and simmer 30-35 minutes or until rice is tender. Add peas and half of the toasted sesame seeds. Mix gently until well distributed and peas are heated through. Salt to taste. Turn into a serving dish and sprinkle with remaining sesame seeds. YIELD: 6 servings.

BROWN RICE-WHEAT PILAF

1 c. brown rice
1 c. chopped green
onion
1 to 2 tbsp. olive oil
1 c. whole wheat kernels
1/2 c. chopped fresh
parsley
1/2 tsp. garlic powder
1/2 tsp. salt

COOK brown rice in 2 c. boiling, salted water. Add rice slowly so boiling does not stop while adding; give a quick stir, cover pan with lid and steam on low heat without peeking for 40-45 min. Rice will be fluffy. Whole wheat kernels should be soaked overnight in water, then cooked in 6 c. gently boiling water for 1-2 hours, or until tender (or cook wheat 20 min. in pressure cooker without pre-soaking). Drain. After rice and wheat are cooked, toss all ingredients together, place in casserole, and bake 30 min. in 350°F oven. Sauteed mushrooms may also be added for variety. Protein per serving: 6 gm. Serves 6.

BUCKWHEAT KASHA

1 c. buckwheat groats
2 c. boiling chicken
   style broth
1 tsp. salt
1 medium onion,
   chopped
1 tbsp margarine or
   olive oil
1/2 c. chopped nuts
1/4 c. parsley
1/2 tsp. basil
1/2 tsp. thyme

COOK buckwheat in chicken style broth for 5 minutes. Saute onion in margarine; stir into buckwheat. Add remaining ingredients, cover, and simmer for 5-10 minutes longer, or until groats are tender and liquid is absorbed. Serves 4.
For chicken style broth, add 2 tsp. chicken seasoning to 2 c. water.
This kasha-like dish makes a very good stuffing holiday meals put into winter squash or pumpkin and baked.

CASHEW NUT CASSEROLE

1/2 c. chopped onions
1/2 c. chopped celery
1 can mushroom soup
1 can water
2 c. raw chopped
   cashews
3/4 large can dry chow
   mein noodles

SAUTE onions and celery. Mix mushroom soup and water. Lightly mix cashews with chow mein noodles. Add the sauted vegetables and the mushroom soup to the cashew mixture and blend. Place in greased casserole dish. Sprinkle rest of chow mein noodles on top. Bake at 350°F for one hour.

CASHEW STUFFING

1 c. diced onions
1 c. finely diced celery
1/3 c. parsley
1/2 c. sliced black olives
3 qts. cubed whole
   wheat bread, toasted
2-1/2 tsp. salt
2 tsp. poultry seasoning
1/2 c. margarine
1 c. chicken style broth
1-1/2 c. coarsely
   chopped cashews

MIX all ingredients together.
Place in greased casserole dish. Bake 45 minutes at 350°F. Serves 6-8.

OR stuff into a whole, half-baked pumpkin or winter squash that has been cleaned out inside. Bake 45 minutes at 350°F. Continue baking until pumpkin is tender when poked with a fork. Makes a beautiful, edible centerpiece for your Thanksgiving dinner table. Serves 6-8.
For chicken style broth, add 1 tsp. chicken seasoning to 1 c. water.

MILLET 'N' VEGETABLES

2 tbsp. vegetable oil
1 c. whole hulled millet
1/2 c. diced carrots
1/2 c. green peas or beans
1/4 c. diced celery
1 tbsp. chopped green
   pepper
1 tsp. salt, or to taste
1/2 tsp. oregano
1/2 tsp. sweet basil
1/4 tsp. chervil or parsley
   flakes
1/4 tsp. summer savory
Water or vegetable broth

HEAT the oil in a deep heavy skillet or saucepan and brown the millet in it, stirring constantly. Add carrots, peas, celery and green pepper and cook 3 minutes.

ADD remaining ingredients including enough water, or broth, to extend 1" above millet-vegetable mixture.

COVER and bring to boil. Reduce heat to simmer and continue cooking until millet is tender, about 30 to 40 minutes. Serves 6.

SAVORY MILLET CASSEROLE

3/4 c. dry millet
2 c. water
1 clove garlic, chopped
1 medium onion, chopped
1/2 c. chopped celery
3 c. V-8 juice or tomato juice
1 (4-1/4 oz.) can sliced olives
1 tsp. salt
1 c. slivered almonds or
   cashew pieces
1/4 tsp. sage
1/4 tsp. summer savory
1 tbsp. sweet basil
2 tbsp. oil

BOIL water and millet 3 minutes; turn heat low; cover tightly and simmer 20 minutes. Stir in remaining ingredients. Put into greased or oiled 8 x 8 x 2" baking dish; cover with lid or foil. Bake at 350°F for 45 min. Turn off heat and let stand 10 min. Serve hot.

Variations: Add one can drained, cooked garbanzo beans. Omit the olives and stir in 1 10-oz. pkg. frozen green peas, thawed, just before baking.
Serves 8.

MILLET PATTIES

1-1/2 c. precooked millet
1 c. wheat germ
1/2 c. rolled oats
2 tbsp. oil
*1/2 c. water
1 medium onion, chopped
   fine
1/4 tsp. celery seed
1 tsp. garlic powder
1 tsp. salt

COMBINE ingredients. SHAPE into round patties on oiled cookie sheet. BROWN in hot oven approximately 25-30 min.

*If patties are too dry, add more water. If too moist, decrease amount.
Serves 4.

BASIC ROAST

Choose one from each of the categories:

2 C. PROTEIN: Cooked & mashed kidney beans, lentils, garbanzos, soybeans, meat analogs, tofu, cottage cheese, etc.

1 C. CARBOHYDRATE: dried whole wheat bread crumbs, uncooked oatmeal, cooked brown rice, crushed cereal flakes, wheat germ, etc.

1/2 C. NUTS (chopped or ground, raw): peanuts, cashews, almonds, walnuts, sunflower seeds, etc.

BINDING AGENTS: 3 tbsp. potato flour or meal, 2 tbsp. soy or garbanzo flour, 1/4 c. dry cream of wheat, 1 egg

LIQUID (1-1/2 c. as needed): tomato sauce or juice, broth from cooked or canned vegetables or from canned meat analogs, milk or soy milk, etc.

SEASONING (1/4 tsp. of one or more): sage, sweet basil, cumin, oregano, thyme, rosemary, Italian seasoning, bouquet garni, parsley, etc.

1 TSP. SALT: salt, soy sauce, Vegex, garlic salt, onion salt, celery salt, etc.

VEGETABLE OIL OR MARGARINE: 2 tbsp.

ONION: 1 chopped

Mix together. Press into an oiled loaf pan. Bake 45 min. to 1 hr. at 350°F Serve with light gravy, if desired. Serves 6.

SAVORY PECAN LOAF

1 c. chopped pecans
1 c. dry bread crumbs
1 small onion
2 medium-sized potatoes
1-1/2 c. milk
1/2 c. chopped celery
1/2 c. soy flour
1 tsp. salt
1 tsp. sage
1/4 tsp. sweet basil
1/8 tsp. thyme
1 tbsp. soy sauce
1/4 c. fresh parsley (or 1
   tbsp. dried)

CHOP onion and potatoes in milk in the blender with a few quick on-off motions. Combine all ingredients in a large mixing bowl. Pour into greased and crumbed loaf pan. Dot the top with small pea-sized pieces of margarine. Bake at 350°F for one hour or until set. Let stand 5-10 minutes before unmolding. Unmold onto serving platter. Garnish with a row of stuffed-olive "coins" down center of loaf and parsley bunches at both ends. Serve in slices with brown gravy and cranberry sauce. Serves 6.

NUT AND RICE LOAF

2 tbsp. oil
2 tbsp. flour
1-1/2 c. milk
2 c. cooked brown rice
2 c. chopped walnuts or
   pecans
1/4 c. chopped green
   peppers
1 small chopped onion or
   2 tbsp. minced dry
   onion
1/2 c. chopped celery
1 c. dry seasoned bread
   crumbs
1 tbsp. Vegex (or bouillon
   cubes)
2 tbsp. soy sauce

MIX all ingredients. Place in greased baking dish or individual molds. Bake at 350°F for 1 hour. Unmold immediately if in individual molds. Garnish with carrot curls, parsley, tomato wedges, etc. Tasty with cranberry sauce. Serves 6-8.

SUNFLOWER SEED ROAST

1 c. ground walnuts
1/2 c. bread crumbs
1/2 c. grated raw potato
1 c. milk
3 tbsp. grated onion
1/2 c. ground sunflower seeds
1 tbsp. oil, 1 tsp. salt

COMBINE all ingredients. Mix well. Pour into casserole. Cover and let stand for 1/2 hour. Bake at 350°F for 1 hour. Serves 6.

CORN TAMALE PIE

1 c. cornmeal (not degerminated)
3/4 c. boiling water
1 c. dry garbanzo beans (2 c. soaked)
3/4 to 1 c. water
1 c. whole-kernel corn
1-3/4 c. tomatoes, cut up
2 onions, chopped
3 cloves garlic, chopped
1 c. ripe olives, pitted and sliced
1/4 c. bell pepper (red & green), chopped
2 tbsp. oil, 1-1/2 tsp. salt
1 tsp. cumin
1/2 tsp. oregano
1 tsp. sweet basil

SOAK garbanzos overnight in water to cover (or soak 2 hours in water that has reached boiling point). Drain. Pour the 3/4 c. boiling water over the cornmeal and mix. (I use my electric mixer with wire whips for this recipe.) Blend soaked garbanzos with the 3/4-1 c. water in electric blender or run through fine blade of meat grinder. Add to cornmeal mixture. Saute chopped onion and garlic. Add to cornmeal-garbanzo mixture along with all other ingredients. (Reserve 2 tbsp. chopped bell pepper and 2 tbsp. sliced olives to garnish top.) Mix thoroughly. Place in flat, greased baking dish. Bake covered for 45 minutes and uncovered for 15-20 minutes at 350°F. Decorate top with olives. Serves 8.

OATMEAL POTATO PATTIES

1 c. cooked oatmeal
1 medium raw potato
4 tsp. vegetable oil
1/2 c. walnuts
1/2 to 1 c. toasted bread crumbs
1/2 tsp. salt
1/3 tsp. sage
1 tsp. Vegex or Marmite
1 tsp. soy flour

GRIND nuts and potato. Add all other ingredients, dissolving Vegex in 1/4 c. hot water. Add enough milk to moisten ingredients. Cover and let set 1/2 hour. Form into patties and brown in small amount of oil on both sides.
Serves 4.

MEATLESS LOAF

1 c. walnuts, finely chopped
1 c. raw potatoes
1 c. raw carrots
1 c. raw onions
1 c. tightly packed whole wheat bread crumbs
1 c. milk
2 tbsp. mayonnaise
1 tsp. salt
1 pkg. George Washington broth seasoning
1/2 can tomato soup, condensed

GRIND potatoes, carrots and onions, and place in bowl. Add other ingredients. Mix well and pour into a greased 9 x 9" square pan. Bake 1-1/2 hours at 350°F. Serve with tomato gravy. Serves 6 - 8.

OATMEAL PATTIES DELUXE (meaty flavor)

1 c. rolled oats
1 c. ground walnuts
3 tbsp. evaporated milk
1 medium onion, minced
1/2 c. soaked garbanzos blended in blender with 1/2 c. water or 2 eggs
1/2 tsp. salt
1 tsp. sage

Broth:
　1 qt. water
　1/3 c. soy sauce
　1 can tomato soup condensed (or homemade tomato soup)

WHIZ garbanzos and water in blender to make a paste (or beat 2 eggs).

COMBINE all ingredients. Drop from spoon to form patties in oiled skillet. BROWN on both sides. Cover with the following broth and simmer 45 minutes to 1 hour.

AFTER the 1 hour, remove patties and thicken the broth to make a gravy. Put patties in casserole dish and pour gravy over them. Can make ahead and heat in oven later. Serves 6.

CURRIED QUINOA

2 tbsp. oil
1 clove garlic, pressed
1 small onion, minced
1/2 c. chopped green
pepper
1/4 tsp. (or to taste)
curry powder (p. 260)
1/2 tsp. salt
1/2 c. raisins
4 c. water
2 c. quinoa (a grain)

HEAT a 2-quart soup pot. Add oil and saute garlic, onion and then pepper. Add curry and salt. Cover and cook for a few minutes. Add raisins and water. Cover and bring to a rapid boil. While water and vegetables are heating, toast the quinoa in a thin skillet for about 10 minutes while stirring continuously. Add quinoa to boiling water. Cover, reduce heat and simmer 15 to 20 minutes. With a damp wooden spoon mix from top to bottom. Cover and allow to rest for an additional 5 to 10 minutes. Serve with your favorite Indian dishes.

STUFFED PUMPKIN

Stuffing:
1 c. cooked whole kernel
wheat (p. 42) or wild rice
2 c. cooked brown rice
4 to 5 c. dry seasoned bread
cubes
1 c. chopped celery
1 c. chopped onion
1 tsp. Vegex, diluted in 1 c.
hot water
1 tsp. garlic salt
1 tsp. sage
2 tbsp. soy sauce
1 c. sauteed mushrooms
(optional)
1 small to medium pumpkin
1 c. nuts (pecans are best)
Optional:
1 c. currants or raisins
Diced Chicken Soyameat

COMBINE and mix all stuffing ingredients thoroughly.

TO PREPARE pumpkin, cut the top out, and clean the inside of seeds and strings. Pour melted margarine into pumpkin and sprinkle the inside with salt. Leave the pumpkin lid off and bake for 30-45 minutes at 350°F.

REMOVE pumpkin from oven and place stuffing inside. Cover pumpkin with its lid and bake an additional 20-40 minutes. Remove pumpkin from oven, garnish and serve.

COTTAGE CHEESE LOAF

1 large onion, chopped fine
3 pkg. George Washington
  Broth Seasoning
1/2 11-oz. pkg. or more
  Special K Cereal
1/4 c. margarine
2 c. low fat cottage cheese
1/2 c. ground nuts
4 large eggs (or see egg
  replacers p. 260)

SAUTE onion and margarine until transparent. Beat eggs slightly, then add other ingredients and mix well. Add sauted onions and mix again.

PLACE in large flat casserole dish and bake at 350°F for about 1 hour. Top will be dark brown when done.

COTTAGE CHEESE PATTIES

1 c. low fat cottage cheese
  or firm tofu, drained
1-1/2 c. quick rolled oats
2 eggs slightly beaten or
  egg replacer (see p. 260)
1 large onion, finely
  chopped
1/2 tsp. salt

MIX quite dry, adding more oats if needed. Drop from spoon to form patties in lightly oiled skillet. Make patties small. Brown on one side, then turn and brown the second side. Place patties in casserole dish and cover with the following mushroom gravy. Bake at 350°F for 30-45 minutes. Serves 6.

MUSHROOM GRAVY

1/2 lb. fresh mushroom,
  thinly sliced
2 cans condensed mush-
  room soup
1 can evaporated milk (or
  1-1/2 c. rich non-dairy
  milk)

SAUTE mushrooms. Add mushroom soup and milk. Mix well. Use over patties in casserole dish.

BASIC HOMEMADE PASTA

Without eggs:
2-1/2 c. semolina flour (made
by grinding durum wheat)
1/2 c. water
2 tbsp. oil
2 tbsp. lecithin granules

With eggs:
2-1/2 c. semolina flour (made
by grinding durum wheat)
4 tbsp. water
2 unbeaten eggs

CHOOSE which recipe at left you will follow.
GRIND approximately 1-1/2 cups durum wheat on "fine"setting of home flour mill to yield 2-1/2 cups semolina flour.
PLACE 2-1/2 c. semolina flour in large mixing bowl. Make a well in the flour and add the water, oil, lecithin OR water and egg. Use your fingers to work these ingredients together swiftly and knead well until smooth. This will take about 10 minutes.

Let the dough rest 10 minutes before rolling out.
Roll out into rectangle on floured surface to desired thickness, from paper-thin to 1/16th inch, turning dough around and over frequently on the floured surface as you roll it out. Pasta swells up during cooking so roll thinner than desired finished product.
Cut into long, noodle length strips or other desired shapes, using pizza cutter or sharp knife.
Cook immediately or lay out to dry or freeze for later use.
TO COOK: Drop into boiling water in large pot to which 1 tbsp. oil and 1 tsp. salt has been added. Cook, uncovered, about 8-10 minutes (less if very thin) or until "al dente" stage (firm to the bite). Keep pushing noodles back under water. Drain and serve immediately with your favorite sauce.
Note: Durum wheat is a variety of wheat grown especially for pasta. The flour is creamy or yellowy white in color. When ground into flour for commercial use the flour is called Semolina flour. It is generally a refined flour as is white flour for bread making. If durum wheat is not available whole wheat bread flour can be substituted. The resulting pasta will be browner and the texture a little softer.

QUICKIE SPAGHETTI SAUCE

1 to 2 small cans of tomato paste
2 to 3 cans water
3 to 4 cloves garlic (chopped fine) or garlic pwd.
1 large onion (finely chopped) or onion powder
Salt to taste
3 tbsp. olive oil
1 tsp. Italian herb seasoning
1/2 tsp. sweet basil

SIMMER 15 minutes. Serve over spaghetti.

GREEN SAUCE (for noodles)

1 large bunch parsley
1 large fresh bunch sweet basil or 2 tbsp. dry basil
3 cloves garlic, minced
1/3 c. olive oil
1/2 tsp. salt or to taste
1 lb. homemade noodles, cooked

CHOP parsley clusters and fresh basil leaves in food processor. In a small saucepan, combine chopped parsley, basil, garlic, olive oil, salt and heat but do not boil. Stir lightly into cooked, drained homemade noodles.
YIELD: 6 servings.

MAMA GLENDA'S RAVIOLI'S IN SAUCE

The secret of true Italian sauces is the long slow cooking. When I serve this Ravioli dish I am always asked for the recipe. The sauce is delicious. It can be made ahead and frozen if desired.
For sauce, saute until clear: 5 to 7 cloves garlic, minced
1/2 c. olive oil, 1 large onion, finely chopped
Add and simmer 4 hours with lid on, stirring occasionally:
1 qt. tomatoes, chopped finely (canned or fresh); 1 (15 oz.) can tomato sauce; 1 tsp. sugar; salt to taste; 1/4 c. parsley chopped.
Serve over ricotta cheese-filled raviolas or large pasta shells.

CREAMED VEGETABLE PASTA
LOW FAT CREAM SAUCE

Make the following low fat cream sauce and toss with fresh cooked pasta and a mixture of fresh or frozen steamed vegetables of your choice.

3/4 c. low fat milk
2 tbsp. flour
1/4 c. cold milk
1/4 tsp. salt
1 tbsp. margarine
1/2 tsp. chicken style seasoning (p. 261)

HEAT 3/4 c. low fat milk (I use tofu milk powder) to lukewarm. (For richer consistency use more powder than when making milk to drink). While milk is heating, mix 2 tbsp. flour and 1/4 c. cold milk to form smooth paste. When milk is warm stir in flour paste with wire whip.

ADD 1/4 tsp. salt. 1 tbsp. margarine and 1/2 tsp. chicken style seasoning. Cook, stirring constantly until thickened. Makes 1 cup.

VEGETARIAN MEAT BALLS (for Pasta)

1 c. crushed cornflakes or wheaties
2 tbsp. Brewer's yeast
1 tbsp. wheat germ
3/4 c. coarsely ground walnuts
2 tbsp. chopped parsley or dry parsley flakes
1 pkg. George Washington Broth
1/2 c. soaked garbanzos whizzed in blender with 1/2 c. water (OR 2 beaten eggs)*
3 tbsp. milk
1 c. small curd cottage cheese or mashed tofu
1/2 medium onion chopped fine

MIX all ingredients together and put in covered bowl for 3 or 4 hours or overnight before cooking. Then shape into balls and brown on both sides in cooking oil, being careful not to burn as these brown quickly. Serves 6.

*NOTE: for other egg replacers, see p. 260.

TOFU LASAGNA

12 lasagna noodles, whole wheat or regular
Tomato sauce (recipe below)
Cashew cheese (recipe below)

PREPARE Tomato Sauce and Cashew Cheese.

COOK noodles till done. Put layer of noodles in long casserole. Spoon tomato sauce over noodles, then cashew cheese mixture. Alternate 3 times.

Bake Lasagne at 350°F until bubbly hot, about 45 minutes. Serves 8 to 10.

TOMATO SAUCE:

2 tbsp. oil
1/2 c. chopped onion
1/4 c. grated carrots
1/2 c. chopped celery
1/4 c. chopped green pepper
*1 c. Vegeburger (optional)
1 clove garlic
1/2 tsp. oregano
1/2 tsp. basil
1 qt. tomatoes

SAUTE vegetables in oil until tender and add Vegeburger. Add tomatoes and simmer for one-half hour.

*Vegeburger is a meatless ground hamburger-like product that is available in many health food stores. It is made of wheat gluten.

CASHEW CHEESE:

1 c. water
1 c. cashews, raw
1/2 tsp. salt
1/4 c. oil
1/3 c. lemon juice
1 4-oz. jar pimientos
1 tsp. onion salt
1 tsp. garlic salt
3 tbsp. Brewer's yeast
1 lb. Tofu, drained

PLACE water, cashews and salt in blender. Whiz thoroughly. Add oil slowly until mixture thickens. Add lemon juice, pimiento, and seasoning and whiz again. Crumble tofu into bowl, pour in the cashew cheese and mix. Use alternately with tomato sauce and noodles. Save some to drizzle on top.

MACARONI AND CASHEW NUT CHEESE

1 c. macaroni, enriched
1 qt. boiling water
1/2 tsp. salt, 1 tbsp. oil

CHEESE SAUCE:

1/2 c. cashew nuts, raw
2 oz. pimentos (2 medium)
1/4 c. lemon juice
3 tbsp. Brewer's flake yeast
1 tsp. salt
1/4 tsp. onion powder
Shake of garlic powder
1-1/2 c. water

CRUMBS:

1/4 c. whole wheat crumbs
1 tbsp. Brewer's flake yeast
1 tbsp. oil
Few drops of butter flavoring
   (Optional)

ADD macaroni to rapidly boiling, salted water in large kettle. Let cook uncovered 15 minutes. Add 1 tbsp. oil to cooked macaroni. Mix lightly. Do not drain.

WHILE macaroni is cooking, combine cheese sauce ingredients and blend in blender until very fine. Add to macaroni. Salt to taste. Put in casserole, cover. Bake at 350°F for 30 min.

SPRINKLE with buttered crumbs, and bake uncovered 15 minutes. Or omit putting in casserole. Cook 15 minutes on low heat after adding cheese mixture.

YIELD: 4 servings.

VEGETABLE SAUTE FETTUCCINE

green beans
zucchini
green or yellow summer
   squash
chopped onions
sliced mushrooms
diced eggplant
tomato
Sweet basil, Italian herbs
Italian herbs, garlic
Optional: cashew pieces,
   sliced almonds, or pinenuts

TO SERVE sauted vegetables over fettuccine, simply saute vegetables in olive oil and a little water until tender. Do not overcook. Serve over fresh-cooked fettuccine.

HOW TO PREPARE AND SERVE IT

Gluten is the protein of wheat. Instead of paying extra money to go out and purchase already prepared meat analogs in the canned, frozen, or dried form, you can make it yourself at home for just a fraction of the cost. Mock meat can be made from whole wheat or white bread flour using the following procedure:

HOW TO MAKE GLUTEN

8 cups hard-wheat flour (high gluten content) (may try using **1 cup gluten flour** with **7 cups white flour** OR **half white flour and half whole wheat flour** OR **all whole wheat**). **3 to 4 cups cold water.**

To the 8 cups flour, add slowly 3-4 cups cold water, and mix into a stiff dough as for bread. Knead well, at least 5 minutes by the clock; or if you prefer to count the strokes, count 250. Kneading develops the gluten and is important.

Cover the dough ball with cold water and let stand for any convenient length of time — 1 hour to overnight. This loosens the starch. Wash out the starch by kneading the dough under water, renewing the water as necessary. Stop washing just before the water is clear.* You will notice the dough is very soft as you wash it, then suddenly becomes firm. That is the time to stop washing. Rinse in clear water and place gluten on a board to drain. Form into a roll and cut with a sharp knife into half-inch slices. Drop into boiling Savory broth. After 3 minutes, reduce heat and simmer 1 hour. Let sit in broth overnight, if possible, to marinate.

Remaining broth may be thickened with 1 tbsp. flour to 1 c. of liquid. When cooked, the gluten is ready to use in loaves, patties, stews, potpies, or as cutlets or "steaks".

The gluten may be ground and used in patties. The pieces may be dipped in breading meal and browned in an oiled skillet, baked or broiled and served with gravy for a meatless main dish.

*(Or tear off a chunk of dough and wash under a slow stream of water as you squeeze in your hand to remove starch and bran.)

SAVORY BROTH I (for dark beef-like color)

8 c. water
1/2 c. soy sauce
1 c. tomato juice
1 tbsp. nutritional food
   yeast flakes
2 tbsp. onion powder or
   2 fresh onions
Vegex or Marmite to
   taste (try 2 tbsp.) or 4
   to 6 bouillon cubes

COMBINE all ingredients in large cooking pot. Bring to boil. Drop cut pieces of gluten into broth. Broth needs to be strongly flavored in order to adequately flavor the gluten pieces. Broth needs to be boiling when gluten pieces are dropped in and then turned lower so broth simmers but does not boil rapidly. Rapidly boiling broth produces tough gluten steaks.

SIMMER gluten in broth for 45 minutes to 1 hour.

SAVORY BROTH II (for light chicken-like color)

1 quart water
1 tbsp. nutritional food
   yeast flakes
1/2 tsp. salt
1/2 tsp. celery seed
1/4 tsp. sage
1/4 tsp. thyme
1/2 tsp. cumin, ground
1/2 tsp. coriander,
   ground
1/4 tsp. garlic powder
1/4 tsp. tarragon
1/4 tsp. rosemary
1/2 tsp. turmeric
2 tbsp. corn oil
1 tsp. chicken style
   seasoning (p. 261)

COMBINE all ingredients in large cooking pot. Bring to boil. Drop cut pieces of gluten into broth and reduce heat so gluten simmers but does not boil rapidly. (Rapidly boiling broth produces tough gluten steaks.) SIMMER gluten in broth for 45 minutes to 1 hour.

BOUQUET GARNI

VEGETARIAN INDIAN CURRY

2 tbsp. margarine
3 to 4 large carrots, cut in julienne strips
1 green pepper, cut in julienne strips
1 large onion, cut in julienne strips
1 tsp. curry powder
1/3 c. flour
3 c. chicken style broth
1 c. half & half or rich soy milk
1 can Worthington Chicken, cut in strips
1 10-oz. pkg. frozen peas

SAUTE carrots, onions and peppers in margarine until half done. Add curry powder and flour. Mix well, Then add chicken broth, half and half, and juice from Soyameat. Cook over low heat until thickened. Add chicken strips and peas. Heat over low heat just until frozen peas are done. Serve over rice (brown). Add toppings at the table.

Toppings to serve at table to go over the curry: currents, diced cucumber, tomato, avocados, olives, salted nuts, etc.

TASTY STEAKS

1 can Worthington Vegetable Steaks or similar product
breading meal
Brewer's Yeast
oil
1 large onion, sliced
flour
2 tsp. Vegex or Marmite
1/2 tsp garlic powder
1 can mushroom soup

ROLL Worthington Steaks in mixture of 1/2 breading meal and 1/2 Brewer's yeast. Fry in oil until brown. Slice and saute onion. In same skillet put more oil and lg. tbsp. of flour and brown. Add 1-1/2 c. water and the Vegex, garlic powder, and mushroom soup into pan with onions. Stir until smooth and pour over steaks. Put in dish in alternate layers with steaks. Put in oven and bake slowly 1 hr. (350°F).

SWISS STYLE "STEAKS"

1 can gluten steaks or homemade gluten
1 chopped onion
1/2 chopped bell pepper
1/2 stalk chopped celery
1 to 2 cans tomato soup

BREAD the steaks in breading meal and fry. Remove from pan. Turn down heat and add onion, green pepper, and celery. Saute until tender, then add tomato soup, undiluted. Return steaks to pan and cover with sauce. Heat until bubbly. Remove to serving dish and serve.

HOLIDAY STUFFING CASSEROLE

No dressing is stuffed into a bird in this holiday entree. The stuffing mixture is layered alternately in a casserole dish with Protose slices.

1 20-oz. can Worthington Protose
2 tbsp. soy sauce
3/4 c. water
1/4 c. margarine
1 chopped onion
1 4-oz. can sliced mushrooms
1 can cream of mushroom soup
1/2 c. sliced black olives
1/2 c. chopped celery
3/4 to 1 pkg. seasoned, cubed stuffing mix

REMOVE Protose from can. (Tip. With can opener cut around both ends of Protose can, run knife all around inside edge of can, then push Protose out, keeping one lid in place to push on.) Cut into 1/4-inch slices, then each slice in half. SAUTE Protose slices in soy sauce, water, and margarine until all liquid is gone, turning to brown on both sides. Mix stuffing mix, onions, mushrooms, olives, celery, and enough water to make the consistency of dressing. (Try 1-1/2 c or so.) Place alternate layers of stuffing mixture and Protose in oblong baking dish. Top with undiluted mushroom soup. Bake 45 min. at 350°F. Serve with cranberry sauce and/or mushroom gravy. Serves 8-10.

STUFFED BELL PEPPERS

6 medium bell peppers
3/4 c. chopped green pepper
1-1/2 c. cooked brown rice
3/4 c. water
1-1/2 tsp. honey
3/4 tsp. celery salt
1/4 tsp. sage
3/4 c. chopped onion
2-1/4 c. Vegeburger* or homemade gluten
1-1/2 c. tomato juice
2 boullion cubes
3/4 tsp. garlic salt

PAR-BOIL peppers 5 minutes. Brown onions, peppers, burger in oil. Combine with other ingredients. Stuff peppers. Bake in oiled pan 1 hour at 350°F.

*A vegetarian hamburger available in some health food stores and super markets. (Or use homemade gluten, see p. 148.)

ONE DISH MEAL (Soyameat and rice)

1 medium onion, diced
1 c. diced celery
1 c. brown rice, uncooked
1 c. Soyameat Chicken
Style (FriChik), diced
1 c. diced carrots
1/2 c. oil
1 tsp. Vegex
2 c. water
3 tbsp. Kitchen Bouquet
1 can mushroom soup

MIX onion, celery, rice, carrots, and Soyameat together and put into casserole. Put oil, Vegex, water, broth, and soup into saucepan and cook for 3 minutes. Pour sauce over casserole and mix gently. Bake in 350°F oven for 1 hour. Serves 6.

BROCCOLI AND GLUTEN OVER RICE

1 bunch broccoli, sliced
and blanched
1 can (2 c.) braised gluten
product
1/4 c. Teriyaki Sauce or
soy sauce
1 tbsp. vegetable oil
1-1/2 tsp. chicken style
seasoning (p. 261)
3 tbsp. water mixed with 1
tsp. cornstarch

DRAIN liquid from 1 can vegetarian gluten product. (I like the Companion brand braised gluten from oriental food markets.) Pull apart or slice into strips and braise in oil and Teriyaki Sauce or soy sauce until liquid is absorbed. Set aside.

WASH, slice, and blanch broccoli. (To blanch, drop broccoli slices into boilding water for 1-2 minutes, then immediately submerge in cold water.) Saute broccoli in oil and season with chicken style seasoning.

PLACE broccoli on serving platter. Arrange braised gluten on top of broccoli. Make thickened sauce of cornstarch and water. Pour over braised gluten. Sprinkle sesame seeds over top. Serve with steamed brown rice.

NOTE: Braised tofu works nicely in place of gluten for this recipe.

Serves 6.

SUKIYAKI (quick one-dish meal)

1 can Multi Grain Cutlets or any vegetarian steak products, sliced and browned in oil
2 stalks celery, sliced slantwise
1/2 lb. fresh or frozen snow peas
2 or 3 fresh mushrooms
3 green onions, cut crosswise
2 c. shredded Chinese cabbage (spinach may be substituted)
1/2 lb. fresh bean sprouts
2 tbsp. soy sauce
2 tbsp. honey

USE an electric fry pan if available, and while still hot from cooking cutlets, add vegetables, layering *in order given.* Add soy sauce and honey, cover with lid, and cook 5 to 7 minutes at 350°F on fry pan control. Serve over cooked brown rice. Serves 6.

VEGETABLE SKALLOPS

Drain **1 can vegetable skallops** and coat with your favorite breading meal or use this nutritious mix for breading. Brown in oiled skillet. Serve with Fresh Tartar Sauce. Serves 6.

BREADING MEAL:
1 c. oatmeal
1 c. food yeast
1 tbsp. chicken style seasoning (p. 261)
Onion or garlic salt (if desired)

WHIZ all ingredients in blender until fine. STORE breading meal in a tightly-covered jar.

FRESH TARTAR SAUCE

1/2 c. low fat mayonnaise
1/2 c. plain yogurt
1/4 c. finely chopped cucumber
1 green onion, finely chopped
1/2 tsp. dill weed
1 tsp. lemon juice

MIX well and chill before serving. YIELD: 1-1/4 cups sauce.

TACOS

1 c. Vita-Burger* soaked in hot water 15 minutes (or 2. c. Vegeburger)
1 onion, chopped
1 clove garlic, chopped
1/8 tsp. oregano or basil
1/8 tsp. cumin
1 tbsp. oil
1/2 c. tomato sauce
1 dozen corn tortillas
Shredded lettuce
Diced tomato, onions, ripe chopped olives
Guacamole sauce

SAUTE onion and garlic until almost done; add burger; stir; cook about 8-10 minutes. Add tomato sauce and cook down until nicely mixed and flavors blended. Crisp taco shells in preheated oven at 450°F for 1-2 minutes. Spoon 2-3 tbsp. burger into each warm taco; top with about 1/2 cup shredded lettuce, diced tomato, onion, 2 tbsp. guacamole sauce, and olives. YIELD: 12 tacos.
*Dry burger granules (meatless).
VARIATION: Use refried beans instead of burger; add lettuce, tomato, guacamole, etc.

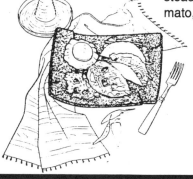

MOCK CHICKEN CASSEROLE

2 c. cooked brown rice
2 to 3 pieces of chicken style soyameat, diced
1/2 c. onion
1 c. celery
1 can mushrooms
1/3 c. juice of mushrooms
1/2 c. homemade mayonnaise
1 can mushroom soup

CHOP onion and celery and saute together. Mix with remaining ingredients. Bake 40-50 minutes at 350°F. Serves 6.

CREAMY CHICKEN SURPRISE
(Served in patty shells)

2 c. fresh mushrooms, or more
1 2-oz. jar diced pimiento
1/4 c. chopped green pepper
1 onion, chopped
3 tbsp. butter or margarine

SAUTE first 5 ingredients together.

1/2 c. sliced almonds
2 c. Chicken Style Soyameat, including liquid, diced
2 cans mushroom or celery soup
1/2 tsp. sage
1/4 tsp. marjoram
1/4 tsp. thyme
1 pkg. frozen green peas (petite)

STIR in remaining ingredients.
HEAT through and serve in patty shells or over toast points.
Serves 8.

STROGANOFF

Saute in 3 tbsp. margarine:
1/2 c. onion (1 medium), chopped
1/2 c. chopped celery
1 clove garlic, minced

SAUTE first 3 ingredients in 3 tbsp. margarine.

1/2 c. dry vegeburger that has been reconstituted with 1/2 c. hot water
1/2 lb. fresh mushrooms, sauted
1 can mushroom soup

ADD remaining ingredients and steam over low heat until done.
ADD sour cream or yogurt. Serve over noodles or brown rice.
Serves 6.

Chapter 8

Meatless Dinner Meals III

Featuring:

- Rice

- Potatoes

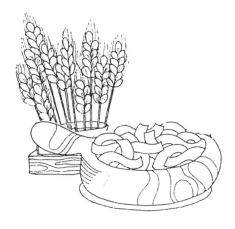

"Wherefore do ye spend money for that which is not bread?
and your labour for that which satisfieth not?
hearken diligently unto me, and eat ye that which is good,
and let your soul delight itself in fatness." Isaiah 55:2

Brown rice is recommended instead of white rice for recipes in our cookbook. Why? White rice has had part of its kernel removed by a milling process. God designed rice, and other grains, to be a complete unit, its three parts working together within our bodies as a team.

Rice, like other grains, is made of three basic parts: the bran (outer covering), the germ, and the endosperm (center portion). When eating white rice, you are eating endosperm. Brown rice is the entire kernel with all 3 parts of the kernel intact.

Science has discovered that in order for the carbohydrate of the endosperm of the grain kernel to be utilized properly by the body, the B-vitamins from the bran and germ portion must be present.

Back in the 1800's when grains were first refined and white breads became more popular than whole wheat, a deficiency disease, beri-beri, became a problem. The team effort of the three parts or the grain kernel had been severed.

To prevent beri-beri, the Federal Government began to require the enriching of white flour. Although the 20 or more vitamins and minerals contained in whole grains are removed with the refining to white flour, four are added back in the enriching process: three B-vitamins: niacin, thiamine and riboflavin; and one mineral: iron. This has been likened to the great grain robbery. How would you feel if someone robbed you of $20 and because of a guilty conscience returned $4? Would you feel enriched?

Brown rice is easy to prepare. Cooking directions follow. There are a number of suggestions in this section for using brown rice as a basis for meatless dinner meals.

Again, we remind you to plan dinner around the carbohydrate dish for the meal. What can be served over or with brown rice or potatoes to make a delicious dinner? Begin with our cookbook suggestions and then start collecting ideas of your own. Try soupy beans, wok cooked vegetables with tofu, curried vegetables with nuts, or creamed vegetables.

Potatoes are a nutritious, starchy vegetable and low in calories and fat, that is, until you add butter, sour cream or gravy. Yams, sweet potatoes and winter squashes are great alternates for variety and add Vitamin A as well.

Try planning a dinner meal around baked potatoes. In this chapter find topping ideas for baked potatoes. Served with a steamed vegetable and fresh green salad the meal is complete.

BROWN RICE

BROWN RICE can be purchased most commonly as Long-Grain Brown Rice and Short-Grain Brown Rice.

LONG-GRAIN RICE is the best choice when you want the finished rice to be flaky, and fluffy—not sticky, such as our Savory Fried Rice recipe and when you are steaming rice for dinner.

SHORT-GRAIN RICE is best when a sticky finished product is needed such as the Holiday Rice Ring here. The mixture will stick together better. Short Grain Rice is also an ideal choice when milling rice into flour for use in baking.

TO COOK BROWN RICE — In a heavy saucepan bring 2 cups water and 1/4 tsp. salt to boil. Add 1 cup brown rice. Cover and when boiling turn heat down to low. Cook 45 minutes without peeking or stirring.

EXTRA FLAKY RICE can be secured by placing the 1 cup brown rice in a dry skillet to lightly brown while water is coming to a boil. Stir constantly over medium heat about 5 minutes. You may hear it crackle and pop. Add to 2 cups boiling water and cook as outlined above. YIELD: 2 cups cooked brown rice.

HOLIDAY RICE RING

2-1/2 c. cooked brown rice, hot
1/2 c. sunflower seeds
1 c. pineapple chunks, cut up
1/4 c. chopped onion
1 tsp. chicken style seasoning (p. 261)
Salt to taste
1/2 c. chopped green pepper
1/2 c. white raisins
1/4 c. soy sauce
4 tbsp. honey
2 tbsp. margarine

COOK rice according to package directions. Saute peppers and onions in margarine. Combine cut-up pineapple chunks, seeds, raisins, soy sauce and seasonings. ADD rice mixture with honey. Press into 1-quart ring mold which has been evenly greased with margarine. Bake at 350°F for 25 minutes. To unmold, run knife around edge and turn onto plate. Fill center with steamed green peas. Serves 6.

SAVORY FRIED RICE

2 carrots, shredded
1 medium onion or 6 green
   onions, chopped
2 cloves garlic, diced
4 c. cooked brown rice
Onion salt to taste
Chicken style seasoning (p. 261)
   or George Washington seasoning, to taste
1 c. frozen peas, thawed
1/2 c. cashews or other nuts
1/2 c. raisins
Turmeric to color
A few shakes Cardamom

SAUTE first three ingredients in a little oil or margarine. Add remaining ingredients, stir and heat through. Serves 6.

ORIENTAL RICE

4 c. cooked brown rice
3 tbsp. margarine
1 small jar pimientos
1/2 c. green pepper
1/2 c. pine nuts or slivered
   almonds
1 bunch green onions, chopped
2 to 4 tbsp. soy sauce, to taste
1 can water chestnuts

MIX together.

BAKE at 350°F for 30 minutes. Serves 6.

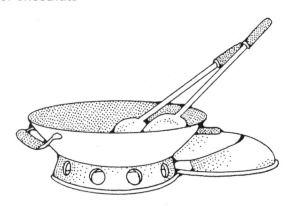

OVER POTATOES

QUICK MEATLESS MEALS — Try these quick ideas for serving a meal over potatoes accompanied with a leafy green salad.

1. Soupy seasoned lentils over baked potatoes.
2. Boston Baked Beans over baked potatoes.
3. Worthington or Loma Linda Vegetarian Chili Beans over baked potatoes.
4. Steamed broccoli chunks and Cashew Pimento Cheese (p. 80) over potatoes.
5. Sauteed fresh mushrooms in olive oil over potatoes.
6. Cottage Cheese over baked potatoes.
7. Creamed peas or mixed vegetables over baked potatoes.
8. Low fat sour cream or yogurt with chives and bacos over potatoes.
9. Cashew Gravy or Mom's White Gravy (p. 256) and scrambled tofu or eggs over potatoes.

BAKED POTATOES, CONVENTIONAL OVEN

WASH potatoes with vegetable brush and remove any blemishes with small paring knife. Prick potatoes with tines of a fork or end of sharp knife in several places and place directly on oven rack in preheated oven. (For soft skinned baked potatoes coat each potato with oil before baking or wrap each potato with foil prior to baking.)
Bake **WHITE POTATOES** in hot oven (425°F) 40 to 60 minutes.
Bake **SWEET POTATOES** in hot oven (425°F) 30 minutes.

BAKED POTATOES, MICROWAVE OVEN

SELECT uniform, medium-size baking potatoes. Scrub potatoes well. Prick each potato through the skin with tines of fork in several places. Arrange potatoes on oven floor. Leave about 1-inch space between potatoes. Using full power, bake as follows:

1 potato	4 to 5 minutes
2 potatoes	5 to 7 minutes
4 potatoes	7 to 9 minutes

These times are approximate and will vary according to the size and variety of potato being cooked. Turn the potatoes over halfway through cooking time.

SAUTEED MUSHROOMS IN OLIVE OIL

Mushrooms
Olive oil
Garlic powder
Baked potatoes

WASH and slice fresh mushrooms. Saute in olive oil. Add garlic powder to season. Serve over baked potatoes instead of sour cream or butter. Optional: chopped green onions or chives.

DUTCH OVEN MEAL

Assortment of
**   vegetables:**
Small red potatoes
Chunks of carrots
Cauliflower
Broccoli
Turnips
Rutabagas or
Beets and onions
1 to 2 cans Worthington
**   Fri-Chik Soymeat with**
**   its liquid**

IN LARGE HEAVY stainless steel or cast iron dutch oven place an assortment of vegetables and cut in large chunks: small red potatoes, chunks of carrots, cauliflower, broccoli, turnips, rutabagas, or beets and onion. Add 1-2 cans Worthington Fri-Chik Soymeat with it's liquid. Cover, bring to boil. TURN heat to low. COOK until just barely tender.
Serves 6 - 8.

COTTAGE BAKED POTATOES

3 large potatoes
Dash of salt
2 tbsp. margarine
1 tbsp. minced onion
1 tbsp. minced parsley
1 c. low fat cottage
**   cheese**
Paprika

SCRUB potatoes thoroughly (so skins can be eaten). Bake at 400°F until tender when pierced with a fork. Cut each in half lengthwise; sprinkle each with salt, margarine, onion, and parsley. Slash each half with a knife a few times for seasonings to penetrate. Cover each half with cottage cheese; sprinkle with paprika. Return to oven long enough to heat the cheese. Serve at once. Serves 6. Per serving (236): 156 calories; 7.7 gram protein; 4.0 gram fat.

OVEN FRENCH FRIES

5 medium potatoes,
  peeled
1 tbsp. oil
Preheat oven to 400°F

CUT the peeled potatoes into 1/2-inch lengthwise strips like French fries. Put the oil and potatoes on a cookie sheet. Stir the potatoes until they are all coated with oil. Bake in the preheated oven for about 20 to 30 minutes. While they are baking, turn with a spatula once. When tender. sprinkle with salt and serve. Serves 4.

OVEN-ROASTED POTATO CHUNKS

2 lbs. potatoes, any
  kind, cut into large
  chunks
1/3 c. olive oil (or less)
1 large onion,
  chopped
1 large green or red
  bell pepper,
  chopped
2 tbsp. chopped
  parsley

PREHEAT oven to 450°F. Saute onion and peppers. Combine all ingredients. Place in shallow baking pan. Bake, stirring occasionally, 40 minutes or until potatoes are tender.

Serves 6-8.

Chapter 9

Vegetables
All Around

- Herbs for Seasoning Vegetables

- Tips for Cooking Vegetables

- Vegetable Dishes

- Sauces and Dressings for Vegetables

"He causeth the grass to grow for the cattle and herb for the service of man: that he may bring forth food out of the earth." Ps 104:14.

As you might guess, we recommend eating lots of vegetables. By consulting the Eating Right Pyramid again you will notice that 3-5 servings of vegetables are recommended each day.

In Biblical Old Testament times, vegetables were a standby. History tells us that 5,000 years ago Babylonians raised turnips, onions, beans, radishes, lettuce, and cucumbers. In the nineteenth century the United States emerged as the world's largest vegetable producer.

Vegetables are blood builders. They carry valuable minerals and vitamins to regulate body processes. Vegetables are high in water content and fiber. They have been called our "protective" foods. We can eat large amounts of vegetables daily to great advantage. It is an ideal plan to keep vegetables at one meal and fruits at another for better digestibility. Our Daily Menu Planner suggests fruits at breakfast time, vegetables for the noon main meal and either a fruit or vegetable dish for supper.

Dark green, leafy and deep yellow vegetables are especially rich in nutrients. For the complete vegetarian who uses no dairy products, steamed leafy greens are one of the best plant sources of calcium.

Choose fresh, crisp vegetables. If they look wilted, shriveled, or limp they are not fresh. If leafy greens have lost their bright green color they are no longer fresh. As vegetables sit, they lose quality both in texture and flavor and also in loss of minerals and viatmins.

If good quality fresh vegetables are not available, frozen vegetables may be a better choice because frozen vegetables are processed quickly from field to freezer.

Have fun experimenting with the tasty vegetable recipes in this chapter as well as your own creations.

A pinch of herbs can perk up any vegetable dish. Taste preferences vary — there are no rules for seasoning. We suggest experimenting, starting with small amounts. There will be happy surprises.

Fresh herbs are the most desirable, especially in salads. Use three times as much as if dried. Rubbing the whole dried leaves between the fingers releases the fresh fragrance — long cooking destroys flavor.

Add herbs about 15 minutes before serving to develop the fresh fragrance you want to enjoy.

Beets:	Tarragon, dill, sweet basil, thyme, bay leaf, cardamom seed
Broccoli:	Tarragon, marjoram, oregano
Brussel sprouts:	Sweet basil, dill, savory, caraway, thyme
Carrots:	Sweet basil, dill, marjoram, thyme, parsley
Cauliflower:	Rosemary, savory, dill, tarragon
Cabbage:	Caraway, celery seed, savory, tarragon, dill
Cucumbers:	Tarragon, sweet basil, savory
Eggplant::	Sweet basil, thyme, oregano, rosemary, sage
Beans (dried):	Sweet basil, oregano, dill, savory, mint, cumin, garlic, parsley, bay leaf
Green beans:	Sweet basil, dill, marjoram, rosemary, thyme, oregano, savory
Lima beans:	Sweet basil, chives, marjoram, savory
Onions:	Oregano, thyme, sweet basil
Peas:	Sweet basil, mint, savory, oregano, dill
Potatoes:	Dill, chives, sweet basil, marjoram, savory, parsley
Squash:	Sweet basil, dill, oregano, savory
Spinach:	Tarragon, thyme, oregano, rosemary
Tomatoes:	Sweet basil, oregano, dill, garlic, savory, parsley, bay leaf
Green salad dressings:	Sweet basil, parsley, chives, tarragon, lemon thyme, dill, marjoram, oregano, rosemary, savory, mint
Cole slaw:	Dill, marjoram, caraway seed, savory, mint
Cottage cheese:	Parsley, sweet basil, chive, sage, marjoram
Fruit salad:	Mint, rosemary, lemon balm
Spaghetti sauce:	Sweet basil, oregano
Chili substitute:	Spanish onions with cumin

COOKING VEGETABLES

Vegetables are most colorful and palatable and will retain more nutrients if these rules are followed in cooking:

1. Cook in as short a time as possible.
2. Cook in a small amount of water. Add the raw vegetables to boiling water, then reduce the heat when boiling resumes. Do not discard the remaining liquid. It will contain water-soluble vitamins and can be used in soup, sauces, gravy, or bread. Refrigerate the liquid quickly in an airtight container.
3. Cook vegetables whole or in large pieces, as more nutrients are lost when more surface area is exposed.
4. Cook only until crispy-tender.
5. Never use soda in the cooking water, as it causes destruction of some of the vitamins—mainly thiamine and ascorbic acid (vitamin C).
6. Add the salt near the end of the cooking time, because salt draws out the juice which carries the vitamins and minerals. Better yet, omit salt.
7. Try to not lift the lid during cooking, as many of the aromatic oils which give vegetables their delightful taste are thus lost.
8. If a meal is delayed after the vegetables are ready to serve, they should be quickly chilled and reheated later, thus preventing continued loss of vitamin C.

COOKING FRESH VEGETABLES

Fresh vegetables are delicious eaten raw or can be cooked by boiling, steaming, stir-frying, pressure-cooking, baking, or microwaving.

BOILING: Wash and prepare vegetables as desired. In a saucepan, add vegetables to a small amount of *boiling* water. Cook, uncovered. Bring the water back to boiling and begin timing. Cover and simmer gently until tender. (After adding green vegetables to boiling water, don't cover till water returns to boiling. Cover for the remaining cooking time. In this way, green vegetables retain their natural green color.)

STEAMING: Place prepared vegetables in the upper compartment of a steamer over rapidly boiling water. Cover steamer tightly and steam just until vegetables are tender.

STIR-FRYING: Use tender vegetables that contain a large percentage of moisture for this method. Place thinly sliced vegetables, usually cut on the diagonal, in a skillet with a small amount of oil and cook until slightly crisp. Stir-frying has been used in oriental cuisines for hundreds of years. To a great many people, stir-fry vegetables are at their peak of palatability.

PRESSURE-COOKING: Pressure cooking greatly speeds up the cooking process. It is a time saver just as a microwave is a time saver. This method is particularly desirable for fresh vegetables that require longer cooking times such as potatoes, beets, carrots, and rutabagas. Follow carefully the directions that accompany the pressure cooker to avoid overcooking the vegetables. Potatoes cook in 5-7 minutes in a pressure cooker which is a lot quicker than on top of the stove. Delicately textured vegetables such as broccoli, cauliflower, summer squash and greens cook so quickly they are not best cooked in the pressure cooker.

BAKING: Baking is ideal for root vegetables. Wash potatoes, winter squash or root vegetables thoroughly. Bake with the skins on or peel and leave whole or cut up. Add a small amount of water for cooking liquid, season, then cover and bake.

MICROWAVING: This method saves time and gives a fresh flavor to all vegetables. Fresh vegetables require a small amount of water to microwave. Frozen vegetables generally do not. Cover during microwaving and follow the microwaving directions on the package of vegetables or that come with your microwave.

COOKING LEAFY GREENS:

Wash greens in cold water at least two times to remove sand and dirt.

Remove damaged leaves. Cut off roots or any tough ends from stems.

Place in saucepan as whole as possible. Add small amount of water in bottom of pan for kale, dandelion and mustard greens. Add no extra water to spinach, swiss chard, beet greens and other tender greens except what clings to the leaves when washing.

Cover and cook over medium high heat few minutes until tender, 3-10 minutes depending upon greens.

        Spinach: 3-5 minutes
        Beet greens: 5 minutes
        Dandelion greens: 10-20 minutes
        Mustard Greens: 10-20 minutes
        Swiss chard: 5-10 minutes

Season with herbs or try drizzling one of our mild herb flavored dressings over steamed greens before serving.

WOK COOKED VEGETABLES

3 to 4 c. vegetables: Broccoli spears, carrots, string beans, snow peas, asparagus, cauliflower, mushrooms, cucumber, zucchini, Chinese cabbage, bok choy, bamboo shoots, water chestnuts, bean sprouts, tomatos, leafy greens, mushrooms, green bell peppers, and always onions and garlic

GLAZE:
1/2 tbsp. soy sauce
1 tsp. George Washington broth powder or chicken style seasoning (p. 261)
1/4 tsp. honey or sugar
1/2 tsp. salt
1/2 c. cold water
2 tsp. cornstarch
Sesame or peanut oil
Protein or meat substitute: Almonds, cashews or tofu cubes
Steamed brown rice

PREPARE vegetables by washing and cutting diagonally. Any vegetables can be used. Make a glaze mixture to pour over vegetables just before serving to give a shiny look without all the cooking oil, to slightly thicken the vegetable juices, and to add seasoning.

GLAZE: In a cup stir together soy sauce plus George Washington broth powder or Chicken Style Seasoning, honey or sugar, salt and cold water plus cornstarch.

HEAT wok to 350°F. Brush with oil (wok cooking oil is ideal). Brown sliced or chopped onions and garlic to golden brown. Add any protein or meat substitute chunks, almonds, cashews or tofu cubes. Sprinkle with soy sauce or teriyaki sauce. Cook and toss 4 minutes. Remove to plate.

USING a small amount of oil again, add vegetables to hot wok. Cook 3-5 minutes, stirring. Start with vegetables that take longer to cook tender, cook a few minutes before adding such vegetables as sprouts, leafy greens, (I add a few drops of water as vegetables are cooking to hasten the cooking.) And do not overcook! Wok vegetables should be crisp.

STIR glaze mixture with spoon and add to hot vegetables. Cook and stir a minute or so. It glazes vegetables and thickens quickly. Add browned nuts or tofu. Toss all lightly and serve immediately with steamed brown rice. This is a whole meal in itself.

YIELD: 4 to 6 servings.

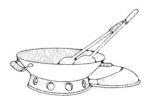

ALMOND VEGETABLES MANDARIN

1 c. thinly sliced carrots
1 c. green beans cut about 1 inch
2 tbsp. salad oil
1 c. thinly sliced cauliflower
1/2 c. sliced green onions
1 c. water
2 tsp. chicken style seasoning (without MSG, p. 261)
2 tsp. cornstarch
Pinch garlic powder
1/2 c. unblanched whole almonds

COOK and stir carrots and beans with salad oil in skillet over medium high heat 2 minutes. Add cauliflower and onion; cook 1 minute longer. Add mixture of water, chicken seasoning, cornstarch, and garlic. Cook and stir until thickened. Vegetables should be crisp-tender. If they need further cooking, reduce heat, cover and steam to desired doneness. Add almonds. Recipe may be doubled only. Do not make larger quantity at one time.
YIELD: 4-6 Servings.

GREEK STYLE GREEN BEANS

1 lb. fresh green beans, sliced French style
2 tsp. oil
1 medium onion, chopped
1/2 c. tomatoes
1 tbsp. fresh chopped dill or 1 tbsp. dill weed, dry
Salt

PREPARE green beans. Saute onions in oil. Add tomatoes and simmer 5 minutes. Add green beans, seasonings, and a few tablespoons of water. Cover and cook on low heat until beans are tender.
YIELD: 6 Servings.

BROCCOLI WITH ALMOND SAUCE

1 large bunch broccoli
2 tbsp. oil or margarine
1/4 c. slivered almonds
2 tbsp. lemon juice
Salt

WASH cut broccoli. Steam over boiling water until tender. Brown slivered almonds in oil. Add lemon juice. Pour over hot drained broccoli. Serve at once.
YIELD: 6 servings.

COMPANY BEETS (or carrots)

2 tbsp. brown sugar or honey
1 tbsp. cornstarch
1/4 tsp. salt
1 tbsp. margarine
1 tbsp. lemon juice
1 1-lb. can sliced beets, drained or 2 c. sliced freshly cooked carrots or beets
1 9-oz. can (2 c.) pineapple tidbits

COMBINE first five ingredients and stir until well mixed. Add last two ingredients and heat. Serve hot. YIELD: 6 to 8 servings.

SESAME EGGPLANT

1 medium eggplant
2 tbsp. sesame seeds
2 tbsp. nutritional yeast flakes
1/2 c. milk (I use soymilk)
Breading meal

MIX sesame seeds and yeast flakes into breading meal. Slice eggplant 1/3" thick; dip in soy milk. Dip eggplant slices into breading meal. Fry in hot oil until tender or bake on oiled flat dish, turning once, until tender.

SESAME SAUCE

Brown: 1/2 c. sesame seeds in
   3 tbsp. olive oil or margarine
Add: Juice of 1 lemon

MIX and serve over broccoli or cauliflower. YIELD: 1/2 cups

EGGPLANT CRUNCH CASSEROLE

1 lb. eggplant, pared and cubed (about 6 c.)
1 c. chopped celery
1/2 c. chopped onion
1/2 c. chopped green pepper
4 tbsp. margarine
1 8-oz. can (1 c.) tomato sauce
1 c. white sauce or mushroom soup
1-1/2 c. coarsely crushed corn chips

IN LARGE SKILLET or sauce-pan, cook eggplant, celery, on-ion, and green pepper in marga-rine till tender, about 15 min. Stir in tomato sauce, mushroom soup, and 1 cup of the crushed corn chips. Turn into 1-1/2 quart cas-serole. Bake, covered, in moder-ate oven (350°F) for 25-30 min-utes, till heated through. Before serving, cover with the remaining 1/2 cup corn chips. Serves 6 to 8.

LEAFY GREENS

1 bunch leafy greens, washed
VARIATION: Kale, collards, swiss chard, turnip greens, mustard, chicory, tender wild dandelions, spinach. Serve with mayonnaise thinned with lemon juice or olive oil-lemon juice dressing (recipe on p. 177) or simply with lemon wedges.

CUT tops off, leaving 2-3 inches of stems. Place in saucepan. Steam in 2-4 tbsp. water over low heat (covered) for a few minutes until tender. (2-3 minutes for spinach; up to 7-12 minutes for collards, kale, mustard greens.)
Don't overcook.

SPRING GREENS

6 c. greens, washed
clean and broken
up roughly
1 onion
2 tbsp oil
2 tbsp. lemon juice
1 tbsp. brown sugar

Note: This recipe can be used for beet or turnip greens, spinach, chard or any of your favorites.

WASH greens thoroughly. Use several waters, lifting greens from the water each time so that sand or dirt will sink to the bottom of the pan. Remove tough stems from kale, mustard greens, etc. as needed. STEAM greens or cook briefly in just the water that clings to the leaves. DRAIN thoroughly and save the liquid to use in soups. Chop greens, somewhat or cut through with a knife.
SLICE onion and saute in oil until golden. In a small bowl, mix lemon juice and brown sugar, then add to the onion and heat thoroughly. Add greens, mix well and heat again. Makes 3-4 servings.

SPINACH ROMAN STYLE

3 lbs. fresh spinach or 2
pkgs. frozen spinach
1/4 to 1/2 tsp. salt
1 tbsp. olive oil
2 cloves garlic, minced
3 tbsp. pine nuts, sliced
almonds, or sesame
seeds
1/4 c. sliced green olives
1/4 c. sliced black olives

If fresh spinach is used, wash and drain. Sprinkle with salt; cook 5 min. then drain and chop. If frozen spinach is used, cook 1 min. less than package directs. Drain and chop. Heat the oil in a skillet; stir in the garlic & nuts until golden. Add the olives, mixing until coated. Mix in the spinach; taste for seasoning. Heat and serve. Serve with lemon wedges. Serves 4-6.

TURNIPS WITH MUSTARD GREENS

This combination of tender-crisp turnip strips and lightly wilted mustard greens goes well on a cold winter day.

2 tsp. sesame seeds
2 turnips 2-1/2" diameter, peeled & cut into 1/8" julienne strips
3 tbsp. each lemon juice, water, and sugar
3 tbsp. olive oil
4 c. lightly packed mustard greens
1 small red bell pepper, seeded, and diced or 1 2-oz. jar pimentos, drained

IN a wide frying pan, combine turnips, red bell pepper, lemon juice, water, and sugar. Cover and bring to a boil over high heat; continue boiling until turnips are tender-crisp to the bite, about 3 min. Remove lid from pan and quickly stir in sesame seeds, oil, and mustard greens. STIR over medium heat just until greens are wilted and tender (10 min. or so). Pour into a shallow serving dish. Serve immediately. Sprinkle with imitation baco chips if desired. Serves 4.

BEAN SPROUTS AND PEA PODS

1/2 lb. fresh bean sprouts or 1 can (1 lb.) sprouts, drained
Soy sauce
1 tbsp. margarine
1 7-oz. pkg. frozen Chinese pea pods or 1/2 lb. small fresh Chinese pea pods
Salt and seasoning to taste

MELT margarine in hot skillet. Add pea pods; saute lightly for 2 min. ADD washed and drained bean sprouts, seasonings, and soy sauce to taste; saute mixture for 5 minutes longer. Serve immediately. Serves 4.

GREEN BEANS SUPREME

1 lb. green beans
2 tbsp. sesame seed or slivered almonds
1 tbsp. oil
Pinch of salt
1 tsp. lemon juice

COOK green beans until crispy tender. Lightly brown 2 tbsp. sesame seed or slivered almonds in 2 tbsp. oil, add a pinch of salt and 1 tsp. lemon juice. Pour over green beans and toss. Serve at once. Also good on broccoli, cauliflower, and squash. Serves 4 - 6.

NUTTY BAKED SQUASH

2 acorn squash
2/3 c. bread crumbs
1/3 c. coarsely chopped
   pecans or walnuts
3 tbsp. melted margarine
3 tbsp. honey
1/2 tsp. salt
1/4 tsp. cardamom or
   cinnamon substitute (p.
   226)

CUT each squash in half. Remove seeds and fibers. Mix remaining ingredients together. Spoon 1/4 of mixture into each squash half. Bake at 400°F in covered dish for 1 hour. Serves 4 - 6.

PEAS AMANDINE

2 tbsp. margarine
1/3 c. slivered almonds
1-1/2 c. cooked green peas
1/8 tsp. salt, or to taste
1/8 tsp. paprika

SAUTE almonds lightly in margarine. Add peas, salt, and paprika and heat through.
YIELD: 4 servings.

PEAS AND MUSHROOMS

1 10-oz. package frozen
   green peas
1/2 c. canned sliced
   mushrooms
1/4 c. chopped green onion
1 tbsp. margarine
1/4 tsp. salt

COOK peas as directed on package. Saute mushrooms & onion in margarine in saucepan until tender. Season with salt & combine with hot peas.
(Note: May be combined with white sauce and served over rice or toast.)
YIELD: 4 servings.

CAULIFLOWER WITH ALMONDS

1 medium (2 lbs.) cooked
   cauliflower (hot)
1/2 c. bread crumbs
2 tbsp. margarine
1/2 c. slivered almonds
1 clove garlic, crushed

SAUTE crumbs in margarine until golden. Add almonds and garlic; mix well. Sprinkle over hot cauliflower and serve. YIELD: 6 servings.

ZUCCHINI CONTINENTAL

Zucchini
Olive oil
Garlic
Lemon juice
Salt

CUT zucchini into lengthwise strips and saute in small amount of olive oil seasoned with garlic until crisp-tender. Sprinkle generously with lemon juice and season to taste with salt.

SUMMER SQUASH DUO

2 green onions, sliced
1 tbsp. oil
2 tbsp. water
1-1/2 c. sliced yellow crook-neck or zucchini squash (1 medium)
1-1/2 c. sliced patty pan squash (1 large)
1 diced tomato, fresh or canned, including only a small amount of liquid
1/4 tsp. salt
1/4 tsp. Italian seasoning or sweet basil

SAUTE onions in the oil about 1 minute. Add remaining ingredients. Bring to a simmer and cook 5 minutes. Serve hot. Serves 4. Per serving (237): 61 calories; 1.1 gm. protein; 4.6 gm. fat.

STUFFED YELLOW SQUASH OR ZUCCHINI

8 squash
5 large mushrooms, chopped or cooked brown rice
3 green onions, chopped
1/4 c. parsley, chopped
1/4 tsp. sweet basil
1/2 c. low fat cottage cheese or tofu
1/4 c. wheat germ
1/2 c. chopped walnuts
1/2 c. bread crumbs
1 tbsp. low fat milk
Pinch of salt
Onion and garlic salt to taste

WASH squash well, cut off ends, and cut in half. Steam until tender, about 8 minutes. In a frypan, saute mushrooms, green onions, parsley and basil.
SCOOP out centers of steamed squash, chop and add to sauted mixture along with all other ingredients.
ARRANGE squash shells in a flat casserole. Lightly salt squash, and fill each shell with sauted mixture. Bake in 350°F oven until hot and bubbly. Serves 4 - 6.

ORANGE-PINEAPPLE YAMS

2 c. orange juice
1 c. pineapple juice
3 tbsp. crushed pineapple
3 tbsp. cornstarch
4 to 6 yams or sweet potatoes

DISSOLVE cornstarch in juices. Bring mixture to a boil and continue to boil 1 minute over medium-high heat, stirring occasionally. Add crushed pineapple. Serve warm over baked yams or baked winter squash. Serves 6.

SCALLOPED CORN

2 cans creamed corn (or fresh corn that has been cut and scraped clean from cob)
1 medium onion, chopped
2 tbsp. margarine (optional for flavor)
1 c. bread crumbs
Salt to taste
2 tbsp. chopped green peppers (optional)
2 tbsp. diced pimiento (optional)

SAUTE onions in margarine until transparent. ADD corn & salt and heat through. Pour half the corn mixture into casserole. Sprinkle on 1/2 c. of bread crumbs. ADD second half of corn mixture and top with second half of bread crumbs. Dot with margarine. BAKE at 350°F until bubbly and golden, 30 minutes. YIELD: 6 servings.

SAUCES AND DRESSINGS FOR VEGETABLES

OLIVE OIL-LEMON JUICE DRESSING

1/2 c. olive oil
1/4 c. lemon juice
1/2 tsp. salt
2 tsp. chervil

COMBINE all ingredients. SPOON over hot vegetables just before serving. YIELD: 3/4 cup.

TARRAGON LEMON BUTTER

2 tbsp. melted margarine
1/4 tsp. tarragon
1 tsp. lemon juice

SERVE over spinach, green beans, or broccoli. MIX together and serve as noted above. YIELD: 2 tbsp.

Chapter 10

Supper Time

- Soups

"Be not among winebibbers; among riotous eaters of flesh: for the drunkard and the glutton shall come to poverty..." Proverbs 23:20,21.

Light and lovely is the key to evening eating. In pleasant surroundings, in a relaxed frame of mind is the ideal way to end the day. Eat like a king for breakfast, like a prince for lunch and like a pauper for supper. This is the wisdom of the ages for longevity and health.

Overeating is the worst of all dietary offenses. Eat the quantity of food which will keep your weight within the desirable range for your height and body build. Be sure you are not eating a big evening meal simply out of habit and to gratify your unnatural appetite. Overeating as well as drinking of alcoholic beverages numbs the brain power and makes wise decision making difficult. Surplus food burdens the body system and produces physical and mental debility; bringing on illness unnecessarily.

Most people are accustomed to eating their largest meal in the evening. But heavy evening meals should be avoided. Easily digested foods like fruits and grains are a great supper choice so the stomach has time to empty before bedtime. For several hours before going to bed, it is best not to eat any food at all. Thus sleep will come easier and the internal body systems can rest during the night and be refreshed for the work of the next day.

A light supper would include:

A soup and bread
or
A salad and bread
or
Fruit and bread

Why not try one of the delicious soup recipes in this chapter for a light supper meal this week?

How does a vegetarian get flavor into a pot of soup without the ham or chicken bone? Making a vegetable stock ahead of time by cooking scraps of vegetables, their peelings, leaves from celery, etc., gives a flavorful soup broth for soups. However, I am often too busy to make stock so just start the soup with plain water and use broth powders and seasoning packets or bouillon cubes for flavor. There are a number of meat-free seasoning products available in natural food stores or you might prefer to make up your own chicken style seasoning base from the recipe on p. 261.

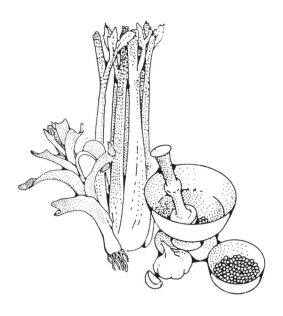

CREAM OF MUSHROOM SOUP

1 c. minced mushrooms
1 c. minced celery
1/2 c. minced onion
1 tbsp. oil
2 tbsp. water
2 tbsp. whole grain flour
2 c. water
2 c. soy milk
1/2 tsp. salt
1/4 c. minced parsley
1/2 tsp. yeast flakes
1/4 tsp. sweet basil

SAUTE first 6 ingredients together until tender. Add remaining ingredients, but do not boil. Serve hot with homemade crackers. YIELD: 4 cups soup.

LENTIL STEW

1/2 c. barley, uncooked
1 lb. dry lentils
1 large potato, cubed
1 large carrot, cubed
1 stalk celery, diced
1 onion, diced
1 clove garlic, through garlic
   press
1 or 2 bay leaves
1 tsp. salt or to taste
1 tbsp. Vegex* or Marmite

SOAK barley overnight and cook with lentils in 8 c. water in large kettle for 1/2 hour on low heat. Add other ingredients, reserving salt until the last half hour of cooking. Then cook another 30 min. or until all is tender. Serves 8.

*Vegex is a nutritional food yeast paste by Worthington Foods.

FAVORITE SPLIT PEA SOUP

1 c. slightly rounded split peas
1 medium onion, grated
4 c. water, or more as needed
1 tsp. salt
1/2 tsp. sweet basil
Optional: herbs, bay leaves,
   garlic
1 carrot chopped
1 stalk celery, chopped

WASH peas. Add to rapidly boiling water. Add onions. Cover. Boil gently until tender. Add seasonings. Just before serving, whiz in blender until smooth. YIELD: 4 servings.

BASIC LENTIL SOUP

Part 1:
1 c. dry lentils
5 c. water
1/8 tsp. thyme
1/8 tsp. oregano
1 to 2 tsp. salt

Part 2:
1 onion or 3 green onions
  chopped
1 carrot, grated
1/4 c. minced parsley
2 tbsp. oil

COOK Part 1 slowly in a covered pan for 15 minutes. Then combine Parts 1 and 2. Add **1 or 2 chopped tomatoes** or a small can of whole tomatoes. Cook all ingredients together for 45 minutes on low heat or until lentils are tender. YIELD: 4 servings.

CREAM OF LENTIL SOUP

4 c. lentils, cooked and
  mashed in blender
1 can condensed tomato
  soup
Seasonings to taste: salt,
  herb seasoning, onion
  powder, margarine
Thin to desired consistency
  with milk

COMBINE all ingredients in saucepan. Heat and simmer 15 minutes to blend flavors.

Serves 6.

CREAM OF TOMATO SOUP

2 c. chopped tomatoes
2 tbsp. chopped onion
2 tbsp. chopped parsley
4 tbsp. margarine
4 tbsp. flour
1/2 tsp. salt
1 c. milk or soy milk

SIMMER tomatoes with onion and parsley. Heat margarine and flour in heavy saucepan with salt. Add milk and simmer until thick. Mix in tomato mixture. Put through sieve or blender if desired. Serves 2 - 3.

MARCELLA'S FAVORITE POTATO SOUP

4-1/2 c. milk (tofu or soy milk)
4 c. cubed, peeled potatoes
1 c. thinly sliced celery
1/2 c. chopped carrots
1/2 c. chopped onion
2 tbsp. snipped fresh parsley
 (1 tbsp. dry)
1-1/2 tbsp. chicken style
 seasoning (p. 261)
1-1/2 tsp. salt
Dash Dillweed
5 tbsp. all-purpose flour
1/2 c. milk
2 tbsp. margarine,
 melted

PLACE milk in large heavy saucepan and slowly heat as you prepare vegetables.

PREPARE vegetables and add to milk in saucepan. (I run them all through the Bosch Food Processor using the French Fry blade.)

ADD seasonings.

COVER and simmer till vegetables are tender, about 15-20 minutes.

PLACE flour and melted margarine in small bowl and gradually add milk, stirring until smooth and no lumps remain.

STIR into soup and cook, stirring constantly till thickened and bubbly.

(If using dairy milk keep heat low and stir occasionally during cooking to prevent sticking to bottom of pan.)

Serves 6.

BOSTON STYLE POTATO SOUP

1 c. chopped green onions
3 c. cubed raw potatoes
1 c. fresh green peas
2 c. water
1 tbsp. chopped parsley
1 tsp. celery seed
2 tbsp. vegetable oil
2 tsp. salt
2 c. soy milk or other milk

COOK onions, potatoes, celery seed, oil, and salt together until almost done. Then add peas and parsley. When peas are done, turn heat to low flame. Add milk; heat, but do not boil. Thicken by stirring a little flour into milk before adding to soup. YIELD: 4 servings.

CREAM OF VEGETABLE SOUP
... for people in a hurry ...

1-1/2 to 2 lb. package of
 frozen mixed or stew pak
 vegetables

Cream sauce:
3 c. low fat milk (tofu milk
 works great)
6 tbsp. flour
1/3 c. cold milk
3 tbsp. margarine
3/4 tsp. salt or to taste
Chicken style seasoning
 (p. 261) instead of salt if
 desired

COOK a 1-1/2 to 2 lb. package of frozen mixed or stew pak vegetables in microwave according to package directions.

WHILE vegetables are cooking, make the following recipe for low fat, medium white sauce in pan on stove. COMBINE steamed vegetables and cream sauce for a delicious creamed soup. Serve with whole grain toast or crackers for a quick winter supper.

HEAT 3 c. low-fat milk (tofu milk works great) in saucepan to luke-warm. Mix 6 tbsp. flour and 1/3 c. cold milk to form smooth paste. Stir flour paste mixture into warm milk. Cook, stirring constantly until thick (gently bubble up for 3 minutes). Season with 3 tbsp. margarine and 3/4 tsp. salt or to taste. Makes 3 cups.

CORN CHOWDER

1 c. diced raw potatoes
1/2 c. diced onion
1/2 c. diced celery
1/4 c. diced green pepper
3/4 c. boiling water
1 pkg. George Washington
 broth seasoning
1 16-oz. can cream style
 corn
1-1/2 c. milk or soy milk
1-1/2 tsp. salt

COMBINE first 6 ingredients. Heat to boiling. Reduce heat; simmer. Do not overcook. Add last 3 ingredients. Heat to boiling point. Serve 4 - 6.

HEARTY VEGETABLE SOUP

2 qts. water
4 to 6 tbsp. chicken style
  seasoning (p. 261) or broth
  powder or vegetable bouillon
  cubes
1 turnip or rutabega
2 to 3 carrots, diced
1 large potato, cubed
1 large onion, chopped
1 pkg. frozen green beans/
  peas
1 pkg. frozen or fresh zucchini,
  sliced
Chopped greens (cabbage,
  spinach, Swiss chard)
2 large tomatoes
1 can garbanzos, cooked
1/2 c. whole pearl barley
3 large bay leaves

COMBINE all ingredients. Simmer slowly on low heat until tender. Can leave out any of the vegetables you wish or can add others.
YIELD: 8-10 servings.

HERBS TO SEASON:
TRY 1/4 tsp. each: dill weed, thyme, sweet basil, marjoram, garlic powder, rosemary. Give taste test and add salt only as needed.

CREAM OF BROCCOLI SOUP

2 bunches fresh broccoli
  (about 2 lbs.)
2 qts. McKay's Chicken
  style broth
1 small onion, chopped
1/2 bunch green onions,
  chopped
2 stalks celery
4 tbsp. butter or marga-
  rine
1/2 c. + 2 tbsp. flour
1 tsp. salt (to taste)
1 bay leaf
1/2 tsp. thyme (to taste)
2 c. half & half or rich
  tofu milk

WASH broccoli and separate into stems and flowerets. Peel the stems carefully and chop into pieces. Gently boil the broccoli stems and half the flowerets, salt, bay leaf, and thyme in chicken broth until tender. (About 15-20 minutes.) Remove bay leaf. Whiz cooked broccoli smooth in blender.
CHOP remaining broccoli flowerets into bite size pieces and steam until just tender so bright green color remains.
SAUTE celery, onion, and green onion in butter in large soup pot. Add the flour and stir well. Combine all ingredients together. Heat and serve. Serves 6.

Chapter 11

Favorite Salads
and Salad Dressings

- Vegetable Salads

- Main Dish Salads

- Fruit Salads

- Salad Dressings and Dips

"A merry heart doeth good like a medicine." Proverbs 17:22

Salads bring colorful beauty, freshness, and nutrition to any meal. There are vegetable salads, fruit salads, potato, pasta and bean salads. There are main dish salads, side dish salads, appetizer salads....cold salads, hot salads, frozen salads, jelled salads....salads for luncheons, dinners and supper time.

In this chapter are presented a variety of salad ideas other than the usual lettuce based salad. Variety is the spice of life and it is fun to use different vegetables in salads other than just the usual lettuce, tomato and cucumbers.

The salad dressing recipes in this chapter feature lemon juice rather than vinegar and sweet herbs to season in place of irritating spices such as black and white pepper. You will enjoy studying the chart showing which seasonings and spices are found to be irritating to the body and which are beneficial (see p. 300).

Vegetable salads are an excellent source of minerals, vitamins, and fiber. Fruits are a source of vitamins A and C. Beans, eggs, tofu, cottage cheese and meat analog products add protein. Salad meals are quick to prepare when time is limited. Salads can be hearty or light.

Most any fruit or vegetable can be eaten raw. Salads need not be elaborate. A single raw vegetable, served attractively, may be enough.

One blessing from eating generously of raw salads is the "full" feeling one experiences before overeating of too many calories. Vegetables and fruit salads contain roughage, bulk, fiber, and water which make them very satisfying. They help to bring regularity to those suffering from constipation. And, remember a simple rule, "the more green or the more yellow a vegetable is, the more Vitamin A is present."

For leafy tossed vegetable salads, purchase only crisp, fresh salad greens. Wash quickly in cold water, dry, and store airtight in the refrigerator. Keeping produce chilled helps save the nutrients.

Be sure to remove most of the water from the leaves after washing so the leaves will not get soggy and spoil quickly. Try wrapping the cleaned lettuce in a dry towel, insert in plastic bag or salad keeper and refrigerate until ready to use.

SALLY'S SALAD BOWL

1 pkg. (2 to 3 c.) alfalfa sprouts
1 diced avocado
1 diced cucumber
3 diced tomatoes

TOSS the above together and serve with your favorite dressing. Serves 4-6.

ASPARAGUS SALAD

20 stalks cooked and chilled
asparagus
4 crisp green lettuce leaves
1 small red onion, cut into rings
1/2 head lettuce, chopped fine

Dressing:
1/2 c. mayonnaise
2 tsp. lemon juice
2 tbsp. tomato paste

LAY one lettuce leaf on each of four salad plates. Divide up the chopped lettuce into four parts and put on salad plates. Divide up the onion and do the same. Lay five stalks of asparagus on the onion and top with dressing. Mix together well. Serves 4.

ZESTY ZUCCHINI SALAD

3 c. thinly sliced and quartered
zucchini, unpeeled
3 large apples, diced unpeeled
1/2 c. diced celery
1/2 c. sliced water chestnuts
1/2 c. toasted almonds, chopped
2 tbsp. sesame seeds
1 c. yogurt
2 tsp. honey
3/4 tsp. salt
1/2 c. mayonnaise
2 tsp. grated orange peel

COMBINE first four ingredients. Toast nuts, then sesame seeds in dry skillet until sesame seeds begin to pop or nuts turn lightly brown. Combine last five ingredients and add to above. Serves 6.

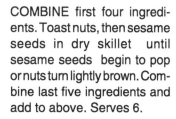

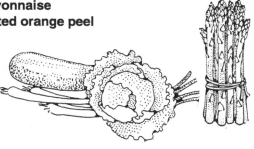

STUFFED TOMATOES

6 medium tomatoes, firm
2 tbsp. minced parsley
1/4 c. ground pecans or
    sunflower seed meal
Mayonnaise to moisten
Salt and garlic powder to
    taste
2 c. mashed tofu or low fat
    cottage cheese

SCOOP out pulp of tomatoes and drain. MIX pulp with remaining ingredients. ADD mayonnaise to moisten and fill tomatoes.

Note: This filling used in large cherry tomatoes makes a delicious appetizer. Or try stuffing this filling into avocado halves. Serves 6.

SPROUT SALAD

2 c. bean sprouts
2 c. alfalfa sprouts
1 c. raw mushrooms, sliced
1/2 c. raw fresh peas
8 dates, pitted, chopped
Avocado dressing

MIX together. Serves 6 or more.

AVOCADO ALFALFA (Delicious!)

1 cubed avocado
2 red tomatoes, cut in
    chunks
Alfalfa sprouts, tender, crisp,
    green

TOSS avocado and tomato with small amount of your favorite dressing. Put on nest of alfalfa sprouts. Serves 4.

GREEK TOMATO SALAD

Cut several tomatoes into
    wedges and add several
    sliced cucumbers
Add chopped fresh onion

TOSS and marinate in a dressing made of equal parts olive oil and lemon juice, salt to taste, and generous sprinkle of herbs such as Italian Herbs, or sweet basil, dill, and garlic powder.

SPINACH SALAD

1 bunch spinach, washed and crisped
6 cauliflower flowerets, thinly sliced lengthwise
1/4 lb. fresh mushrooms, washed & sliced
Tomato wedges & red onion rings to garnish

TEAR spinach into bite-sized pieces, discarding stems. Toss with the mushrooms and cauliflower slices and top with Italian Salad Dressing or other dressing of your choice. Serves 6.

CHINESE CABBAGE SALAD

1/4 c. butter or margarine
1/2 c. slivered almonds
1/4 c. sesame seeds
Noodles from 2 pkgs. of Top Ramen Soup
1 head shredded cabbage

LIGHTLY brown in 1/4 cup butter the almonds, sesame seeds and dry noodles. (Do not use seasoning packet.) COOL. ADD to 1 head shredded cabbage. Toss with the following dressing.

Dressing:
1/2 c. oil
1/4 c. sugar
1/4 c. lemon juice
1 tbsp. soy sauce

STIR well and pour over cabbage. Toss well.

Serves 6 - 8.

MARINATED CAULIFLOWER SALAD

1/3 c. salad oil
2/3 c. lemon juice
1/2 tsp. salt
1/2 tsp. oregano
1/2 tsp. basil
1/2 tsp. garlic salt
1 large head cauliflower, sliced
1 (5-1/2 or 7-oz.) can pitted ripe olives, drained and sliced
1 medium green bell pepper, chopped

MIX together. Serve in a lettuce lined salad bowl. Serves 4-6.

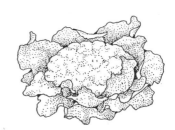

POTATO SALAD

4 large cooked potatoes, sliced
1/2 c. celery, diced fine
1/2 c. green onions, chopped fine
2 tbsp. lemon juice
1/4 c. chopped parsley
1 c. mayonnaise
1 tsp. salt
Few lettuce leaves
Dill weed (optional)

MIX together the potato, celery, onions, parsley and salt. Sprinkle over this the lemon juice. Stir in salt, few shakes of dill weed, and mayonnaise. Give it the taste test for salt., and mayonnaise. Turn out into lettuce-lined salad bowl. Serves 6.

TABOULI SALAD

1/4 c. chopped parsley
1/2 c. chopped green onions
1/4 c. olive oil
1/4 c. lemon juice
1 c. cooked triticale or wheat
   berries or 1 c. soaked bulgar
   wheat
1 c. chopped fresh tomatoes
1/2 c. garbanzo beans (optional)
Dash garlic powder
Salt to taste (1/2 tsp. or so)

MIX and marinate for 1-2 hours. Serves 4.

To soak bulgar wheat: pour boiling water over and let stand to absorb.

BEAN SALAD

1 can garbanzos, drained
1 can small red kidney beans,
   drained
1 or 2 chopped green onions
1 thinly sliced cucumber
1/4 c. lemon juice
1/4 c. oil
1 clove garlic or garlic salt
Italian seasoning (start with 1 tsp.)
Salt to taste

COMBINE and chill. Serves 6.

ORIENTAL SALAD

1 c. fresh bean sprouts (about 3 oz.)
4 c. cubed Worthington Chickettes (frozen) or Chicken Style Soymeat (canned)
2 c. cold cooked brown rice
1 c. thinly sliced celery
1/2 c. thinly sliced green onions
3/4 c. mayonnaise
1/4 c. fresh lime or lemon juice
1 clove garlic, minced or mashed
1 tbsp. soy sauce
3 c. shredded Chinese cabbage

RINSE the bean sprouts well and drain thoroughly. In a large bowl COMBINE the Chickettes, rice, celery, and all but 1 tbsp. of the green onions and bean sprouts. Also STIR TOGETHER the mayonnaise, lime juice, garlic, and soy sauce. COVER and chill separately the salad and dressing over the Chickettes mixture and mix well. Line a large serving plate (or individual salad plates) with the cabbage and mound the Chickettes mixture on top. Garnish with the remaining green onion. This is an excellent meal-in-one dish. Serves 6. Protein: 25.7 gm./serving; Calories: 422 gm./serving.

FRUIT SALADS

WALDORF SALAD

3 red or green apples, diced
1/2 c. chopped peanuts or walnuts
1/2 c. crushed pineapple, drained
1/4 to 1/2 c. chopped dates
1/2 c. dressing (yogurt or mayonnaise, honey, lemon juice)
6 lettuce leaves
6 cherries or grapes to garnish

MIX together carefully. Serve in lettuce cups garnished with a cherry or grape. Serves 4-6.

GRAPEFRUIT/AVOCADO/BANANA SALAD

6 grapefruit
4 avocados
4 bananas
1 tbsp. celery seed
4 tbsp. of lemon
  juice
1/2 c. honey (or to
  taste)
2 tbsp. vegetable oil

LIGHTLY toss fruit (with lemon juice, honey, and oil). Sprinkle celery seed over all. Serve on lettuce leaves or spinach greens.

This is a very easy and lovely salad. If desired, you can sprinkle finely-ground nuts and add a dollup of whipped topping and serve it as a dessert. It is a good first course for a meal, and different. Serves 6.

SALAD DRESSINGS AND DIPS

INSTANT MAYONNAISE

1 c. water (purified or dis-
  tilled)
1/2 c. soy milk powder
1/2 tsp. salt
2 to 3 tbsp. fresh lemon juice
*2 tbsp. instant Clear Gel

Optional ingredients:
1 to 2 tbsp. oil
Dash or two homemade
  curry powder (p. 260)
Dill weed, onion and garlic
  powder

WHIZ all ingredients in blender, adding Clear Gel last. Blend until smooth. Store in refrigerator 1-1/2-2 weeks. Purified water is bacteria-free; therefore the mayonnaise will keep fresh longer. YIELD: 1-1/2 cups. Calories: 10/ tbsp.
*Instant Clear Gel is a precooked cornstarch product available from bakery wholesalers. It is great for making instant jams and pie fillings with fruit juices and for thickening salad dressings without oil.

OLIVE BRANCH MAYONNAISE

1-1/4 c. water
1/2 c. unbleached white
  flour

BLEND water and flour until smooth. Place in saucepan. COOK and stir until thick. Cool to lukewarm.

1 to 2 tbsp. lemon juice
1-1/2 tsp. honey
1/2 tsp. salt
Optional (to taste): Garlic,
  onion powder, herbs, dill
  weed, homemade curry
  powder (p. 260)
Optional: 1/2 c. oil

Return to blender and add remaining ingredients. Blend until creamy. Store in refrigerator. Optional 1/2 c. oil can be added last at high blender speed. YIELD: 1-3/4 to 2 cups mayonnaise.

AVOCADO SALAD DRESSING

1 c. buttermilk or yogurt
1 medium avocado
Juice of 1 medium lemon
1/2 tsp. dill weed
1/2 tsp. thyme
1/2 tsp. salt
Dash garlic salt

WHIZ in blender and refrigerate.
YIELD: 1-1/2 cups dressing.

CELERY SEED DRESSING

1 6-oz. can unsweetened
  pineapple juice
2 tbsp. honey
2 tbsp. lemon juice
2 tsp. cornstarch
1/2 tsp. celery seed

COMBINE in saucepan. Heat to boiling, stirring constantly. YIELD: 1 cup dressing.

CASHEW MAYONNAISE

1-1/4 c. boiling water
3/4 c. raw cashews
1 tbsp. honey
1 tsp. salt
3 to 4 tbsp. lemon juice

WHIZ in blender until creamy-smooth all ingredients except lemon juice. Briefly whiz lemon juice in last.
NOTE: Adding boiling water cooks cashews somewhat, giving them more thickening properties, so fewer cashews can be used and the mayonnaise does not separate.
Calories: 16 per tbsp. YIELD: 2 cups mayonnaise.

SESAME SEED DRESSING

1/4 c. toasted sesame
  seeds
2 tbsp. soy sauce
1/4 c. lemon juice
1/4 c. oil, 1 tsp. honey

PUT all in blender and blend until well mixed. Serve on any green salad. YIELD: 1/2 cup dressing.

HOUSE DRESSING

**2 c. mayonnaise or yogurt
and mayonnaise
2 tbsp. tomato puree
3 tbsp. chopped green onion
2 tbsp. chopped parsley
2 tsp. lemon juice
1 tsp. sweet basil
1/2 tsp. chervil
1/8 tsp. garlic powder
1/2 tsp. tarragon
1/2 tsp. maggi seasoning
Dash salt**

MIX together. Store in refrigerator. Good over salads or sandwiches. YIELD: 2-1/4 cups dressing.

TOFU MAYONNAISE

**1 lb. tofu
1 tbsp. soy sauce
Juice of 2 lemons
1/8 tsp. garlic powder
1 tsp. onion powder
1 tsp. dill weed
1/2 tsp. ground sweet basil
1/4 tsp. salt**

PUT in blender and blend till smooth. If you want a thinner consistency, add 2 tbsp. of water. YIELD: 2-1/2 to 3 cups dressing.

FRUIT SALAD DRESSING

**2 tbsp. cornstarch
1/4 c. orange juice
1 c. pineapple
juice**

MIX cornstarch with orange juice until smooth. BRING pineapple juice to boiling and stir a small amount into cornstarch mixture, then add to the boiling pineapple juice; stir constantly as it cooks slowly about 2 minutes; cool. COVER and REFRIGERATE until used. MIX with fruit for fruit salad.

NOTE: Because this fruit salad dressing contains two high vitamin C fruit juices, it will keep fresh fruits such as apples, bananas, pears, and peaches from turning brown. This dressing keeps well in the refrigerator.
YIELD: 1-1/4 cups dressing.

RIVIERA FRENCH DRESSING

1/4 c. oil
1/4 c. water
1 tsp. salt
2 tbsp. lemon juice
1 tsp. honey
1 slice lemon
2 sprigs parsley
1 pimiento
1 strip green pepper

WHIZ all ingredients in blender until smooth. Add garlic and onion powder, celery salt or herbs as desired for variation.
YIELD: 2/3 cup dressing.

YOGURT HERB DRESSING

1/2 c. mayonnaise
1/2 c. yogurt
1/4 c. parsley, chopped fresh
2 green onions, chopped
2 tsp. dried chives
1 tsp. tarragon
1/2 tsp. garlic salt or powder
1/2 tsp. salt

COMBINE and chill before serving.
YIELD: 1-1/4 cups dressing.

YOGURT LEMON DRESSING

1/2 c. yogurt (plain, unflavored)
1/4 c. low fat mayonnaise
1 tbsp. lemon juice
Salt to taste
Chopped chives (optional)
Variation:
1/4 tsp. dill weed
1/4 tsp. chervil
2 tsp. parsley flakes
3 tbsp. tomato puree

MIX all ingredients together. For low calorie dressing, omit the mayonnaise.
YIELD: 3/4 cup dressing.

ZERO SALAD DRESSING (Low Calorie)

1/2 c. tomato juice
2 tbsp. lemon juice
1 tsp. onion powder
1 tsp. dry parsley flakes
1/4 tsp. salt
1 tsp. nutritional food yeast
   flakes such as Brewer's
   yeast
1/2 tsp. celery salt
1/2 tsp. vegetable powder*

COMBINE all ingredients in jar with lid and shake well before using. YIELD: 1/2 cup dressing.

*Vegetable seasoning powder, available in health food stores is dried vegetables ground into powder.

HIDDEN VALLEY RANCH DRESSING
(for salads, baked potatoes, vegetables, sandwiches)

1 c. buttermilk
1 c. mayonnaise
1/4 c. lemon juice
1 tsp. onion salt
1/2 tsp. garlic salt
1 tbsp. food yeast flakes
1 tsp. sweet basil
1/4 tsp. dill weed
Other herbs as desired to
   season

MIX and let stand 15 minutes to develop flavors.
YIELD: 2 cups dressing.

ITALIAN DRESSING (Oil free)

1/2 c. lemon juice
1/2 c. water
2 tsp. Italian herb seasoning
1 tsp. salt
1/8 tsp. garlic salt
1-1/2 to 2 tbsp. fruit pectin
   (Surejell or MCP)
1 tbsp. honey, if desired

SHAKE together. CHILL.
YIELD: 1 cup dressing.

SUNFLOWER-YOGURT DIP OR SALAD DRESSING

1 c. plain yogurt
1/2 c. sunflower seeds, roasted and ground
1/4 c. chopped scallion tops or chives
1/2 tsp. salt or 2 tbsp. soy sauce (if you use soy sauce, use less yogurt — 3/4 c.)

MIX all ingredients together.
YIELD: 1-1/2 cups dip/dressing.

SUNFLOWER SOUR CREAM OR DRESSING

1-1/3 c. sunflower seeds
1-2/3 c. water
1 tsp. salt
1/3 c. lemon juice (to taste)
1/4 tsp. garlic powder
1/2 tsp. onion powder

BLEND all ingredients in blender. Use over baked potato. With finely chopped avocado or tomato, makes an excellent salad dressing.
YIELD: 3 cups dressing.

CREAMY CABBAGE SLAW DRESSING

1 c. mayonnaise
2 tbsp. honey or sugar
2 tbsp. lemon juice
2 tsp. celery seed
1 tsp. salt

COMBINE all ingredients and stir until well blended. Pour over a mixture of shredded cabbage and sliced green onions.
YIELD: 1 cup dressing.

CREAMLESS SOUR CREAM

1 c. low fat cottage cheese
3 tbsp. plain yogurt or buttermilk
Pinch salt

BLEND at high speed in blender to make smooth.
Variation: Add chopped green onion and parsley or chives.
Excellent as a topping for baked potatoes, as a dip, or as a salad dressing. (Only 9 calories per tablespoon.) YIELD: 1-1/4 cups.

FRESH TARTAR SAUCE

1/2 c. low fat mayonnaise
1/2 c. plain yogurt
1/4 c. finely chopped cucumber
1 green onion, finely chopped
1/2 tsp. dill weed
1 tsp. lemon juice

MIX well and chill before serving.
YIELD: 1-1/4 cups sauce.

PIMIENTO DIP SPREAD

1 c. cashews
1/2 c. water (use part liquid from pimientos)
1 small jar pimientos (2 whole)
2 small green onions with tops
1/2 tsp. salt
Lemon juice

BLEND all ingredients well in blender for 2 min. until smooth. Stir in small amount of fresh lemon juice to taste. Delicious on avocado, cucumbers, tomato and cabbage slaw. Good spread for sandwiches or crackers. Great for stuffing celery.
YIELD: 1-1/2 cups spread.

SPINACH DIP

1 10-1/2 oz. pkg. frozen spinach
2 c. plain yogurt (low fat)
1 tsp. minced garlic
1-1/2 tsp. lime or lemon juice
1/2 tsp. salt
1/4 tsp. paprika

COOK spinach. Drain and press out all moisture. Then chop very finely and chill. Combine with remaining ingredients.
YIELD: 2-1/2 cups dip.

GUACAMOLE

2 avocados
1 medium tomato
Fresh onion, grated (optional)
3 tbsp. lemon juice (or to taste)
1 tsp garlic salt

PEEL avocados and mash. Peel tomato and cut small.
COMBINE all ingredients and chill. Serve on tostados or tacos or as a dip. Serves 4-6.

Chapter 12

The Blessing of
Fresh Fruit

"And he shewed me a pure river of water of life, clear as crystal, proceeding out of the throne of God and of the Lamb... In the midst of the street of it, and on either side of the river, was there the tree of life, which bare twelve manner of fruits, and yielded her fruit every month: and the leaves of the tree were for the healing of the nations."
Revelation 22:1, 2

"An apple a day keeps the doctor away" contains more truth than you might think. Fruits are known as our protective foods. They protect us from certain illnesses in a number of ways.

Fruits play a major role in cooking by God's Book. Fruits help keep us well in the following ways.

1. Fruits are appetizers. Their juicy, attractive appearance and flavor tempt the appetite. Food eaten with relish is digested quickly. The mouth's watering for a food means that the digestive juices are being stimulated. This stimulation prepares the stomach for food so that digestion begins at once.

2. Fruits are low in calories and high in fiber. They contain a large amount of water. Fruits have been called blood cleansers or purifers.

3. Fruits are one of our best sources of vitamins.

4. Fruits are a good source of minerals.

5. Fruits are a natural sweetener for healthful desserts.

6. Fruits are good regulators. One of the fundamental health rules is a regular bowel movement. Fruit has a most wholesome effect on the intestines and elimination process. Both the fiber and the acids which fruits contain produce a laxative effect.

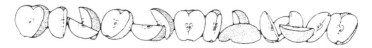

7. Fruits contain energy value.

8. Fruits are an important part of a weight watchers diet due to their low calorie-high water content.

9. A substance in fruit called pectin has a cholesterol reducing effect.

The National Academy of Sciences recommends consuming 2-4 servings of fruits each day. Select fresh fruits that are crisp, free of decay, and not shriveled. Wash thoroughly with a few drops soap in cold water to remove germs and pesticide sprays. Rinse and dry. If fresh fruits are unripe store at room temperature to continue ripening. If ripe enough, store fruits in refrigerator until eaten.

Frozen fruits are a good choice when fresh fruits are not available. When purchasing canned fruits, read the label. Select those that are sweetened with fruit juice or light syrup. Transfer canned fruits to glass jars or bowls for storage rather than leave fruit in opened metal cans in refrigerator.

Because of pesticide sprays, be sure to wash fruits and vegetables with soap and water, then rinse well before eating.

FRESH FRUIT PLATE

Try to use some unusual fruit, such as:
Kiwi
Papaya, etc.
Raspberries
Blueberries
Honeydew
Pineapple, etc.

INSTEAD OF a rich, high fat and sugar dessert try fresh fruit. Choose 2 or 3 different colored fruits. Slice and arrange attractively on pretty dessert plates. Use lace paper dollie or green leaf under fruit or garnish with mint leaf, sprinkle of shredded coconut, chopped nuts, etc.

BLUEBERRIES WITH CREAM

Put unsweetened blueberries (frozen) in a dessert dish and pour over them enough cream to almost cover them. The cream freezes around the berries and makes an interesting dessert.

HAWAIIAN SUNSET

4 to 5 bananas, diced
3/4 c. orange juice
1 c. crushed pineapple
6 fresh strawberries, sliced (optional)

MIX ingredients carefully. VARIATION: Diced papaya, berries, or other fresh fruit in season can be used. Serves 6.

FRESH APPLESAUCE

Place quartered, cored, unpeeled apples in blender. Add pineapple juice enough to blend. Add more or less as needed to yield desired thickness. Golden Delicious apples don't turn dark as fast. This makes a simple, light dessert. Chill before serving.

STUFFED BAKED APPLES

6 large Rome Beauty apples, Golden Delicious, or other baking apples
3 tbsp. raisins
3 tbsp. chopped walnuts or other nuts
1/4 c. honey or brown sugar
1 tsp. ground coriander or cinnamon substitute (p. 226)
1 tbsp. lemon juice
Water to cover bottom of baking pan 1/4-inch deep

WASH and core apples; peel or slit around center; place in deep baking dish.
MIX raisins and walnuts; put a tablespoon of mixture in center of each apple.

MIX honey, coriander, and lemon juice; pour a teaspoonful into center of each apple.

MIX a cup of water with rest of the honey mixture; pour over apples in baking pan; pour more water over apples to make about 1/4 inch deep; cover with lid or foil.

BAKE at 375°F until tender when pierced with a fork (about 45 minutes), depending on size and type of apples.

SERVE hot or at room temperature; plain or with about 2 tbsp. yogurt or cream for light dessert.

NOTE: Honey mixture may be mixed with the water for a syrup and poured over apples. Amount of honey may be varied according to sweetness of apples.
Serves 6.

PER SERVING:
210 calories
1.2 gram protein
3.8 grams fat

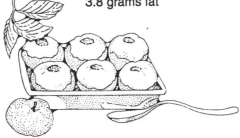

INDIVIDUAL FRUIT PLATE

16 slices apple, peeled
8 sections oranges
8 sections grapefruit
6 balls honeydew melon
Lettuce
Parsley
4 ripe olives
Cream mayonnaise

WASH and quarter a large red apple. REMOVE core and cut in thin slices. PEEL a large orange with sharp knife, cutting out the sections so they are free from pulp and membrane. Prepare grapefruit sections in same way. CUT balls from honeydew melon with melon ball tool. When ready to serve, place a bed of lettuce on a chilled salad plate and make a mound of shredded lettuce in the center as a base for the fruit. Around this mound arrange alternate sections of orange and grapefruit. Slip a slice of apple between sections. Top with balls of honey-dew, and parsley. GARNISH the edge of the salad with ripe olives, balls of honeydew, and parsley. Accompany with cream mayonnaise made by folding 1/2 cup whipped topping into each cup of mayonnaise.

AVOCADO FRUIT SALAD

2 large oranges, peeled
1 avocado, peeled
1/4 c. French Dressing
1/2 head lettuce
24 balls honeydew melon

SEPARATE the oranges into membrane-free sections. Slice the avocado lengthwise.
ARRANGE an outer border of avocado on lettuce, then a circle of orange sections.
FILL the center with melon balls.
SPRINKLE with French Dressing. Approximate yield: 6 salads.

COTTAGE CHEESE LUNCHEON PLATE I

4 oranges
1/2 pound cottage cheese
1/2 c. salted peanuts
2 c. honeydew melon balls
16 strawberries
2 tbsp. chopped romaine
  lettuce
2 tsp. chopped mint
French Dressing

PEEL oranges, separate in membrane-free sections. Combine cottage cheese and nuts, place mounds on individual salad plates. ARRANGE melon balls on cheese to simulate bunches of grapes. SLICE berries. Arrange orange sections and berries on lettuce around melon balls.
GARNISH with dressing mixed with mint.
YIELD: Approximately 4 salads.

COTTAGE CHEESE LUNCHEON PLATE II

1 c. diced raw apples
1 c. diced pineapple
1 c. diced peaches
dates
pecan halves
whipped topping
1 c. cottage cheese

MIX apples, pineapple, and peaches together. PLACE mound on center of lettuce leaves. On one side put a small amount of cottage cheese. On opposite side put a spoonful of whipped topping. DECORATE with dates and pecan halves.
YIELD: Approximately 4 salads.

FRESH FRUIT CUP

SELECT medium sized, well colored **oranges and apples,** or a **pineapple**.
CUT off the top about 1/4 inch thick.
SCOOP out the fruit and cut into cubes.
ADD diced **bananas** and a few ripe **strawberries** if available.
ADD **lemon** sauce to season and fill the shells, having them well rounded with fruit. Serve.

PINEAPPLE-ORANGE SALAD

PLACE sliced **pineapple** on crisp lettuce. BUILD wedges of **orange** sections around pineapple.
PLACE **apricot** half, hollow side up, in center, and fill with chopped **dates**. Serve with Lemon Sauce.

PEAR AND CHERRY SALAD

1/2 pear
1 tbsp. cottage cheese
3 pitted cherries
lettuce leaves

CUT pear in thirds and arrange on lettuce leaves.
PLACE cottage cheese in center and cherries on top.
SERVE with mayonnaise.
YIELD: 1 salad.

DATE FRUIT CUP

1c. orange sections
1 c. thin slices of
  unpeeled apple
1/2 c. dates, chopped
  fine
2 tbsp. lemon juice
3/4 c. orange juice

COMBINE the orange sections, apple slices,and dates.
POUR the mixed orange and lemon juice over all.
CHILL thoroughly.
YIELD: Approximately 6 servings.

APPLE AND BANANA

2 c. sweet apples, diced
1 large banana, cut in
  half length-wise and
  sliced
6 finely cut dates
fruit sauce

MIX the ingredients lightly, and serve on a lettuce leaf, or with Lemon Sauce (p. 226).

GRAPE, PINEAPPLE, AND FIG

2 c. diced pineapple
1-1/2 c. seeded grapes
1/2 c. figs, cut into small pieces

MIX the fruit, serve in sherbet glasses, with or without nuts on top. A sprinkling of coconut makes an attractive garnish also.

PRUNE TAPIOCA

1 c. prune pulp
1-1/2 c. water
1 c. prune juice
1/4 tsp. salt
1/2 c. Minute Tapioca
Juice of half a lemon

SELECT prunes that are near one size. PUT them to soak overnight in hot water. Next morning, cook slowly 15 minutes. When done drain off the juice. PUT the prune juice, lemon juice, and salt in top of double boiler. BRING to a boil, add the tapioca, and stir until transparent. PLACE in bottom of double boiler, let cook for 30 minutes. THOROUGHLY MASH the prune pulp, and fold into the above mixture. Cool and serve.

STEWED DRIED APRICOTS

WASH **dried apricots** thoroughly in warm water, and let soak in hot water overnight or until as soft as fresh fruit. If properly soaked, apricots will not require any cooking. SERVE either hot or cold.

ORANGE APRICOTS

1 pound dried apricots
1 orange

PREPARE apricots as above. STRAIN and add juice of 1 orange.

DATES AND APRICOTS

1 pound pitted dates
1-3/4 c. apricots,
   drained and soaked
1/2 c. honey
2 tbsp. liquid drained
   from apricots

BLEND fruit with honey and liquid in a saucepan. This may be eaten as a sauce or used as a sandwich filling if desired.

APRICOT AND BANANA SALAD

2 c. shredded lettuce
   leaves
1 c. sliced bananas
lemon juice
6 stewed apricots
whipped topping

ON EACH PLATE arrange a bed of shredded lettuce, and on it place a layer of sliced ripe bananas which have been dipped in lemon juice. TOP with the halves of an apricot. SERVE with whipped topping. YIELD: 4 to 6 salads.

BANANA AND NUT SALAD

3 well-ripened bananas
lemon juice
1/2 c. chopped nuts
6 lettuce leaves
1/2 c. mayonnaise

PEEL bananas and halve lengthwise. ROLL each half in lemon juice and then in nut meats.
PLACE on lettuce leaf and garnish with dressing. Equal parts of dressing and whipped topping may be used. YIELD: 6 small salads.

BANANA SALAD

Yellow-ripe **bananas** make an attractive and healthful salad. After peeling off the skin, slice the fruit down the center lengthwise or cut it into slices. DIP in **lemon juice** to keep it from turning dark.

COMBINE it with other fruits, such as **strawberries, pineapple**, or **grapefruit**. SERVE on **lettuce leaf.**

Chapter 13

Sugar-Less Desserts

- Fruit Desserts

- Puddings, Pies and Pastries

- Cakes

- Cookies and Candies

- Jams and Jellies

- Fruit Canning Without Sugar

"If you find honey, eat just enough,
too much of it and you will vomit." Proverbs 25:16

Because evidence shows that excessive intake of refined sugars and fats as found in rich desserts is a factor in many major diseases of modern times we are featuring a selection of low-sugar and no-sugar dessert recipes.

Using sugars within their original product, such as in eating an apple, is the way God originally intended them for our use. We can eat generously of sweet fruits with beneficial results. Pulling the sugar out and using it freely in its pure state brings an imbalance within the human machine.

Refined sugars used in popular dessert recipes come from sugar beets and sugar cane. Did you know that it takes a three foot length of sugar cane to yield just one teaspoon of white sugar? If you were to chew on a piece of sugar cane, you would find it is not very sweet. It is fibrous and somewhat juicy.

God's way of eating is to use whole foods just as they come from the land with all their parts intact. It is difficult to overeat using these guidelines and overweight is almost non-existent. Whole plant foods contain good fiber that makes one feel full before overeating.

Become a label reader whenever you shop for packaged foods. Check to see if sugar and other sweeteners are high on the list. Buy foods with no sugar or with low amount added. Some manufacturers use several kinds of sugar in a product so as not to show sugar as the number one ingredient on the package label.

Sugar comes in a multiplicity of names on package labels. All of the following terms are various names for sugars: raw sugar, brown sugar, dextrose, sucrose, glucose, fructose, corn syrup, corn sweeteners, honey, and molasses. All need to be used sparingly in the diet.

A small amount of fruit as a light dessert is a better choice than to overeat of rich desserts. And, remember that dried fruits used in recipes, although nutritious, contain concentrated calories. Make these serving sizes smaller.

SUGGESTIONS FOR CONTROLLING SUGAR INTAKE

1. Do not put sugar on the table. Try using raisins, dates, or some other fruit for a natural sweetener instead of sugar.

2. Use dark brown sugar, molasses, honey and dried fruits with as little white or raw sugar as possible. Be sparing with *all* concentrated sweets.

3. When serving a dessert high in calories, plan for it in the meal by serving less calories in the main part of the meal.

4. Build up a supply of recipes using little or no sugar. In many desserts the quantity of sugar can be cut in half, and the dessert will be acceptable.

5. Buy no sugar-coated breakfast food.

6. Avoid desserts that use large quantities of milk, sugar and eggs together (like puddings.)

7. Learn to make desserts without the use of soda.

8. Let desserts be a special treat—not served every day of the week!

9. Use unsweetened fruit juices rather than heavily sugared ones.

10. Many fruit recipes do not need any sugar at all. Use more fresh fruit and frozen fruit without added or large amount of sugar added. If you buy canned fruit, purchase it with light syrup rather than heavy syrup. Well prepared fruit dishes can take the place of the concentrated, refined sweets so freely eaten by children (and adults).

11. Take sweet foods chiefly at the end of a meal.

12. Do not eat candy or other sweets between meals.

13. Avoid large amounts of sugar and milk in combination.

14. If today's diet is to provide thiamine and niacin as the wholesome diet of a former era did, we will have to give as hard a look at sugar as we did at roller-milled white flour.

    We are eating huge amounts of sugar in candy, desserts, breakfast sweets, and beverages that have no nutritional significance, only extra calories.

15. Keep the total amount of sugar in the diet low, and take only small amounts of concentrated sweets.

DON'T DESERT THE DESSERTS

SIMPLE DESSERTS

A successful dessert is one that completes the meal but does not dominate it. A successful dessert should also make its contribution of nutrients. Serve your family beautiful fresh fruits such as strawberries and melons when they are in season. Apples, oranges, and bananas are available the whole year round. An apple raw or baked can be just as desirable as a serving of apple pie.

In planning the dessert, remember that nature's sweets are the most wholesome and the most delicious, as well as the most attractive. Fruits served fresh or in simple recipes cannot be surpassed. If properly cared for and prepared, they will contribute materially to the vitamin content of the diet, particularly vitamin C and vitamin A. Melons of various kinds are both luscious and healthful. Crunchy cookies made of healthful ingredients, wafers and sticks of various kinds served with a glass of milk or fruit nectar make a simple and healthful dessert. If pies or cakes appear on our tables on rare occasions, let us be sure that they are simple and wholesome.

The amount of sugar specified in dessert recipes is not always necessary for a satisfactory product. Extremely sweet desserts can become a habit. The sugar in the desserts covers the flavors of other ingredients, so that the only taste is extreme sweetness. *In many dessert recipes the sugar content could be changed to one half or less of the original amount specified and still give good results.*

FRUIT DESSERTS

FRUIT JUICE TAPIOCA (Jello-like desserts)

MIX **1/4 cup minute tapioca, fruit juice** and **honey** as listed below. Let stand 5 minutes. Bring to boil at medium heat, stirring frequently. Cool and refrigerate. It thickens upon cooling. Serves 4.

Apple Tapioca:	2-1/3 c. apple juice + 2 tbsp. honey
Orange Tapioca:	2 to 2-1/2 c. orange juice + 3 tbsp. honey
Grape Tapioca:	2 c. grape juice + 1/3 c. water + 2 tbsp. lemon juice + 2 tbsp. honey

LAYERED APPLESAUCE

Make layers in pretty stemware dessert glasses as follows:
Layer of chilled applesauce
Layer of granola-type cold cereal or Crunchy Oat Topping (recipe below)
Layer of whipped topping such as Cashew Cream Topping (recipe below)
Garnish with mint leaf and orange slice, twisted over top. Serves 8 - 10.

CRUNCHY OAT TOPPING

2 c. uncooked quick rolled oats
2 tbsp. date sugar or brown sugar
1 c. chopped nuts
1/4 to 1/2 c. orange juice (or other)

IN dry skillet, toast quick oats, stirring constantly, until golden brown (medium heat). Stir in date sugar and nuts. Stir in 1/4-1/2 c. (as needed) orange juice to give the wet look. Continue to heat a few more minutes to dry mixture. When cool, store in covered jar in refrigerator or freezer. Then you will be ready for a quick dessert. Good topping for apple crisp or apple pie too.

CASHEW CREAM TOPPING

1 c. raw cashews
1 c. hot water
1/3 c. soy milk powder (Soyagen or Soyamel)
2 tsp. vanilla
2 to 4 tbsp. honey, as desired

BLEND cashews and hot water in blender until very smooth. Add soy milk powder, vanilla, and honey. Blend until smooth. Chill in refrigerator. Will thicken upon chilling.

SOUTH-OF-THE-BORDER BANANZA

6 ripe bananas, sliced
1 c. peanuts, roasted, unsalted
1-1/2 c. shredded coconut
1/2 to 1 c. orange juice concentrate
1 c. plain yogurt or pina colada flavor
3 tbsp. date sugar or brown sugar

COMBINE all ingredients and sprinkle with sugar. Chill for 1 hour before serving for a delicious light dessert. Serves 6 - 8.

JANUARY FRESH FRUIT WHIP

1 ripe avocado
1 pear
1 banana
2 tbsp. raw honey
Pineapple or lemon juice

BLEND in blender just until smooth. Serve in sherbet glasses with whipped topping and a red berry from your freezer. YIELD: 4 servings.

PERSIMMON DESSERT

Place in blender jar in order listed:
Juice of 1 orange
3 persimmons, peeled and cut up
1 Jonathan apple, cut up

RUN machine until contents are well blended. Serve topped with whipped topping. YIELD: 4 servings.

PERSIMMON PARFAITS

1-1/2 c. thawed persimmon pulp or 1-1/2 c. fresh pulp with 2 tsp. lemon juice
1 tsp. grated lime peel
3 tbsp. lime juice
2 tbsp. honey
1c. whipped topping sweetened
1/4 tsp. vanilla

COMBINE first 4 ingredients. Cover. Chill. Fold in whipped topping.
TOP with toasted sliced almonds or cashews. Serves 4.

QUICK PERSIMMON PARFAITS

MIX equal parts of persimmon pulp and whipped topping.
SERVE in sherbet glasses.
TOP with mint leaf and a berry or toasted nuts.

HI "C" FRUIT DELIGHT

Toss some sliced bananas in a small amount of undiluted frozen orange juice concentrate. Spoon mixture into pretty sherbet glasses. Top with fresh or frozen strawberries (unsweetened) that have first been whizzed in blender to make a sauce. Sweeten with honey, if needed. Garnish with a dollop of whipped topping and a whole berry.

TUTTI-FRUTTI ICE CREAM

4 tbsp. raw cashews
*4 tbsp. soy milk powder
2 c. unsweetened pineapple
   juice
4 heaping tbsp. frozen orange
   juice concentrate
2 ripe bananas
1 c. unsweetened crushed
   pineapple

PLACE cashews, soy milk powder, and pineapple juice in blender; blend until smooth. Add orange juice concentrate; blend. With blender running, add bananas and crushed pineapple. Pour into old-fashioned ice cream freezer and freeze until soft ice cream consistency. YIELD: 2 quarts. Repeat mixture for a one-gallon ice cream freezer.

VARIATIONS:
Pineapple/strawberry/banana
Pineapple/peach/banana
Use your imagination

NOTE: Raw cashews should be washed thoroughly in hot water and heated through in oven (but not browned) before use.

*Available in natural food stores. Use nonfat dairy milk powder in a pinch.

BLUEBERRY SAUCE OVER BANANA SLICES

1 lb. (3 to 4 c.) frozen
    unsweetened blueber-
    ries
3 tbsp. honey
1/4 c. water

SIMMER for 3 min. in a saucepan. Cool. Serve as topping for banana slices as is. Or whiz in blender. Cool. Serve in sherbet dish topped with vanilla yogurt (or plain yogurt sweetened with honey). Garnish with almond slices or pine nuts.

YOGURT POPSICLES

1 pint yogurt
1 small can frozen orange
    juice
2 tsp. vanilla

BLEND together 1 pint yogurt, 1 small can frozen orange juice, 2 tsp. vanilla. Blend together and freeze. If desired, add 1/4 cup milk.

BANANA MILKSHAKE

2 to 3 c. milk
1/2 tsp. vanilla
3 bananas (frozen)
1 tbsp. honey

PLACE in blender 2-3 cups milk and 1/2 tsp. vanilla. Turn on blender and gradually add frozen bananas until thickness desired is reached (about 3 bananas). Can add a tablespoon honey if not sweet enough.
YIELD: 3 - 4 c.

APRICOT WHIP

2 c. dried apricots
Water to cover
1/4 tsp. vanilla
1/2 c. dates, chopped
2 tbsp. honey
1 c. whipping cream or
    cashew whipped top-
    ping
1/2 c. pecans, chopped
Flaked coconut (optional)

SIMMER apricots and honey in enough water to cover for 10-20 minutes. Let cool. Whip the cream, adding vanilla. Fold in the chopped, drained, stewed apricots and the chopped dates. Pecans may be folded in or used as a topping. Top with coconut if desired. Serves 4 - 6.

GLORIFIED RICE

1 c. whipped topping
1 c. cold cooked brown rice
1/2 c. honey (or less)
1-1/2 c. crushed pineapple, drained
1-1/2 c. shredded coconut
1/2 c. chopped walnuts

COMBINE all ingredients. Chill before serving. Heap into sherbet dishes and top with a cherry. Serves 4 - 6.

MILLET-DATE PUDDING

(delicious served with lemon sauce, p. 226)
3/4 c. raw millet
4 c. water
1/4 tsp. salt
1 c. soy milk powder
4 tbsp. honey
1 tsp. vanilla
1 tsp. lemon juice
1/2 c. grated coconut
1/2 c. chopped dates or raisins

COMBINE soy milk powder and water. Add millet and salt and bring to a boil. Add remaining ingredients. Pour mixture into casserole dish. Cover casserole and bake, stirring occasionally, at 350°F for 1 hour. Serves 6.

NO-SUGAR APPLE PIE

6 c. peeled and sliced sweet eating apples such as Golden Delicious
1 12-oz. can frozen unsweetened apple juice concentrate undiluted
3 tbsp. arrowroot powder, cornstarch, or minute tapioca
Pinch of salt
1 tsp. cinnamon substitute (p. 226)

MIX the 3 tbsp. arrowroot powder and cinnamon substitute with 1/4 of the apple juice and set aside. Simmer sliced apples and remainder of apple juice together in large saucepan until apples begin to look transparent. Add arrowroot mixture and stir briefly until thickened and clear. Pour into unbaked whole wheat pie crust. Top with Crumb Topping (p. 221) or second crust. Bake at 350°F for 45 minutes or until done. YIELD: 1 9-inch pie.

EASY WHOLE WHEAT PIE CRUST

*1-1/2 c. fine whole wheat flour (whole wheat pastry flour is best)
1/2 tsp. salt
1/3 c. oil
4 tbsp. very cold water

IN MIXING BOWL combine the flour and salt. Combine the water and oil and add all at once to the flour mixture. Stir briefly until mixed and then gather together into a ball. Roll out between two sheets of waxed paper with rolling pin (or pat out by hand directly in pie plate).

REMOVE top piece of waxed paper with rolling pin. Lift pie crust and bottom waxed paper up together and invert over pie plate. Peel off the waxed paper. Fit the pie crust down into the pie plate and trim edges. For fruit pie do not bake ahead, just fill with cooked fruit mixture. For lemon cream pies or fresh fruit pies, bake crust in advance in a 425°F oven for 10 min., pricking crust well before placing in the oven.
*In place of soft wheat flour use 1 cup barley flour plus 1/2 c. whole wheat flour.
YIELD: 1 9-inch pie shell.

GRANOLA PIE CRUST

1-1/2 c. granola
1/4 to 1/3 c. fruit juice

WHIZ granola in blender until fine. Add fruit juice with wire whips of mixer or hands until crumbly. Press into pie shell and bake at 400°F approximately 8 minutes.

CRUMB TOPPING

1/3 c. rolled oats
1/4 c. date sugar or brown sugar
2 tbsp. chopped nuts
1/3 c. flour (whole wheat)
2 tbsp. wheat germ
1/8 tsp. salt
2 to 3 tbsp. orange juice

COMBINE all dry ingredients. Mix in orange juice until all is moistened.

SPRINKLE over any fruit pie.

FRUIT GLAZE (for fresh fruit pie)

1 c. liquid (water in which several pieces of fruit have been blended, then strained). For red color, use a little beet juice; for yellow color use a little carrot juice.
1 tbsp. cornstarch
2 tbsp. honey

BRING to boil while stirring and boil until clarified. Remove from heat. ADD **1 tsp. vanilla** and **2 tbsp. lemon juice.** SPOON over fruit that is already arranged in your pre-baked crust. YIELD: Glaze for one pie

CAROB CREAM PIE

2 c. soy or other milk
1/2 tsp. vanilla
1/3 c. honey or 3/4 c. pitted dates + 1/4 c. water
1/4 c. oil or 1/2 c. cashews
1/4 tsp. salt
4 tbsp. cornstarch
1/4 c. carob powder

MIX ingredients in blender. Cook in double boiler over medium heat (not high). Stir until quite thick. Place in baked pie shell. Top with whipped cream or Soy Whipped Topping. YIELD: 1 pie.

PINEAPPLE WHIPPED TOPPING

Use recipe for Soy Whipped Topping (next page) but omit half the vanilla and add 3 tbsp. crushed pineapple.

LOW FAT WHIPPED TOPPING

1/2 c. evaporated milk, chilled several hours
1-1/2 tsp. lemon juice
1 tbsp. honey
1/4 tsp. vanilla
Dash of salt

MEASURE evaporated milk and chill with mixing bowl and beaters 1 hour or longer. BEAT milk to consistency of whipped cream using hand or electric beaters but not a blender; quickly add remaining ingredients while continuing to beat. Work quickly so topping does not warm to room temperature. SERVE immediately or FREEZE immediately. Per tbsp.: 6 calories; 0.2 gram protein; 0.2 gram fat. YIELD: 2-1/2 cups.

NO-SUGAR LEMON PIE FILLING

1 c. pineapple juice
1 c. fresh orange juice
4 tbsp. fresh lemon juice
10 dates
1 tbsp. cashew nuts
1/4 c. water
1/3 c. + 1 tbsp. arrowroot powder (or cornstarch)
1/4 tsp. salt
1 to 2 tbsp. grated lemon peel

PLACE all ingredients in blender and blend until smooth. Cook on low heat, stirring constantly until mixture thickens. Let cool and pour into baked pie crust. If stronger lemon flavor is desired, use 3/4 c. orange juice and 1/2 c. lemon juice. Serve with whipped cream or cashew cream over top or folded in.

ADD 1/4 c. honey if need sweeter taste. YIELD: 1 pie filling.

SOY WHIPPED TOPPING

(Since Emes gelatin is slow in setting, this recipe should be made at least several hours before serving time.)

1 tbsp. Emes unflavored gelatin
1/4 c. water
1/2 c. boiling water
4 c. soy or other milk
3/4 c. raw cashews
1 rounded tbsp. honey
1 tsp. vanilla
Pinch of salt

SOAK gelatin in the 1/4 c. water in liquefier for several minutes. Pour boiling water over soaked gelatin. Whiz briefly to dissolve. Add 1 c. soy milk, cashews, and flavorings. Liquefy thoroughly.

ADD remaining 3 c. soy milk. Whiz to blend. Pour in bowl and refrigerate until mixture has set and is the consistency of a light custard.

WHIP in liquefier and return to refrigerator. It isn't necessary to whip in the liquefier again before serving. However, it can be beaten with a spoon before serving to make it more frothy.

YIELD: 5-6 cups, depending on how frothy the mixture becomes.

POLY WHIPPED TOPPING

(This polyunsaturated substitute has a taste and consistency closely resembling whipped cream, but it has no saturated fat.)

1 tsp. gelatin	CHILL a small mixing bowl. Soften gelatin with 2
2 tsp. cold	tsp. of cold water, then add the boiling water,
water	stirring until gelatin is completely dissolved. Cool
3 tbsp. boiling	until tepid. Place ice water and nonfat dry milk in the
water	chilled mixing bowl. Beat at high speed until the
1/2 c. ice water	mixture forms stiff peaks. Add the sugar, still beat-
1/2 c. nonfat	ing, then the oil and the gelatin. Place in freezer for
dry milk	about 15 minutes, then transfer to the refrigerator
3 tbsp. sugar	until ready for use. Stir before using to retain a
3 tbsp. oil	creamy texture. YIELD: 2 cups. Approximate calo-
	ries per serving: 1 cup = 320; 1 tbsp. = 20. (Source:
	American Heart Association Cookbook.)

CONNIE'S TOFU PIE

Crust (for 9" pie pan)

3/4 c. whole wheat	PREHEAT oven to 350°F. Combine dry
pastry flour	ingredients. Add oil and mix well into
3/4 c. rolled oats	mixture. Add water and mix well—let
1/4 tsp. salt	stand for about 3 minutes. Press mix-
1/4 c. oil (sesame) or	ture into lightly oiled pie pan to form
other vegetable oil	crust. Bake crust 15 minutes.
2 tbsp. water	

Filling for Connie's Tofu Pie

1 lb. 5 oz. Tofu	BLEND all ingredients in blender until
4 tbsp. maple syrup	creamy. Pour into pre-baked pie crust.
1 tbsp. of grated lemon	TOP with topping on next page.
rind	
1/4 c. apple juice con-	
centrate (frozen)	
1 tbsp. sesame butter	
1/2 tsp. vanilla	

Topping for Connie's Tofu Pie

1 c. raisins	SIMMER in saucepan for about 3-5 min-
1/2 c. apple juice	utes. Then puree in blender. Spread
	over filling. Bake 30 minutes at 350°F.
	Let cool. Refrigerate and serve cold.

COCONUT PIE CRUST

1-1/2 c. macaroon (fine) unsweetened coconut
1-1/2 tbsp. whole wheat flour
Enough milk (dairy, soy or nut milk) to moisten enough to pat mixture into pie plate.

Mix well. Form into crust with fingers. If your pie filling is to be baked in shell, as for a pumpkin pie — don't bake crust first. If your pie filling is pre-cooked, as a lemon pie or custard pie, bake crust first at 325°F for 15 minutes or until golden brown. Fill. Cool. This is a yummy crust for a banana cream pie or a carob cream pie.

CAKE

APPLE CAKE

1/2 c. brown sugar
1/2 c. raisins
2 c. shredded apples (3 apples)
1/2 c. chopped nuts
1/4 c. oil
1 egg white, Ener-G Egg replacer, or other egg replacer (see p. 260)
1 c. whole wheat flour
1-1/2 tsp. cinnamon substitute (p. 226)
1 tbsp. yeast
1/4 c. warm juice or water
1/2 tsp. salt

PUT yeast to dissolving in 1/4 c. warm juice with 1/2 tsp. brown sugar. Grind 1 c. wheat in flour mill on fine. Chop 1/2 c. walnuts into mixer bowl using coarse shredding disc. Follow with the shredding of 3 apples with the same coarse blade. Remove shredder. Put wire whips on. Add sugar and raisins. Mix briefly.

ADD oil and egg. Mix again briefly. Add yeast mixture and all dry ingredients and blend in gently with low speed.

PLACE in greased 9 x 9-inch cake pan. Cover and let rise in warm place 45 minutes. Bake at 350°F for 1 hour. Serve with whipped cream or lemon sauce.

LEMON SAUCE

1 c. pineapple juice (or water)
1-1/2 tbsp. cornstarch
pinch salt
2 tbsp. lemon juice
1 tsp. lemon rind
1/3 c. honey

WHIZ juice, cornstarch and salt together in blender. Pour mixture into saucepan and simmer till clear over low heat. When thick, remove from heat and add lemon juice, lemon rind, and honey. Lemon sauce may be used on steamed puddings, cakes, brownies, rice puddings, gingerbread, fruit dishes. If thicker sauce is desired, add 1/2 tbsp. more cornstarch. YIELD: 1 cup sauce.

COOKIES AND CANDIES

KITCHEN SINK COOKIES

1 c. whole wheat flour
1/4 c. soy flour
1-1/3 c. rolled oats
3/4 c. unsweetened coconut
1/4 c. milk powder (1/3 c. if instant)
1/2 tsp. salt
1-1/2 tsp. cinnamon substitute (below)
2/3 c. raisins
2/3 c. carob chips (optional)
1/4 c. chopped nuts
1/3 c. sunflower seeds
1/4 c. oil
1/4 c. molasses
1/4 c. honey
*2 egg whites, beaten, or egg replacer

STIR all dry ingredients together in a bowl. Beat egg whites, oil, honey, and molasses together well in small bowl. Pour liquids into dry ingredients until moistened. If too dry add milk or water to drop-cookie consistency. Drop cookies onto lightly oiled cookie sheet. Bake at 350°F for 10-12 min. YIELD: 4 dozen cookies. 3 grams usable protein in 2 cookies.

*or 1/2 c. of a paste made of garbanzo or soy flour mixed with water. For other egg replacers, see p. 260.

CINNAMON SUBSTITUTE

2 parts coriander
1 part cardamom

GRIND together. Use in recipes calling for cinnamon.

RAISIN-NUT OAT COOKIES

1/2 c. brown sugar
*1 egg or 2 egg whites
1 tsp. safflower oil
1/4 tsp. salt
1/2 c. rolled oats
1/2 c. unsweetened
   shredded coconut
1/2 c. chopped nuts
1/2 c. raisins
1/2 tsp. vanilla

PREHEAT the oven to 375°F. Beat the sugar and egg together until light and fluffy. Add remaining ingredients and mix well. Drop by teaspoonfuls, 2" apart, on oiled baking sheet and bake 10 minutes or until tops are golden. Cool on baking sheet several minutes, then carefully remove to a rack. Makes about 1-1/2 dozen.

*Or use 1/4 c. of a paste made of soy or garbanzo flour mixed with water or Ener-G Egg Replacer. For other egg replacers, see p. 260.

POLYNESIAN BARS

3/4 c. whole wheat flour
   (fine)
3/4 c. rolled or quick
   rolled oats
1/4 tsp. salt
Orange or pineapple
   juice to moisten
1/4 c. unsweetened
   shredded coconut
   (optional)
1/4 c. chopped nuts
   (optional)

FOR the crumb mixture, mix ingredients together using just enough orange juice to hold dry ingredients together.
PAT half of crumb mixture into greased pyrex baking dish 8" x 8". Cover with date filling mixture, then rest of crumbs. PAT down well. Bake 30 minutes at 350°F. Let cool and cut into squares. YIELD: 1-1/2 dozen bars.

Date Filling for Polynesian Bars

2 c. chopped dates
6 tbsp. water
1 c. crushed pineapple,
   undrained
1/2 tsp. vanilla

COOK ingredients together until thick and smooth in saucepan over medium heat. Use as filling for Polynesian bars. YIELD: 1-1/2 dozen bars.

GRANOLA MACAROONS

3 tbsp. honey
Dash of salt
*1 egg white, well beaten
1/4 c. whole wheat flour
1 c. grated coconut
1 c. granola

COMBINE all ingredients. Drop from spoon onto oiled baking sheet. Bake 12 minutes at 325°F or until slightly brown.
YIELD: 1-1/2 dozen macaroons.
*For egg replacers, see p. 260.

SIMPLE SIMON FRUIT CRUNCH

1 double recipe of Crumb Topping (p. 221)
3 c. canned or frozen fruit thickened with 1/3 c. cornstarch and sweetened with honey as needed
1 tbsp. lemon juice
1/4 tsp. almond extract

SPREAD half of crumb topping in greased baking dish (9 x 13). Spread thickened fruit evenly over crumb topping. Sprinkle remaining crumb topping over the top. Gently pat down.
BAKE at 350°F for 30 minutes.
SERVE warm or cool, cut in squares. Top with whipped topping or a scoop of ice cream if desired.
YIELD: 12 servings.

TAHINI COOKIES

6 tbsp. tahini (sesame seed butter)
1/2 c. honey
1/2 tsp. cinnamon substitute (see p. 226)
1/2 c. chopped walnuts or peanuts
1-1/2 c. quick rolled oats

STIR honey and tahini together; add nuts. Add quick oats mixed with cinnamon substitute until blended. Drop by teaspoonfuls onto oiled cookie sheet. Bake at 350°F for 10 minutes or until edges are brown. As a variation, add chopped apples, raisins or dates.
YIELD: 1 dozen cookies.

CAROB CHIP COOKIES

1/4 c. oil
1/2 c. chopped nuts
1/2 tsp. salt
1/2 tsp. vanilla
3/4 c. carob chips
1 c. whole wheat flour
1/2 c. date sugar or brown sugar
1/2 c. coconut
3/4 c. rolled oats or quick oats
1/2 c. crushed pineapple
  (unsweetened)
1/2 c. wheat germ
1/4 c. applesauce

CREAM oil and sugar. Add vanilla, pineapple, and blend. Add flour and salt and then beat. Add oatmeal and wheat germ and beat well again. Blend in remaining ingredients. Drop from spoon onto greased cookie sheet and spread to desired shape. Bake at 350°F until brown (15 minutes or so). These cookies are chewy and delicious. YIELD: 3 to 4 dozen cookies.

FRUIT CRISPS

A cross between a cookie and a cracker with a yummy fruit filling between.

2 c. whole wheat flour,
  finely ground
1/2 tsp. salt
3 tbsp. date sugar
2-1/2 tbsp. oil
1/2 c. water
2 c. raisins
1/2 c. chopped nuts

WASH raisins in hot water; let stand and then lift out of water and grind through food grinder. Mix dry ingredients; add oil and mix again. Add water slowly, only sufficient to mix into stiff dough. Place half of dough on greased cookie sheet, cover with waxed paper and roll with rolling pin. Spread fruit evenly and sprinkle with chopped or ground nuts.

ROLL other half of dough between waxed paper and place on top of raisins, stretching in place. Roll the rolling pin over dough and score into squares. Prick with fork.

MIX 2 tbsp. rich soy milk and 1 tsp. honey. Brush lightly over top crust to brown nicely. Bake at 350°F for 5 minutes and then 300°F for 10-15 minutes until lightly browned (before fruit cooks too much). May need to cook longer. Variations for fillings: Try dried prunes, figs or apricots with crushed pineapple. YIELD: 1-1/2 dozen.

HAYSTACKS

4 c. unsweetened, shredded coconut
3/4 c. whole wheat pastry flour
1/3 c. rolled oats, old-fashioned
3 c. chopped dates
1/3 tsp. salt
1/4 c. honey or orange juice
1-2/3 c. chopped walnuts
3/4 c. cold water

(This is a cookie that you mound into a haystack with an ice cream scoop. Kids love them in their school lunch boxes. Coconut is used for the "straw.") MIX all ingredients together. Scoop onto ungreased cookie sheet with ice cream scoop. Bake until browned—about 20 minutes at 350°F.
YIELD: 18 to 24.

CAROB SUPER FUDGE

1/2 c. water
1/2 c. carob powder
1 c. peanut butter
1/2 c. coconut, shredded
1 c. date butter (1 c. chopped dates cooked in 1/2 c. water until very soft)
1 c. walnuts, chopped
1 tsp. vanilla

BOIL the carob in water, stirring, for 5 minutes until a smooth paste. Mix all ingredients and press into square pan. Refrigerate. May add 2-3 tbsp. honey if needed for added sweetness. Cut into squares to serve. Decorate with walnut half on top. YIELD: 2 dozen pieces.

DATE-NUT CLUSTERS

MELT **carob chips** in top of double boiler, thinning with a little hot water if the melted candy is too thick. Stuff **dates** with **walnuts** and roll in the melted carob chips. When clusters begin to set, put on oiled plater. Place in refrigerator until completely set.

MARTHA'S CANDY LOGS

1 c. ground or finely chopped nuts
1 c. ground raisins or dates
Molasses or honey to mold (or orange juice)

ROLL in finely chopped nuts or coconut after shaping the mixture into an oblong log. Refrigerate the log, wrapped in wax paper or Saran wrap.

CUT slices off the log as desired. Nice for lunch boxes. Other combinations to try:

Pecans with dates or raisins
Try other dried fruits and nuts

ALMOST ALMOND ROCA

1 c. walnuts, ground
1 c. raw almonds, ground
1 c. coconut, ground
1/2 c. dates, ground
3 tbsp. carob powder
1/4 c. honey
1/2 c. orange juice
3 tbsp. minute tapioca
1 tsp. butter flavoring
1 tsp. vanilla
Ground nuts for rolling

GRIND nuts and dates through coarse blade of food grinder. Place nuts, dates, coconut, and carob powder in mixing bowl. Combine in small saucepan the orange juice, honey, butter flavoring and tapioca. COOK and stir over medium heat until tapioca is clear, about 6-8 minutes. Add vanilla. Combine all ingredients and mix thoroughly (fingers work best). Roll small portions between palms of hands into logs, about 1-1/2 inches in length. Roll logs in ground nuts. Chill until firm. YIELD: 2-3 dozen pieces. Store in refrigerator.

CAROB-COATED PEANUT BUTTER KISSES

(Tastes like Reeses Peanut Butter Cups)

1 c. peanut butter
1 c. chopped walnuts or
  other nuts
1 c. chopped dates
1 c. wheat germ, toasted
1/2 c. date sugar (or omit
  and increase chopped
  dates to 1-1/2 c.)
1/2 c. nonfat milk powder
2 to 3 tbsp. fruit juice to
  moisten if needed
1 lb. package carob chips

MIX first 7 ingredients together with hands. Roll into balls or small rectangular shapes. Melt carob chips in top of double boiler over hot (not boiling) water. Using 2 forks or tongs, dip candy pieces into melted carob to coat.

YIELD: approximately 3 dozen pieces. Store in refrigerator or freezer.

OLD-FASHIONED FRUIT CANDY

1 c. (about 1/4 lb.) dried figs
1 c. pitted dates
1 c. raisins
1 c. dried apricots
1 c. nuts (walnuts, pecans, almonds)
1 tsp. grated lemon or orange rind
3 tbsp. lemon juice

GRIND fruits and nuts together through fine blade of food grinder. Then add juice and rind. Line a pan with wax paper. Pack fruit mixture well, and smooth the top. Place a weight on top and let stand for a few hours. Then cut into squares. Decorate tops with shredded coconut or walnut halves. Optional additions: May add 1 cup peanut butter, 1/2 cup wheat germ, or 1 cup granola-type cereal fruit after grinding. For added sweetness add 2 tbsp. honey. Store in refrigerator or freezer. YIELD: 4 cups.

SESAME SEED DROPS

1 c. sesame seeds
honey to taste
1/4 tsp. almond extract
1/2 c. raisins
18 walnut halves, approximately

PLACE the seeds in an electric blender and blend until they are a smooth mass. Turn onto a board and gradually knead in a little honey. (The seeds are fairly sweet alone.) Knead in the extract. Work in raisins, and when mixture is a compact ball, pinch off small pieces and shape into flat rounds. Press half a walnut into each candy. Store covered in refrigerator. YIELD: approximately 18 candies.

BAKED FIG JAM

4 c. sliced figs (fresh)
1 6-oz. can apple juice
concentrate (frozen)
1/8 tsp. salt
1 tbsp. orange rind

COMBINE figs and apple juice concentrate. Add salt. Blend at high speed to pulverize seeds. Bake in flat pyrex baking pan at 250°F for an hour, or until as thick as desired. Stir occasionally. Add grated orange rind just before removing from oven. YIELD: 2 cups jam.

APPLE-DATE SPREAD

1 qt. apples, finely
chopped
1 qt. dates, cut small
1-1/2 c. water
Pinch salt
1 can unsweetened
crushed pineapple
(optional)

BOIL gently together until soft and consistency of jam. Add more water if necessary. YIELD: 6 to 7 cups spread.

FROZEN FRUIT JAM

SIMPLY thicken frozen berries or other fruit with cornstarch or sweet rice flour or arrowroot powder over medium heat in a saucepan.
Example: 1 package unsweetened blueberries takes about 4 tbsp. thickening. Can add a little sugar if needed. Can whiz or grind fruit first if desired. Store in covered jars in refrigerator.

DRIED FRUIT JAM

REHYDRATE dried apples, pears, peaches, etc. or any combination of these with just enough water to cover the fruit. Simmer until soft or soak overnight. Put in blender and whiz until smooth. Store in refrigerator. Will keep at least a week. Increase sweetness by adding dates simmered in small amount of water until soft. Blend until smooth.

APPLE BUTTER

1 qt. applesauce
1 6-oz. can frozen apple juice
  concentrate
1/2 tsp. cardamom or cinnamon substitute (p. 226)

MIX and place in oblong, flat pyrex baking dish. Bake at 275° to 300°F until it is of desired thickness. Stir occasionally. Takes several hours. YIELD: 2 cups.

DATE JAM

2/3 c. dried apricots
1-1/2 c. apple or pineapple
  juice
2/3 c. soft dates, chopped

SOAK apricots overnight in juice. Bring to a boil and simmer in juice until soft, or just tender. Whiz all ingredients in blender. Serve on toast, waffles, etc. Store in refrigerator. YIELD: 1-1/2 cups jam.

MARMALADE AMBROSIA

1 lb. dried apricots
1 lb. dried prunes
1 lb. dried peaches or pears
1 20-oz. can crushed pineapple (or 2-1/2 c.)
honey enough to sweeten

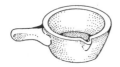

WASH and soak dried fruit overnight, using only enough water to soften the fruit. Lift out all but prunes. Cook prunes in water in which they were soaked. Cool enough to remove pits. Put all these fruits except pineapple through food grinder. Add crushed pineapple and honey. Mix thoroughly.
Note: This mixture may be brought to a boil and canned. Other combinations of fruit may be used.
YIELD: 4 cups.

BAKED FRUIT JAM

WHIZ one quart home canned fruit in blender. Place in flat pyrex baking dish. Bake at 250° to 275°F until baked down to jam consistency. Stir occasionally. Add lemon or orange rind as desired. YIELD: 2 cups jam.

DATE BUTTER

1 c. pitted dates, cut twice
3/4 c. water

COOK dates and water 6-8 minutes, stirring constantly until a smooth consistency. Use on toast instead of jam or jelly. Mixed with peanut butter it is a good sandwich filling. Can mix half and half with applesauce for muffins or pancakes. YIELD: 1 cup.

MARMALADE DELUXE

1 c. dried apricots
1 c. pitted dates
1 tbsp. lemon juice
** (optional)**
1-3/4 c. water or pineapple
** juice**

WASH and soak fruit overnight in liquid. Liquefy in blender after soaking. Use in place of jams, jellies, or preserves. Dried pears, peaches, or prunes may be used instead of the apricots, or only a portion may be replaced. YIELD: 2 cups.

NATURAL FRUIT-JUICE JELLY OR SAUCE

1 c. grape juice or any
** other kind of juice**
1 to 2 tbsp. cornstarch or
** tapioca**
Sprinkle of salt

MIX with a wire whip. Cook until thickened, stirring almost constantly. Use hot on waffles and cereals or pour into jelly jars, refrigerate, and use on toast. YIELD: 1 cup.

INSTANT GEL JAM

WHIZ any fresh, frozen or canned fruit (drained) in blender until smooth. Add Instant Clear Gel until desired thickness is achieved. (Use approximately 1 tbsp. Clear Gel per cup of pureed fruit.)

INSTANT Clear Gel is a precooked cornstarch product available from bakery wholesalers. It is great for making instant jams, pie fillings, and for thickening soy mayonnaise and salad dressings.

Harvesting and preserving fruit is a big family project at our house that begins in late May or early June with strawberries and ends in December with persimmons.

Of the basic foods that make up a good diet, fruits and vegetables are often the most neglected. They are our "protective" foods in that they are rich sources of minerals and vitamins. We ought to include at least 6 to 10 servings of them every day.

Most of us are neither fortunate enough to have a year-round supply of fresh fruits nor rich enough to afford them, so home preserving of fruits in as natural and healthful a manner as possible is well worth the effort required.

A method for home canning of fruits using fruit juices instead of sugar.

STEP 1:
Use tree ripened fruit for the best flavor and natural sweetness. Let pears and apples box ripen to bring out as much sweetness as possible.

STEP 2:
Watch for specials on unsweetened fruit juices (canned or frozen) such as pineapple, apple, orange, grape. You will be adding only about one cup per quart, so a little will go a long way. White grape juice is my favorite, we purchase it fresh from a local winery in late summer and bottle it ourselves at very inexpensive prices.

STEP 3:
Follow the usual recommended procedures for cold-packing fruits EXCEPT that in place of the boiling hot sugar syrup you will use hot fruit juice brought to the boiling point. Place prepared fruit in jars. Pour hot juice over the fruit in the jar just as you would the sugar

syrup and screw the lids on tightly as usual. Process by the cold-pack method according to recommended timetables. I tend to shorten the time somewhat since the fruits are tree ripened. This saves both flavor and nutrients. However, you need to process enough to allow the jars to take a good seal.

STEP 4:

Which kind of juice for which fruits? Half the fun is experiencing new flavor combinations. Combining two juices together mutes their flavors so that the fruit's own flavor predominates. Here are some combinations that we like:

For all fruits:	white grape juice alone
For apricots and peaches:	equal parts pineapple and apple juice
For pears:	equal parts orange and pineapple juice or apple/pineapple
For cherries and prunes:	apple or grape juice
For applesauce:	no juice needed

Fruits that are home canned with fruit juices are sweet and delicious, and you will ask yourself why anyone ever adds additional sugar!

Chapter 14

Beverages

- The Ideal Beverage

- Fruit Drinks

- Milk Drinks

- Shakes and Smoothies

"Wine is a mocker, strong drink is raging: and whosoever is deceived thereby is not wise." Proverbs 20:1

CARBONATED soft drinks, both sweetened and unsweetened, caffeinated and caffeine-free, abound the world around. They long ago surpassed water as the beverage of choice to satisfy thirst.

Whatever happened to good plain water as the ideal refreshment and replenisher of body fluids? King Solomon in the Bible recommends a thirst quencher: "If he be thirsty, give him water to drink." Proverbs 25:21.

Pure, naturally soft water (not softened water, which is high in sodium) is nature's choice beverage. It has the advantages of no calories, sugar, artificial flavorings, preservatives, colorings, caffeine, or sodium. Water is indispensable to the body and, next to air, is the most important factor for our very survival. Adequate water intake is one law of good health to remember! Try drinking 6-8 glasses of water daily besides other fluids as God's ideal beverage. (But not at mealtime.)

Hot cereal beverages, made of roasted grains, provide the relaxing, soothing effect of a hot beverage without drug effects. Some trade names are Postum, Cafix, Pero, Pioneer, and Roma.

Certain herb teas, such as alfalfa, clover blossom, and mint, are not known to be harmful; hop and catnip teas have sedative effects and may be undesirable if used too freely.

Carob powder is made from the pods of the carob tree. The flavor of carob powder is often compared to that of chocolate, but it is more subtle and delicate. Free of stimulating drugs such as caffeine, it is a good alternative for people who are allergic to chocolate. On a weight basis, it is lower in calories, protein, and fat than is cocoa. Since carob contains natural sugars, you may reduce the sweetening when replacing cocoa in beverages and desserts.

	Cal.	Pro.	Fat	CHO.	Ca.	Pho.
carob flour, 1 oz.	49	1.4	0.4	22.8	98	21
cocoa, 1 oz.	75	4.9	5.4	14.6	35	184
high medium fat						

—USDA Handbook No. 456

Alcoholic beverages cause intoxication, loss of judgment and self-control, and damage to the liver and the brain.

Carbonated beverages and imitation fruit juices contribute little more than sugar to the diet and, when used frequently, join candy and other sweets to increase the risk of dental caries and obesity.

Coffee and cola drinks contain caffeine, a drug that strongly stimulates the central nervous system; the effect is followed by depression. Habitual use of caffeine-containing beverages contributes to fatigue, an unbalanced nervous system, and loss of self-control. When habitual use is discontinued, drug withdrawal symptoms, such as headaches, usually occur, but typically these disappear after a few days of abstinence.

Decaffeinated coffee does not produce significant caffeine effects. It has all the other ingredients of coffee, one of which is caffeol, which gives the characteristic aroma and flavor of coffee. Caffeol is an irritant to the stomach and digestive tract.

Tea (green or black) and iced tea contain caffeine as well as tannic acid, which slows digestion.

Caffeine Content of approximately 6 ounces of Selected Beverages*

Brewed Coffee	100-150 mg. caffeine
Instant Coffee	30-75 mg. caffeine
Decaffeinated Coffee	2-6 mg. caffeine
Tea	70-90 mg. caffeine
Cola-type beverages	26-30 mg. caffeine

Chocolate and Cocoa contain a questionable amount of caffeine, but a larger amount of theobromine, a substance related to caffeine, but virtually inactive as a central nervous system stimulant. It is a weak diuretic.** Chocolate contains a hard saturated fat believed to aggravate acne in some people. Cocoa is chocolate made into powder after most of the cocoa butter (hard fat) has been removed. However, the amount of sugar used to make it palatable may be more harmful than the chocolate itself.

*Seventh-day Adventist Dietetic Association, Box 75, Loma Linda, California 92354.

**L.S. Goodman and A. Gilman, editors, *The Pharmacological Basis of Therapeutics,* 5th edition, 1975, pp. 367-376.

On those occasions when tasty drinkables are desired try one of our refreshing fruit juice beverages.

FRUIT COOLER

Keep a variety of frozen unsweetened fruit juices in your freezer for quick summer stir-ups.
Place in blender: 3/4 c. water; 1 heaping tbsp. each of frozen apple juice, pineapple juice, orange juice. Blend just enough to mix.

MIX 'N' MATCH FRUIT DRINKS

A variety of thick fruit smoothie drinks: Combine the basic mixture and one variation of your choice in an electric blender and whiz until smooth.

Basic Mixture:
   2 c. unsweetened pineapple juice or orange juice
   1 c. crushed ice.
Variation No. 1:   1 apple, diced; 1 banana; 1 pear, diced;
                   1 orange, peeled and sliced.
Variation No. 2:   6 apricots, 2 peaches, 1 banana
Variation No. 3:   10 pitted dates, 1 banana, 8 apricots
Variation No. 4:   1 medium cantaloupe, sliced
Variation No. 5:   1 banana, 12 almonds
Variation No. 6:   1 c. mixed fresh fruits, 3 tbsp. lemon juice
Variation No. 7:   1 banana, a few fresh strawberries
Now use your imagination to create your own drinkables!

CALIFORNIA CITRUS PUNCH

1 c. each freshly squeezed orange juice,
   grapefruit, and tangerine juice
Add 1/2 c. pineapple juice
1 bottle chilled mineral water or
   Hansen's lemon-lime soda

Serve over ice. Serves 4 - 6.

ORANGE FROSTIE

Liquefy in blender until smooth:
1 c. orange juice
1 tsp. vanilla
1/4 c. raw cashews, almonds,
   or dry milk powder
2 tbsp. unsweetened flake
   coconut

ADD and whiz:
1 c. more orange juice or
   pineapple juice
4 ice cubes
honey to taste if needed—
   rounded teaspoon
Serves 2 to 3.

ROOT BEER SLUSH

1 6-oz. can apple juice concen-
   trate, frozen
1/8 tbsp. lemon juice
1/2 tsp. Root Beer extract
6 ice cubes
2 c. mineral water

PUT all except mineral water in
blender. Whiz until slushy. Add
mineral water.
Serves 4.

FROSTY COOLER

2-1/4 c. grapefruit juice
2-1/4 c. pineapple juice
2-1/4 c. grape juice (or berries
   whizzed)
1/4 c. honey, if needed

COMBINE all ingredients; stir
until dissolved. Serve chilled
over ice cubes with a sprig of
mint for garnish.
Serves 7.

PINK PUNCH

1 12-oz. can frozen pink lemon-
   ade diluted according to
   directions.
1 pkg. strawberries, fresh or
   frozen whizzed in blender
1 bottle sparkling mineral water

COMBINE all ingredients and
chill.
Serves 8 to 10.

CRANBERRY ORANGE SPARKLE

2 c. cranberry juice cocktail, chilled

3/4 c. frozen orange juice, concentrated, thawed (6-oz. can)

1 c. lemon-lime sparkling mineral water (7 oz. bottle)

IN BLENDER container combine cranberry juice and orange juice. Cover and blend at highest speed until frothy, about 20 seconds. Pour into six 5 or 6 oz. glasses. Pour a small amount of sparkling water into each glass, mixing with an up and down motion.
YIELD: 6 servings.

MILK DRINKS

RUSSIAN MOCK CHOC

1 c. hot water

2 tbsp. Postum* or other roasted cereal beverage

2 tbsp. carob powder

4 tsp. honey or sugar to taste

3 c. low fat milk

1/2 c. evaporated milk

1/2 tsp. vanilla

Dash of salt

ADD Postum, carob, and honey to the hot water and beat well. ADD remaining ingredients. SERVE hot or cold for breakfast or any meal of the day.
Serves 6.

NATURE'S MILK

	2 qts.	1 qt.	2 cups
Cashews	1 c.	1/2 c.	1/4 c.
Almonds	1/2 c.	1/4 c.	2 tbsp.
Warm water	1-1/2 c.	3/4 c.	1/3 c.
Soy milk powder	4 tbsp.	2 tbsp.	1 tbsp.
Honey	4 tbsp.	2 tbsp.	1 tbsp.
Vanilla	2 tsp.	1 tsp.	1/2 tsp.
Cool water	6 c.	3 c.	1-1/2 c.

Directions:
1. Soak first 3 ingredients for about 10 minutes. Blend well in blender.
2. Add next 3 ingredients and blend.
3. Continue blending and add water.
4. Squeeze through clean cloth to remove pulp, if desired.

MOCK HOT CHOCOLATE

1 c. soy milk powder
1/2 c. carob powder
1 c. honey
1 tsp. vanilla

TO USE:
Place 2-3 tbsp. of the mix into cup and add hot or cold water to fill. Stir.
MIX together and store in jar.

SHAKES AND SMOOTHIES

Just by whirling fruit, yogurt, and ice in a blender, you can make frosty drinks that are tasty, nutritious, and low in calories.

TROPICAL ICE CAP

1-1/2 c. milk
1 6-oz. can frozen tangerine juice concentrate
1-1/2 c. cubed fresh pineapple
1 fresh and ripe banana (about 8 inches long)
6 or 7 ice cubes
Orange and banana slices to garnish

COMBINE milk, frozen tangerine juice, pineapple, banana and ice in an electric blender. Whir until thick and velvety. Garnish glasses with orange and banana slices, as desired.
YIELD: 1 quart or about 4 (8 oz.) servings.

CRANBERRY HAILSTORM

1 c. milk
1/3 c. frozen cranberry juice concentrate
1 tbsp. lemon juice
5 ice cubes

COMBINE all ingredients in electric blender. Whir until thick and frothy.
YIELD: 2-2/3 cups or about 3 (7 oz.) servings.

STRAWBERRY SNOWDRIFT

1 c. milk
9 or 10 medium size fresh or
frozen strawberries
2 tbsp. honey
2 tbsp. lime juice
5 or 6 ice cubes
1 lemon or lime wedge

COMBINE first 5 ingredients in electric blender until smooth and frothy. Garnish with lemon or lime wedge to serve.
Serves 2 - 3.

MILK SHAKE REFRESHER

1 c. buttermilk
1 banana
1/2 c. milk powder
Vanilla to taste
Frozen pineapple chunks

WHIZ in blender, adding pineapple chunks until shake is thick.

STRAWBERRY-BANANA SMOOTHIE

1 c. unflavored yogurt
2 c. strawberries
1/2 large banana
2 tbsp. honey
1 c. cracked ice

WHIZ until smooth.
Serves 3-4.

TROPICAL COOLER

1 8-oz. can unsweetened
pineapple (drained)
1 c. each unflavored yogurt
and cracked ice
1 banana
2 tbsp. honey
2 tbsp. shredded coconut
(optional)

WHIZ until smooth.
Serves 2.

PEACH FROSTY

2 c. sliced peaches
1 c. each cracked ice and
  unflavored yogurt
3/4 c. milk
2 drops almond extract
2 tbsp. honey

WHIZ until smooth.
Serves 2.

ORANGE JULIUS

2 c. low fat milk
1 6-oz. can frozen orange juice
  concentrate
2 tbsp. honey
1 tsp. vanilla
6 - 8 ice cubes

WHIZ until smooth.
Serves 2.

PINA COLADA

1 small carton (1 c.) strawberry
  yogurt
1 small carton (1 c.) pina colada
  yogurt
1 15-oz. can pineapple slices
  chilled
1 banana

WHIZ all together in blender.
Serves 2.

Chapter 15

Sprouting

SPROUTING BASICS

"The seed is the word of God. Be ye doers of the word."
Luke 8:11; James 1:22

SEEDS THAT WILL SPROUT

Almost any whole natural seed will sprout. Alfalfa, lentils, mung beans, soy beans, wheat, sunflower, peas, garbanzos, and almost all grains—rye, oats, corn, wheat (red or hard variety, not white wheat)—can be used. Fenugreek seed makes nutritious sprouts also.

Radish seed sprouts are very mild and have a delicious flavor, making them suitable for salads. Radish seeds may be mixed with alfalfa seeds and sprouted together. This is very rich in vitamin C.

Red clover sprouts are much like alfalfa except their taste is "stronger." Obtain your seeds from local merchants, seed houses, or health food stores. Be sure the seed is of good quality, free from insects, and that it has not been treated by harmful chemicals or sterilizing heat. Heat-treated seeds sometimes sold in grocery stores do not sprout.

Broken seeds are worthless for sprouting and for that reason hulled seeds do not always sprout well, for many of the seeds may be broken or bruised. Pick out all broken or shriveled seeds, for they will not sprout.

Seeds	Amount in Quart Jar	Sprouting Time	Best Length
Lentils, dry	3/4 cup	3 days	1/2-1"
Sunflower, whole	1 cup	2 days	1/4"
Garbanzos, whole	1 cup	3 days	1"
Mung beans, whole	3/4 cup	2-3 days	2-3"
Fava beans, whole	1 cup	3 days	1/2-3/4"
Alfalfa	3 tbsp.	3-4 days	1-2"
Soy beans	1 cup	3 days	1/2-3/4"
Wheat, whole	1 cup	2 days	1/4-1/2"
Alfalfa	(large pan method)	5 days	1-1/2-2"

METHODS OF GROWING SPROUTS

JAR METHOD: This is the simplest of all. All you need is a wide-mouthed jar, wire screen or old nylon stocking, and whole, unsprayed seeds.

1. Soak seeds in plenty of water overnight.
2. Drain water from jar (through screen or stocking) and rinse seeds well.
3. Turn jar upside down (in a bowl or wire stand) and put in dark, warm place.
4. Rinse seeds through screen 2 times a day (3 in summer). Keep jar inverted.
5. Most sprouts are ready to use when they are 1/4-1/2" long. Alfalfa sprouts are best a little longer. After 2 days put in sun to develop bright green color (vitamin A and chlorophyll).

PAN METHOD:
1. Start seeds in jar (especially alfalfa seeds) using method given above.
2. After the second day spread seeds thinly, but evenly, on bottom of glass pan.
3. Sprinkle generously with water 2-3 times a day. Cover with wet cheesecloth.
4. In about 5 days your alfalfa or other sprouts will look like a green carpet. They are ready to eat and so delicious.

STRAINER METHOD:
1. Line a colander or wire strainer with cheese cloth.
2. Put in soaked seeds and then cover with cloth. Put in dark, warm place.
3. Run warm water over them or sprinkle generously 2-3 times a day.

RAG DOLL METHOD:
1. Spread soaked seeds on terry cloth, keeping enough cloth to spread over seeds.
2. Roll up and keep well dampened in a dark, warm place.
3. Using this method the sprouts should be used before they get too long. (Mildew will develop more quickly than in some of the other methods.)

NOTE: When sprouts have grown to the desired stage, put them in a closed jar in the refrigerator. They will keep for a few days, like any other fresh vegetable, if properly covered.

WHY SPROUT SEEDS?

When a seed sprouts, its food value is slightly increased. Vitamin C materializes as if by magic, and other nutrients also increase. The starches turn to sugar, so the flavor is quite sweet.

This is the reason why many sprouts may be eaten raw. Those sprouts requiring cooking—such as the larger beans (soybeans, fava, etc.), will be ready to eat after 15-30 minutes of tenderizing (steaming) even though they may be the kind that usually require hours of cooking to get them done.

Sprouting is one of the fastest ways to improve the nutritional value of foods. Sprouted beans are no longer gas-forming.

WHAT SEEDS WILL SPROUT?

Almost any whole natural seed will sprout. Alfalfa (king of sprouts) are rated the best. Others are lentils, mung beans, soybeans, wheat, sunflower, peas, garbanzos, and almost all grains—rye, oats, corn, wheat (red or hard variety, not white wheat). Fenugreek seed make nutritious sprouts.

Try radish seeds or radish seeds mixed with alfalfa seeds. Radish seed sprouts are very mild and have a delicious flavor, making them suitable for salads and are very rich in vitamin C.

Obtain your seeds from local merchants, seed houses, or health food stores. Be sure that the seed is of good quality, free from insects and has not been treated by harmful chemicals or sterilizing heat. Heat treated seeds sometimes sold in grocery stores do not sprout.

WAYS TO SERVE SPROUTS

Whenever possible, use them without cooking. Alfalfa sprouts should never be cooked. Sunflower seed sprouts are delicious if eaten when no longer than the seed. Wheat sprouts can be ground and used raw in healthy desserts.

BEVERAGES: Try liquefying them with tomato juice, fruits, or milk. Drinks made with sprouts are highly nutritious. Pineapple juice with sprouted sunflower seeds; tomato juice with alfalfa sprouts; carrot or celery juice with alfalfa sprouts; prune juice with wheat sprouts; hot carob with sunflower seeds sprouts.

SOUPS: Blend sprouts with creamed soups, or add a handful just before serving.

SALADS: Tossed salads, all vegetable combination salads, and fruit salads are made delicious with sprouts. Mung bean sprouts are crisp and take the place of celery in salads. Lentil sprouts may be tenderized and added to vegetable salads. Alfalfa sprouts are delicious any way. Sprouted wheat and sunflower seeds are good in fruit salads. They may be added to jellied or molded salads just before they begin to set.

MAIN DISHES: See the recipes given here and then use your imagination.

SALAD DRESSINGS: Blend tender sprouts in blender while making favorite salad dressings.

BREADS: Add ground wheat sprouts to bread and rolls.

SPROUTED LENTIL CASSEROLE

TO SPROUT LENTILS: soak in a jar 2 cups of dry lentils overnight well-covered with water. In the morning rinse lentils and invert jar. (Use nylon stocking or screen to fit top of gallon jar.) Keep sprouts in a dark, cool place and rinse 2 times a day. Sprouts are ready to use when they are 1/2-1" long (2-3 days).

Sprouted lentils
2 c. diced celery with leaves
2 c. chopped onions
2 tbsp. oil
1/2 tsp. salt
3 to 4 tbsp. soy sauce

TO COOK: In a skillet combine sprouted lentils and other ingredients. Toss with a fork and tenderize sprouts 10 to 15 minutes. Add garlic powder if desired. This makes a delicious main dish for any dinner meal. Serves 8 - 10.

BARLEY BURGERS

2 c. whole barley, steamed or
sprouted and steamed
2 tsp. onion powder (or 1 chopped
onion)
1/2 c. finely ground walnuts or
pumpkin seeds
1/4 c. grated raw potato
1/4 c. minced green pepper
2 tbsp. oil
1/4 tsp. thyme
Salt to taste
Seasoned bread crumbs to form
stiff burgers

GRIND barley through food grinder. Add rest of ingredients. Mix well. Shape into flat burgers and brown in heavy skillet. Serve between burger buns with homemade mayonnaise. Serves 4.

SPROUTED LENTIL CREAM SOUP

SPROUT lentils to 1/2-inch long. Tenderize in skillet with little oil, salt, and onion powder. Add some soy sauce. Make a thin white sauce and heat to thicken. Combine white sauce with tenderized lentils and serve.

SPROUTED WHEAT BURGERS

2 c. sprouted wheat or cooked
wheat
1/2 c. sunflower seeds, ground or
chopped
1/2 c. pumpkin seeds, ground or
chopped
2 c. steamed barley or millet
2 tbsp. peanut or cashew butter
2 tbsp. oil
2 tbsp. soy sauce
1 tbsp. onion powder or 1/4 c.
chopped raw onion
1/2 tsp. each thyme, salt, sage
Bread crumbs, soft (approx. 1/2 c.)

MOLD with hands to form patties.
BROWN in a skillet on both sides. Place between burger buns and serve with homemade mayonnaise, catsup, and all the trimmings. May also be served with gravy as a meatless main dish. Serves 6-8.

SPROUTED GARBANZOS

In skillet tenderize for 10-15 minutes with a lid on tightly:
**3 c. sprouted garbanzos put
 through food grinder**
2 tbsp. oil
1/2 c. water
1/2 tsp. salt
1/2 tsp. onion powder

In another skillet:
2 c. chopped onions
2 c. fresh chopped parsley
2 tbsp. oil
Salt to taste

COMBINE all ingredients together. Serve with a tossed salad for a meatless dinner. A little chicken style seasoning (p. 261) gives a good flavor. Serves 6.

ALFALFA SPROUTS

1. Soak 1 tbsp. seeds in wide-mouth quart jar overnight in water to cover.

2. Cover jar with screen or piece of nylon stocking and drain water, rinsing well.

3. Shake seeds as evenly as possible around sides of jar and place on its side in a dark, warm place.

4. Rinse the seeds through screen twice a day.

5. After 2 days place sprouts in a shallow dish in the light. Cover lightly with plastic wrap and keep moist. They will be ready to use when the leaves are green.

Chapter 16

Gravies and Sauces

"Delight thyself also in the Lord; and he shall give thee the desires of thine heart."
Psalms 37:4

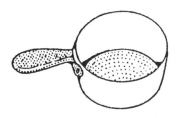

CASHEW GRAVY

1/2 c. raw cashews
2 c. hot water
2 tsp. arrowroot powder
  (or cornstarch)
2 tsp. onion powder
2 tsp. soy sauce
1 tbsp. brewer's yeast
  flakes
Salt to taste

LIQUEFY all ingredients in blender until smooth. Transfer to saucepan and stir over low heat or in double boiler until thickened. Serves 6-8. YIELD: 2 cups.

CHICKEN GRAVY

2-1/2 c. water
1/2 c. evaporated or rich
  soy milk
*5 tbsp. browned flour
2-1/2 tsp. chicken style
  seasoning (p. 261)
1/4 tsp. salt, or less

DISSOLVE flour in cold liquid in saucepan. Bring all ingredients to a boil over medium heat and continue to boil 1 minute or until thick and creamy, stirring frequently. YIELD: 2-1/2 cups. VARIATION: For "Deluxe Chicken Gravy" simmer 2/3 c. fresh chopped mushrooms and 1/2 c. chopped onion in part of water.

MOM'S WHITE GRAVY

1-1/2 c. milk
1/2 c. water
*5 tbsp. browned flour
2 tsp. chicken style
  seasoning (p. 261)
1/2 tsp. Bakon Yeast
1/4 tsp. celery salt
1/4 tsp. salt

DISSOLVE flour in cold liquid in saucepan. Bring all ingredients to a boil over medium heat and continue to boil 1 minute or until thick and creamy, stirring frequently. YIELD: 2 cups.
Bakon yeast is a hickory-smoked food yeast available at certain health food stores.
*Browned flour is made by stirring flour in a dry skillet over medium heat until lightly browned. Store browned flour in a jar for gravy making.

BROWN GRAVY

1-1/2 c. water
2 tbsp. chopped onion
1/2 c. milk
*3 tbsp. browned flour
1 tbsp. soy sauce
**1 tsp. Vegex
2/3 tsp. lemon juice
1/2 tsp. Kitchen Bouquet
  (optional)
1/4 tsp. paprika
1/4 tsp. salt

BRING onion and water to a boil in saucepan. Reduce heat and simmer covered until onion is tender. Dissolve flour in milk in 2-cup measuring cup. Pour into saucepan, stirring vigorously. Add remaining ingredients except lemon juice. Bring mixture to a boil over medium heat and continue to boil 1 minute or until thick and creamy, stirring frequently. Add lemon juice. Serve. YIELD: 2 cups.
*Browned flour is made by stirring flour in a dry skillet over medium heat until lightly browned. Store browned flour in a jar for gravy making.
**Vegex is an extract of Brewer's Yeast available at most health food stores.

WHITE SAUCE

	Thin	Medium	Thick
Oil or margarine	1 tbsp.	1 tbsp.	1 tbsp.
Flour	1 tbsp.	2 tbsp.	1/4 c.
Salt	1/4 tsp.	1/4 tsp.	1/4 tsp.
Milk	1 c.	1 c.	1 c.

HEAT milk in saucepan to lukewarm. Mix flour and small amount of cold milk to form smooth paste. Remove warm milk from heat. Stir in flour mixture; cook, stirring constantly until thick (boil 3 minutes). Season with margarine and salt. YIELD: 1 cup.

DILL SAUCE

Delicious mixed into homemade noodles.

Make medium white
  sauce (above)
Add: 1 tsp. dill weed or
  1/2 tsp. dill seeds

Mix into noodles.

ITALIAN SPAGHETTI SAUCE

1 tbsp. olive oil
1 medium minced onion
2 6-oz. cans tomato paste
Water
1 clove garlic, through
   garlic press
1 tbsp. oregano
1-1/2 tsp. sweet basil
1/4 tsp. anise seed
Salt to taste

SAUTE onion in oil. Add tomato paste and water until a thin consistency. Add herbs, rubbing between fingers. Add garlic. Simmer over low heat to sauce consistency. Serve over noodles or brown rice.

NOTE: This sauce has many uses — with rice, noodles, macaroni, spaghetti, beans, garbanzos, lentils, summer squash, eggplant, broccoli; for pizza, sliced vegetable protein, analogs, simmered or baked, and in many other ways.

QUICK TOMATO GRAVY

1 can undiluted tomato
   soup or 2 cans tomato
   sauce
1/4 tsp. onion powder or
   1 small onion, chopped
1/4 tsp. Italian Seasoning
1/4 tsp. cumin

HEAT and serve over patties or loaves.

TOMATO GRAVY

1 tbsp. oil
2 tbsp. flour
1/2 tsp. salt
1 c. tomato juice
1/4 tsp. garlic powder
1/4 tsp. onion powder
1/4 tsp. cumin
1/2 tsp. Italian seasoning

BROWN oil, flour and salt in skillet, stirring almost constantly.
ADD remaining ingredients and cook until thickened. (If too thick, thin slightly with water.) Tomato gravy is delicious served over lentil or other bean type patties or loaves.

Chapter 17

Miscellaneous

"If you put an end to oppression, to every gesture of comtempt, and to every evil word; if you give food to the hungry and satisfy those who are in need, then the darkness around you will turn to the brightness of noon. And I will always guide you and satisfy your needs. I will keep you strong and well. You will be like a garden that has plenty of water, like a spring of water that never goes dry." Isaiah 58:9-11

EGG REPLACEMENT (BINDERS)
(for binding vegetarian loaves and patties)

To replace 1 egg in a recipe, use one of the following:

3 tbsp. potato flour or potato flakes
2 tbsp. soy flour
2 tbsp. garbanzo flour + water to yield a paste
2 tbsp. rolled oats whizzed in blender
2 to 3 tbsp. gluten flour
1/4 c. soaked garbanzos whizzed smooth with 1/4 c. water
Commercial product called Ener-G Egg Replacer (in health food stores).

CHILI POWDER SUBSTITUTE (non-irritating)

2 tbsp. paprika
1 tbsp. parsley flakes
1 tsp. ground oregano
1 tbsp. dried bell pepper
1/4 tsp. dill weed
1 tsp. onion powder
1/4 tsp. savory
1/4 tsp. garlic powder
2 bay leaves
2 tsp. cumin
1/2 tsp. sweet basil

GRIND all ingredients together in blender.

CURRY (non-irritating)

1 tbsp. turmeric
1 tbsp. cumin
1 tbsp. coriander
1 tbsp. garlic powder

MIX thoroughly and store airtight.

CHICKEN STYLE SEASONING (no MSG)

4 tsp. celery salt
1 tsp. turmeric
4 tsp. onion powder
1/2 tsp. garlic powder
1/4 tsp. marjoram
4 tsp. parsley flakes, ground
Pinch savory
1/4 c. salt
1 tsp. brown sugar

ONE tsp. of this seasoning may be substituted for one packet of George Washington Seasoning (Golden). When substituting for McKay's Chicken Seasoning, use less salt in recipe. FOR 1 c. chicken style broth, add 1 tsp. chicken style seasoning to 1 c. water.

DO-IT-YOURSELF SEASONED SALT

2 tbsp. salt
2 tbsp. paprika
1 tsp. onion powder
1 tsp. celery salt
1 tsp. garlic powder
1 tsp. chicken style seasoning
   (above)
1 tsp. bacon flavored Brewer's
   Yeast

MIX thoroughly.
Store in airtight container.

BREADING MEAL

1-2/3 c. potato meal (or flour) or
   rolled oats (whizzed)
1/3 c. Brewer's Yeast flakes
2 tbsp. chicken style seasoning
   (above
1-2 envelopes George Washington
   broth powder
2 tsp. Bakon Yeast
1 tsp. garlic powder
2 tsp. fine herbs
1 tsp. onion powder

MIX all together.
YIELD: about 1 pint.

TO MAKE BREAD CRUMBS

DRY out your whole grain bread, mix bread heels and stale bread leftovers in 200°F oven. Break up and whiz in blender to crumb consistency.

SEASONED BREAD CRUMBS OR BREAD CUBES

**1 c. dry bread crumbs or
  3 c. dry bread cubes
1/3 c. food yeast flakes
1 tsp. sage
1/2 tsp. celery salt
1/2 tsp. onion powder
1/4 tsp. garlic powder
1 tbsp. oil (optional)**

MIX and use as:
(1) Crumb topping on casseroles
(2) In recipes calling for crumbs
(3) To "crumb" pans in which entrees are baked
(4) As a breading meal
(5) As whole wheat stuffing mix
YIELD: 1-1/3 cups.

HOME-STYLE MUSTARD RELISH

**1 c. mayonnaise
2 tsp. turmeric
2 tsp. onion juice (grate
  onion on finest grater or
  scrape with paring knife)
2 tbsp. chopped parsley
1 tbsp. lemon juice
Dash of paprika, garlic, and
  onion salt**

MIX ingredients together in a small bowl.
YIELD: 1 cup.

QUICK PIZZA SAUCE

**1 5-oz. can tomato paste
1 tomato paste can of water
1 tsp. oregano
1 tsp. sweet basil
1/2 tsp. salt
2 tbsp. olive oil
1 tsp. onion powder**

COMBINE all ingredients.
YIELD: Sauce for 1 extra large pizza.

NOTE: See p. 80 for homemade pizza recipe.

QUICK CATSUP

1 c. tomato puree or equivalent of tomato paste
Salt to taste
1/4 c. lemon juice
1/2 tsp. onion powder
1/4 tsp. garlic powder
3 tbsp. honey or 4 tbsp.
  date butter
1/4 tsp. paprika
1/8 tsp. cumin
1/2 tsp. celery seed ground
  fine (optional)

COMBINE all ingredients. Chill.
YIELD: 1-1/4 cups.

Date Butter: Soften dates in microwave with small amount of water
until mashed to a thick paste.

LEMON JUICE CATSUP (Cooked)
(unstrained, makes tomato relish)

1 28-oz. can tomatoes
1/2 6-oz. can plain tomato
  paste
4 tbsp. brown sugar
1-1/2 tsp. salt
*1 tsp. Vegex
1 medium onion, chopped
  fine
1 large stalk celery, diced
3 sprigs parsley, chopped
1 clove garlic, minced
1/2 pimiento, diced
1 bay leaf
1/2 tsp. basil
1/4 c. or more lemon juice

SIMMER first 5 ingredients in heavy
saucepan while preparing vegetables. Add the vegetables and all
remaining ingredients except lemon
juice. Simmer until vegetables are
crispy tender. Remove bay leaf.
This makes a tomato relish. If used
for catsup, whiz in blender or press
through a sieve. Cool. Add lemon
juice. Store in refrigerator. May be
canned.
YIELD: 2 to 3 cups.
* Vegex is a dark colored seasoning
paste made from Brewer's yeast.

SOY CHEESE WHIZ

(Use over pizza, cauliflower, or where a cheese sauce is desired.)

1 c. water
1 tsp. salt
2 tbsp. lemon juice
2 tbsp. nutritional yeast
   flakes
1/3 c. oil
1 c. soy powder
1 clove garlic
1 4-oz. jar pimientos
1 tbsp. sesame tahini

LIQUEFY water, soy powder, salt, and garlic in blender. Add lemon juice, pimiento, yeast flakes, and tahini and blend. Add oil slowly to thicken. YIELD: 1-1/2 cups.

ZESTY TOMATO RELISH

2 large tomatoes, chopped
5 dates, minced
1 small minced onion
1 tbsp. fresh lemon juice
1/2 tsp. salt
1/2 tsp. celery seed
1/2 tsp. sweet basil

SIMMER together the tomatoes, dates, and onion 15 minutes. Add lemon juice, salt, celery seed and sweet basil. Serve with main dishes or as a relish or sandwiches. YIELD: 1-1/2 to 2 cups.

Chapter 18

Menu Planning

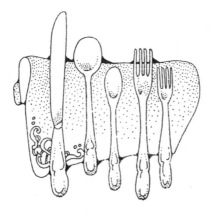

"Commit to the Lord all that you do, and your plans will be fulfilled."
Proverbs 16:3

Planning menus in advance is an important key to your success in cooking "By the Book." Using grains and beans as the backbone for main dishes is not difficult, but different cooking procedures are needed. Planning ahead will help you remember to do such jobs as cooking rice, beans or potatoes in the morning for use at the evening meal. By writing out menus in advance, your meals will become more interesting and contain a wider variety of good foods throughout the week and the month.

Try the one-week menu planner included on p. 273. It makes meal planning quick and simple. Set aside 15-20 minutes once a week to plan the following week's menus.

You will notice that the one-week menu planner has a suggested daily menu guide on the left side of the sheet (p. 272). All you have to do is create menus using this basic pattern of eating. Watch grocery ads for weekly specials to save money on the weekly food budget and plan menus using fruits and vegetables that are "in" season. As you plan the week's menus, make a grocery list as well. Shopping from a written list just once a week saves over-spending, saves impulse buying of unneeded and unhealthy snack foods, and saves time-consuming trips to the grocery store.

As the week progresses, check your menu-planner to remind if beans, rice, or other foods need to be cooked in advance. I often put a pot of rice on to cook first thing in the morning before going to work so it will be ready when we come home in the evening. Or I will put some dry beans to soak one day, cook them the next, and serve them a third day.

Again, let me remind you that cooking "from scratch" is not difficult, but does require thinking ahead. It just doesn't work to walk in the front door at 5:30 PM and say to yourself, "Now, what shall we have for supper?" You will end up resorting to "fast foods" or packaged mixes that are high in fat, more refined and much more costly. A homemade pot of soup can be made the day ahead and is much more tasty and lower in sodium and spices than commercially canned or packaged soups.

Ideally the evening meal should be eaten 4 hours before going to bed which means soon after getting home from work.

When planning menus for the week, study the Daily Guide to Food Choices (Vegetarian Food Pyramid) on pp. 269-271. Eat from "the bottom up" is its message. The eating pyramid illustrates the concept that the base of our daily diet should be grains/cereals followed by vegetables and fruits with lesser amounts of dairy and protein foods.

Eat the following number of daily servings:

6-11 servings whole grains: breads, rice, pasta
3-5 servings vegetables
2-4 servings fruits
2-3 servings low fat dairy or fortified alternates
2-3 servings protein foods (beans, nuts, seeds, tofu, etc.)
Sparingly fats, oils, and sweets

Daily Calories

"How many calories a day are needed?" you ask. The U.S. Department of Agriculture Nutrition Guidelines offers the following suggestions for calorie intake:

- Eat enough calories to maintain ideal weight
- 1600 calories is about right for many sedentary (inactive) women and some older adults.
- 2200 calories is about right for most children, teenage girls, active women, and many sedentary men. Women who are pregnant or breastfeeding may need more.
- 2800 calories is about right for teenage boys, many active men, and some very active women.

When planning menus for the week, try to use a variety of foods. Eating the same foods over and over, meal after meal or day after day, does not provide as good a balance of nutrition. Vary the type of grains used for cereal. Vary the kinds of fruits and vegetables as much as possible. If you use potatoes as the starch dish for dinner one day, then use brown rice the next, followed by pasta the third day. Use sweet potatoes part of the time, or other yellow winter squash. For breakfast, use oatmeal cereal one day, then wheat or barley the next, and so forth.

Lastly, remember that we first eat with our eyes. Make food look attractive. The first impression that family members feel when called to mealtime is from the looks of the food set before them. Plan menus that include different colors. Use a sprig of parsley, a tomato wedge, or a slice of orange or lemon on the plate for added color and interest. Provide one dish that is crunchy and crispy. Don't serve all soft foods or all chopped up foods at the same meal. A menu of mashed potatoes, steamed cauliflower, cottage cheese, and bread is pretty dull looking with its all-white color even though nutritionally sound.

Provide a variety of textures. If serving mashed potatoes, then don't serve mashed yellow squash as the vegetable and soft tofu. This provides too many soft textures. Try large broccoli spears and nut patties and tomato gravy with the mashed potatoes instead.

Be sure to serve hot foods hot and cold foods cold. Do not hold hot foods hot for long periods of time while waiting for family members to arrive. If the meal cannot be served immediately, let foods cool off. Then reheat as needed. Bacteria grow when foods are kept warm for long periods and precious vitamins and minerals are destroyed.

Cold foods left for long periods out of refrigeration will wilt and bacteria will multiply. Refrigerate cold foods if not eaten soon after prepared.

THE VEGETARIAN FOOD PYRAMID

FATS, OILS, AND SWEETS
EAT SPARINGLY

A DAILY GUIDE TO FOOD CHOICES

LOW-FAT OR NON-FAT,
MILK, YOGURT, FRESH CHEESE,
AND/OR FORTIFIED
ALTERNATIVES

2-3 SERVINGS

EAT MODERATELY

BEANS, NUTS, SEEDS, AND
MEAT ALTERNATIVES
2-3 SERVINGS

EAT MODERATELY

VEGETABLES
3-5 SERVINGS

**EAT
GENEROUSLY**

FRUITS
2-4 SERVINGS
EAT GENEROUSLY

WHOLE GRAINS:
BREADS,
CEREALS, RICE,
AND PASTA

6-11
SERVINGS

**EAT
LIBERALLY**

Source: General Conference Nutrition Council
Order from: The Health Connection: 1-800-548-8700 or 301-790-9735.

ILLUSTRATION BY MERLE POIRIER

A DAILY GUIDE TO FOOD CHOICES

FOOD PYRAMID (Cont.)

Choose from a variety of whole grains, fruits, and vegetables.
Select relative portions to meet your caloric need.

Food Groups	One Serving Equals One Item	Nutrient Contributions	Number of Servings — Sample Diet (Calories)			Food Choice Examples
			1600	2200	2800	
Whole Grains and Legumes **Eat Liberally** 6-11 Servings daily	1 slice bread ½ cup hot cereal ¾ cup dry cereal ¼ cup granola ½ cup rice or pasta 1 tortilla 1 chapati ½ bagel or English Muffin 3-4 crackers ½ muffin ½ cup cooked beans	Complex CHO Fiber Protein Vitamin B_1 (Thiamine) Vitamin B_2 (Riboflavin) Vitamin B_6 and Niacin Iron Magnesium Calcium Trace minerals	6	9	11	Grains: oats, brown rice, barley, millet, bulgar wheat, rye, corn, wheat, multi-grain, etc. Legumes: (see list below)
Vegetables **Eat Generously** 3-5 Servings daily	1 cup raw, leafy vegetable salad ½ cup cooked vegetables ½ cup chopped raw vegetables ¾ cup vegetable juice	Fiber Potassium Beta-Carotene Folate Vitamin C Calcium Magnesium	3	4	5	Vegetables: broccoli, kale, cabbage, collards, spinach, pumpkin, carrots, winter squash, sweet potatoes, potatoes, parsnips, rutabagas, turnips, tomatoes, beets, eggplant, okra, summer squash, cauliflower
Fruits **Eat Generously** 2-4 Servings daily	1 medium, whole fruit ½ cup canned fruit ¼ cup dried fruit 1 cup berries ¾ cup fruit juice	Vitamin C Beta-Carotene Fiber Potassium Folate Magnesium	2	3	4	Fruits: oranges, grapefruit, lemons, apricots, peaches, nectarines, plums, persimmons, apples, pears, kiwi, papaya, mango, pineapple, bananas, strawberries, raspberries, blueberries Dried Fruits: raisins, dates, pears, pineapple, prunes, peaches, figs

FOOD PYRAMID (Cont.)

Limit foods high in fat, cholesterol, sugar, and salt.

Eat Moderately — Legumes, Nuts, Seeds, Meat Alternatives
2-3 Servings daily

Food	Nutrients	Number of Servings			Examples
½ cup cooked beans or peas 1/3 cup nuts (1 oz.) ½ cup tofu 2 Tbsp nut butter (1 oz.) ¼ cup seeds ¼ cup meat alternative 2 egg whites	Protein Zinc Iron Fiber Calcium Vitamin B_6 Vitamin E Niacin (B_3) Linoelic Acid	2	2-3	3	Legumes: pinto, black, white navy, soybeans, garbanzoes, lentils, blackeye, green pea, split pea, peanuts Nuts: almonds, walnuts, filberts, chestnuts, brazil, pecans, cashews Seeds: pine nuts, sesame, sunflower, pumpkin Alternatives: tofu, meat alternatives

Eat Moderately — Dairy Products and/or Fortified Alternatives
2-3 Servings daily

Food	Nutrients	Number of Servings			Examples
1 cup milk, nonfat or lowfat 1 cup soymilk (fortified) ¾ cup lowfat cottage cheese ½ cup soy cheese 1½ oz. fresh cheese 1 cup low-fat or non-fat yogurt	Calcium Protein Vitamins A and D Riboflavin (B_2) Vitamin B_{12}	2	2-3	3	Dairy: milk, yogurt, cottage cheese, ricotta, other fresh cheeses Alternatives: soy or tofu milk, soy cheese

Eat Sparingly — Fats, Oils, Sugar, Salt

The small tip of the Pyramid shows fats, oils, salt, and sweets. These foods such as salad dressings and oils, cream, butter, margarine, sour cream, cream cheese, sugars, soft drinks, candies, and sweet desserts provide calories and are low in nutrients. Oils contain essential fatty acids. Most people should use these sparingly. For every tablespoon of fat added to a 2200 calorie diet, you increase the percentage of calories as fat by approximately five percent. Every tablespoon of sugar adds twice calories as sugar.

- Use visible fats sparingly.
- Limit desserts to two or three per week.
- Use honey, jams, jelly, corn syrups, molasses, sugar sparingly
- Use soft drinks and candies very sparingly, if at all.
- Limit foods high in salt.

1 tsp salt (5 gm table salt) = 2000 mg sodium
1 T oil = 13.6 gm fat   120.0 calories
1 tsp oil = 4.5 gm fat   40.1 calories

1 T margarine	= 11.4 gm fat	102 calories
1 T mayonnaise	= 11.0 gm fat	99 calories
1 T sour cream	= 3.0 gm fat	30 calories
1 T cream cheese	= 5.0 gm fat	52 calories
1 T sugar	= 12 gm	48 calories
1 tsp sugar	= 4 gm	16 calories
1 T honey	= 21 gm	64 calories
1 tsp honey	= 7 gm	21 calories

Daily Menu Planner

Water: One or two 8-ounce glasses upon arising
(not at mealtime)

BREAKFAST

1 slice whole-grain bread
1 teaspoon nut butter or bread spread
1/2 to 1 cup whole-grain cereal or other protein food
2 fruits
1 glass (8 ounces) milk

Water: Two 8-ounce glasses (not at mealtime)

NOON MEAL

1 entree
1 green leafy vegetable
1 other vegetable
1 raw vegetable salad
1 slice whole-grain bread
1/2 tsp. soft margarine, nut butter, or other spread
1 glass (8 ounces) milk

Water: Two 8-ounce glasses (between the meals)

EVENING MEAL

(if eaten)
1 serving fruit or vegetable soup or salad
1 slice whole-grain bread or 3-4 whole grain crackers

Water: Two 8-ounce glasses (not with the meal)

WEEKLY MENU PLANNER

Menu Suggestions	Sunday	Monday	Tuesday	Wednesday	Thursday	Friday	Saturday
BREAKFAST Breadstuff 1 Vit. C fruit 1 other fruit Whole-grain Cereal 　or Protein Food Milk or equiv.							
MAIN MEAL Entree 1 leafy green veg. 1 other vegetable 1 veg. salad Bread/Spread Milk or equiv. Simple Dessert							
SUPPER (or lunch) Fruit or Soup Bread/Crackers							

BREAKFAST MENUS

1. Cooked Hot Cereal Blend w/ raisins
   Melon slices
   Cashews
   Whole wheat toast/margarine
   Milk

2. Thickened Berries over toast
   La Loma Little Links
   Grapefruit
   Milk

3. Orange Juice
   Brown rice w/honey and milk
   Almonds
   Canned apricots
   Whole wheat toast/margarine
   Milk

4. Pineapple juice
   Creamed Boiled eggs over toast
   Stewed prunes
   Whole wheat muffin/margarine
   Milk

5. Tomato juice
   Oatmeal w/raisins
   Peaches
   Whole wheat toast/margarine
   Milk

6. Cream of Rye cereal
   Whole orange
   Whole wheat toast with peanut butter topped with applesauce
   Milk

7. Cooked wheat nuggets with dates
   Strawberries
   Whole wheat toast/margarine
   Milk

8. Orange juice
   Waffles
   Strawberry Orange Sauce
   La Loma Little Links
   Hot milk drink

9. Apricot nectar
   Cooked whole wheat cereal
   Almonds
   Orange sections
   Raisin nut toast/margarine
   Milk

10. Grapefruit juice
    Hash brown potatoes
    Scrambled Tofu
    Peach slices
    Hot drink

11. Grape juice
    Golden Grain Granola
    Pear
    Pumpernickel toast/margarine
    Milk

12. Orange juice
    Oatmeal
    Boiled egg or handful nuts
    Fruit cocktail
    Whole wheat toast/margarine
    Milk

13. Strawberries
    Roman Meal cereal
    Whole wheat toast with peanut butter and applesauce
    Milk

14. Dry cereal with bananas/raisins
    Nuts
    Cantaloupe
    Blueberry muffins/margarine
    Milk

15. Breakfast Millet served with
    raisins
    Soy Milk
    Whole Wheat Toast
    Fresh Fruit

16. Sunflower Seed-Oat Waffles
    served with Orange or Apple
    Syrup
    Fresh Fruit
    Milk

17. Tahini French Toast Breakfast
    or Garbanzo French Toast
    served with Orange or Apple
    Syrup
    Fresh Fruit

18. Eggless Wheat-Oat Crepes
    served with Strawberry Slices or
    Bananas and whipped topping

19. Hurry-Up Hearty Hash
    Toast
    Fruit
    Milk

20. Make-Ahead Pancake Mix
    Breakfast served with boiled egg
    Hot Thickened Fruit

21. Cheery Rice Breakfast
    Steamed Brown Rice
    Chopped Red Apple
    Sunflower Seeds
    Milk
    Honey

22. Millet Breakfast
    Steamed Whole Millet
    Chopped Apples
    Raisins
    Milk
    Honey

23. Soy-Oat Waffles served with
    Orange or Apple Syrup
    Whipped Butter
    Fresh Fruit
    Milk

24. Familia Breakfast Cereal (A
    meal in one)
    Fresh Fruit
    Milk

25. The Instant Meal on the Run
    Hurry-Up Breakfast Drink
    Piece of fresh fruit

26. Creamed Green Peas Over
    Toast
    Grapefruit Halves
    Whole Wheat Biscuits
    Tomato Juice

A MONTH'S SUGGESTIONS FOR PACK-IT LUNCHES

	Something Hearty	Something Crisp	Something Toothsome	Something Drinkable	Something to to Surprise (Opt.)
First Week					
Mon.	Peanut butter	Carrot strips	Applesauce	Potato soup (cream)	Dried fruit
Tue.	Tomato Nuttose	Cucumber sticks	Orange quartered	Milk	Date bar
Wed.	Egg sandwich	Celery sticks	Apple quartered	Milk	Fruit candy
Thur.	Savory soy pattie	Assorted relishes	Fruit salad	Tomato juice	Oatmeal cookie
Fri.	Avocado, tomato & lettuce sandwich	Olives	Half banana	Noodle soup	Bag of peanuts
Second Week					
Mon.	Tofu sandwich	Cucumber sticks	Apple quartered	Tomato soup (cream)	Oatmeal cookie
Tue.	Vegetarian burger	Lettuce wedge	Jel fruit salad cookie	Milk	Peanut butter
Wed.	Garbanzo spread	Olives	Apricots, fresh, dried or canned	Fruit juice	Wheat brownie
Thur.	Sweet Filling	Stuffed celery	Half banana	Milk	Mixed nuts
Fri.	Lentil pattie	Carrot sticks	Berries, fresh or frozen	Lentil rice soup	Carrot cake

Third Week

Mon.	Vegetarian wiener on bun	Nuts	Cherries, fresh or canned	Corn chowder	Dried fruit
Tue.	Millet pattie	Olives	Orange quartered	Milk	Stuffed prunes
Wed.	Cottage cheese	Crackers	Tomato quartered	Vegetable soup	Molasses cookie
Thur.	Browned tofu sandwich	Celery curls	Ripe pear	Milk	Fruit whip
Fri.	Savory Garbanzo sandwich	Carrot sticks	Pineapple chunks	Milk	Dates

Fourth Week

Mon.	Hard boiled egg (deviled)	Assorted relishes	Potato salad crackers	Milk	Dried fruit
Tue.	Vegeburger on bun	Carrot strips	Peaches fresh/canned	Vegetable soup	Pudding
Wed.	Bean pattie	Stuffed celery	Melon, peeled & sliced	Milk	Coconut cookie
Thur.	Peanut butter sandwich	Olives	Grapes	Fruit juice	Rice pudding
Fri.	Garbanzo Falafel	Lettuce wedge sandwich	Half banana	Tomato soup	Dried fruit (cream)

DINNER MENUS

1. Pot 'O Beans
   Baked potato
   Parsleyed carrots
   Tossed green salad/dressing

2. Stroganoff over noodles
   Fresh steamed beets
   Broccoli
   Carrot & celery sticks
   Whole wheat bread/margarine
   V-8 Juice

3. Tofu Oatmeal Patties with gravy
   Baked sweet potato
   Green peas
   Cabbage slaw
   Rye bread/margarine
   Milk

4. Italian Lentils
   Oven French Fries
   Spinach
   Grated carrot salad/dressing
   Whole wheat bread/margarine
   Milk

5. Busy-day Stew
   Frozen green limas, steamed
   Tossed salad with dressing
   Whole wheat bread/margarine
   Apple juice

6. Delicious Blackege Peas
   Baked potato
   Turnip greens
   Sliced tomatoes
   Whole wheat bread/margarine
   Milk

7. Vegetarian meat balls
   Mashed potatoes/margarine
   Green peas
   Relish plate—olives, celery,
      turnips, tomato wedges
   Pumpkin pie
   Whole wheat rolls/margarine
   Fruit punch

8. Spaghetti with homemade sauce
   French style green beans
   Marinated Cauliflower Salad
   Whole wheat French bread/
      margarine
   Milk

9. Savory Pecan Loaf
   Sweet potato
   Peas
   Tossed salad
   No-Sugar Lemon Pie
   Pumpernickel Bread/margarine
   Fruit Punch

10. Sesame Seed Pilaf with Rice
    Carrots
    Lettuce wedges
    Whole wheat dinner rolls
    Milk

11. Savory Soy Patties
    Baked potatoes
    Spinach Roman Style
    Tossed salad
    Dinner rolls/margarine
    Milk

12. Dutch Oven Meal
    Waldorf salad
    Oatmeal cookies
    Corn bread
    Milk

13. Black Beans over Rice
    Spinach Salad
    Layered Applesauce Dessert
    Dinner Rolls/margarine
    Apple juice

14. Lentil Loaf
    Parsleyed Potatoes
    Peas
    Tossed Salad
    Rye bread/margarine
    Ice cream
    Cranberry Juice Cocktail

SUPPER MENUS

1. Sprout Salad with Avocado Dressing
   Bran Muffins

2. Vegetable Soup
   Rye or whole wheat crackers

3. Fruit Plate
   Whole wheat sticks

4. Cream of Tomato Soup
   Avocado-grapefruit salad
   Old Fashioned Hoecakes

5. Creamed Asparagus on toast
   Date muffins

6. Corn chowder
   Whole wheat Bread/margarine

7. Fruit bowls—canned sliced peaches, pear
   halves, pineapple chunks, sliced banana
   Ezekiel's bread

8. Greek Tomato Salad
   Whole Wheat bread/margarine

9. Cream of Vegetable Soup
   Cornbread/margarine/honey

10. Baked apples
    Muffins

11. Watermelon or fruit in season
    Pumpernickel bread/margarine

12. Glorified Rice
    Fresh fruit slices

13. Creamed Peas over toast
    Yeast Biscuits/margarine

14. Fruit Salad with yogurt
    Old Fashioned Corn Pones

FAST MEATLESS MENUS FOR PEOPLE IN A HURRY

1. Wok vegetables & Tofu
   over Steamed Brown Rice or
   Noodles

2. Vegetarian chili beans
   Cole slaw salad
   Rolled up warm tortillas

3. Island soybeans over Baked or boiled potatoes
   Greek tomato/cucumber salad
   Steamed green vegetables from freezer

4. Quick Garbanzo pot pie with Whole wheat biscuits
   Sliced tomatoes & cucumbers
   Steamed green vegetables

5. Crunchy vegetable salad with
   Cottage cheese or yogurt
   Whole grain bran muffins

6. Creamed vegetables over toast or in patty shells

7. Fried rice
   Green vegetable, steamed
   Brown tofu slices
   Carrot-apple salad

8. Bean salad served in lettuce cups
   Garnish of finger food vegetables
   Whole grain bread or rolls

9. Tacos made with refried beans or
   Vegetarian chili beans
   Shredded lettuce, chopped tomatoes
   Chopped onions, shredded cheese

10. Taco boats: corn chips on plate
    Topped with layers of hot chili beans
    Shredded lettuce, chopped tomatoes
    Onions, shredded cheese

11. English muffin tostados:
    toast English muffins
    Top with hot vege chili or
    Refried beans, then shredded lettuce and
    Other chopped vegetables.
    Top with Guacamole.

12. Baked Garbanzo casserole
    Mashed potatoes or baked
    Sweet potatoes
    Steamed green vegetable
    Tossed vegetable salad
    Whole wheat bread or rolls

13. Big Mac patties with all the
    Traditional trimmings
    Oven baked fries
    Fruit salad

14. Millet 'n vegetables casserole
    Fresh green salad
    Whole wheat bread or rolls

15. Pot 'O Lentils stew
    Tossed salad
    Whole wheat bread or rolls

16. Busy-day stew (steam 1 pkg. frozen vegetables
    Add chopped vegetarian meat product)
    Whole grain bread or crackers
    Tossed green salad

17. Fast cream of vegetable soup
    (Use 1 pkg. frozen mixed vegetables or
    First blend and add a cream sauce)
    Whole grain bread or muffins

18. Pasta salad pastina
    (A frozen vegetable/pasta mix is available in supermarket.
    Cook. Cool. Add dressing of your choice)
    Whole grain French bread

19. Dutch oven meal
    (Steam together all in one heavy pot:
    Small red potatoes, carrot chunks, zucchini pieces,
    Worthington Fry Chik type meatless product)

20. Sloppy Joes
    (Vegetarian chili served over buttered whole wheat toast)
    Raw vegetable finger foods

21. Spaghetti with meatless sauce
    Worthington meatless meatballs
    Vegetable salad
    Whole grain French rolls

22. Soupy beans served over
    Baked potato, green vegetables
    Steamed carrot salad

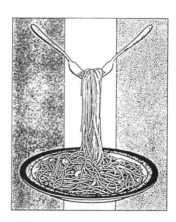

Chapter 19

Weight Control

"I can do all things through Christ which strengtheneth me."
Philippians 4:13

IF WEIGHT IS A PROBLEM

Why Lose Weight?

Being overweight adds unnecessary strain to your body. (If you don't believe it, try carrying a 50 pound bag all day!) Overweight people also are more likely to get certain diseases—heart, kidney, circulatory diseases, and diabetes. Being overweight is dangerous!

How did the fat get there? All foods contain calories.

Some foods are higher in calories than others. Your body breaks down foods so the calories can be used for energy. You need energy just to keep you alive— e.g., to breathe, for your heart to beat, and to maintain muscle tone.

You will **stay** at the same weight if you eat as many calories as your body uses for energy.

You will **gain weight** if you eat more than your body can use because your body stores extra calories as fat.

You will **lose weight** if you eat less food than your body requires because your body will burn your stored fat for energy. Attack the fat from two sides: Consume fewer calories and increase your physical activity.

How can I lose weight?

Before you begin any weight reduction program, get your doctor's approval. Then follow these guidelines:

- Eat foods from the Eating Right Pyramid in the recommended amounts.
- Avoid foods high in sugar and fat; avoid alcohol consumption.
- Eat meals regularly and exercise regularly. (Good exercises for seniors are walking, calisthenics, deep breathing and stretching.)
- Be determined to change your eating habits permanently. You can't cure fat, but **you can** control it.

CHOOSE TO LOSE

Here's how to start...

According to a Harvard Medical School Health Letter, December 1980, an estimated 20 million Americans are on a "serious" diet at any given time; yet Americans on the average are reported to be gaining weight. If there were easy formulas for appetite control or weight loss, the record would be a little better. The fact that it isn't should make you very suspicious of  special diets, highly visible commercial weight-control products, and hard-sell programs offering to make you into a sex symbol in a few easy weeks.

Many "quick weight loss" diets have been popular. Such diets aren't recommended. They neither effect a permanent change in eating habits, nor do they result in a significant reduction in the amount of stored body fat.

There are myriads of myths about weight control. Here are some of them:

1. "It's better to smoke than to be fat.." False
2. "Calories don't count." Meaningless. The only thing that counts *is* calories.
3. "Some foods, such as boiled eggs or grapefruit, burn up calories." Wrong.
4. "A crash diet is a good way to begin a weight-loss program." A bad idea. Crash diets produce rapid fluid loss, but the fluid is easily regained when the diet is abandoned.
5. "Exercise is a relatively unimportant factor in weight control." Probably the reverse of the truth.
6. "Everyone gains weight with equal ease." Not so.

To prevent weight gain is the only successful defense against obesity. A behavioral modification program in which you begin to *change your basic life-style and overall eating habits is the only long-lasting, effective weight-loss program..*

BEGIN TONIGHT... Eat nothing before you hit the sack. Set your alarm for 30 minutes earlier than usual. Walk every morning for 30 minutes *before* you eat. This will help to whet the appetite for breakfast. **THEN...**

EAT A SUBSTANTIAL BREAKFAST. Feature whole grain cereals with skim milk and fresh fruits. Eat no added oil or fat and no sugar, jams or honey and no coffee. This is the most important meal of the day. Don't slight it or forget it!

BEGIN TO BREAK UP THOSE OLD HABIT PATTERNS. Eat NOTHING between meals. Your stomach needs to rest after it has digested your breakfast. You should allow four to five hours between meals. Some diets allow low-calorie snack foods. We don't. You must begin to break that habit of eating five (or ten?) times a day.

TO HELP YOU REMEMBER...Stay out of the kitchen as much as possible. The sights and smells of food are too much for you at this stage. Do your grocery shopping on a full stomach, not when you are hungry.

SET A REGULAR TIME FOR YOUR NOON MEAL. Follow a wholesome low-calorie menu plan. (Menu suggestions follow). If possible, take a 15-minute walk after you eat. AT NIGHT—WATCH OUT! Here's where you usually get into trouble! Limit yourself to the menu suggestions and to eating only at mealtime. You will need to get away from the kitchen.

FOR A WHILE...YOUR STOMACH MAY GROAN. But in a week both you and your stomach will adjust. BEFORE BEDTIME—no snacks. Try another 15-minute walk before you hit the hay.

WHEN YOUR STOMACH SAYS
I choose to eat . . . YOU SAY RIGHT BACK . . .
I choose to lose!

Remember—this weight-control program is launching you into a permanent change of life-style. Old habits are being replaced with new habits. So keep at it! Be faithful with this program. Read and reread each step and determine to follow it exactly. Remember to say often, "I choose to lose!"

REMEMBER TO EXERCISE REGULARLY. We ask you to walk 30-45 minutes every day. Why? Normally a physiological mechanism in the body called the appestat balances what we eat with what we burn up. But unfortunately, the sedentary life most of us lead has suppressed this mechanism. If we exercise regularly, the appestat will once again control how much we choose to eat. Dieting will still be necessary in order to lose weight, but dieting with exercise is much easier. Regular moderate exercise will pay dividends also in increased energy and greater freedom from fatigue. Regular exercise is an excellent way to relieve stress, tension and discouragement—which are reasons why some people overeat in the first place.

DIVINE AID. The power of God in your life makes the battle of overeating completely different. There is a direct relationship between how we eat and our spiritual life. When we don't have the willpower to carry our good intentions through to good behavior, we become frustrated and discouraged with ourselves.

It may surprise you to know that there is a spiritual problem behind the majority of fat problems. As we look around us, we notice that most people please *self*. They eat what they want, when they want it. It seems like freedom to please self, but it turns out to be total slavery.

But there is a solution. We may go to Jesus and confess that we have made wrong choices and are now willing to please *Him*, Then we may ask for His power to operate in our lives to keep us from overeating. Then God is working in us! It is no longer our fight. As long as we give our will to God, the battle is His. Then we begin to eat to His glory. As long as we do this, we will experience victory.

If long-range success is to be accomplished in weight control, you must pay attention to basic eating habits and dietary principles. Calorie counting may be OK for short-term diets, but most people who have a weight problem need to make some real changes in their eating habits. Therefore, we suggest you adopt the following dietary guidelines.

If you can't be bothered with endless record keeping and calorie counting, you'll love this simple weight-loss program.

1. Eat all the fruit and vegetables you want, but don't juice them, sweeten them or butter them. Be sure you get one vitamin-C-rich and one vitamin-A-rich fruit or vegetable per day.

2. Eat two servings of bread or cereal per meal making certain it is whole grain and does not contain sugar or sweetener. You must count any fat that you eat with it within the limits of no 4. Potato, sweet potato and corn count as bread.

3. Eat one from the following at each meal:
   a. A combination of bread or cereal with legumes (beans, peas).
   b. A combination of legumes with nuts (Keep nuts within the limits of no. 4.)
   c. A combination of bread or cereal with nuts. (See no. 4)
   d. A serving of skim milk or low fat cottage cheese.
   e. One egg (limit to three per week). (See no. 4.)
   f. One small serving soya meat analog or nut meat. (See no. 4.)

4. Eat two fat units per meal. The following foods equal one fat unit:
   a. 1 tsp. oil (any kind).
   b. 1 tsp margarine (soft, tub margarine is best).
   c. 4 medium olives.
   d. 1 tbsp. nuts or seeds (any variety).
   e. 1 -1/2 tsp. peanut or other nut butter.
   f. 1 tsp. unsweetened dried coconut.
   g. 2 tsp. fresh coconut or 1 piece 1x1x3/8 inch.
   h. 1 oz. avocado (1/6 of a medium fruit).
   i. 1 whole egg (limit to three per week).
   j. 1/4 cup creamed cottage cheese (low-fat cottage cheese doesn't count as fat).
   k. 1 serving soya meat analog or nut meat.

5. Eat a hearty breakfast and a light supper.

6. Let no morsel of food or drink (except water) be swallowed except at meal time. Limit meals to three per day. (Two is ideal, if you space them properly.)
7. Walk at least 30 to 60 minutes per day.
8. Eat absolutely no refined sugar, honey or syrup.
9. Eat no refined flour, cereals or bread.

If you stick to these few restrictions, you may relax and lose weight. You won't have to count to more than two in your head. Now hurry up and get started so you can see your new trim figure sooner.

Suggested Body Weights

| Height[a] | Range of Acceptable Weight (lb) | |
	Men	Women
4'10"		92-119
4'11"		94-122
5'0"		96-125
5'1"		99-128
5'2"	112-141	102-131
5'3"	115-144	105-134
5'4"	118-148	108-138
5'5"	121-152	111-142
5'6"	124-156	114-146
5'7"	128-161	118-150
5'8"	132-166	122-154
5'9"	136-170	126-158
5'10"	140-174	130-163
5'11"	144-179	134-168
6'0"	148-184	138-173
6'1"	152-189	
6'2"	156-194	
6'3"	160-199	
6'4"	164-204	

Source: G. Bray, ed., "Obesity in America" (Washington, D.C.: United States Government Printing Office, 1979), National Institutes of Health Publication No. 79-359, p. 7.

[a]Height is measured without shoes; weight is measured without clothes.

Chapter 20

Healthful
Eating
Principles

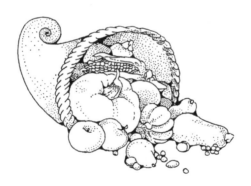

Principles of Healthful Eating

- Eat a hearty breakfast and make the evening meal your lightest meal of the day so that the stomach and digestive system will be at rest when retiring. Avoid heavy late suppers.

- Two or three regularly scheduled meals a day in a relaxed frame of mind, as the digestive juices come into action at the expected meal time. Allow 20 minutes minimum for each meal.

- Allow at least 5 hours between each meal to allow one meal's food to digest before introducing the next.

- Eat nothing between meals or late at night. By this plan the stomach is in condition to digest the next meal.

- Take time to chew your food thoroughly in order that the saliva may be properly mixed with the food, and the digestive fluids called into action.

- Do not wash food down with liquid at mealtime. The more liquid taken with the meal the more difficult for the food to digest, for liquid must be absorbed before digestion can begin.

- Drink plenty of water (at least 6 glasses per day) but not during meals. A glassful or two on awakening and again in a little while before each meal is an excellent plan.

- Keep the meals simple, serving only 2,3, or 4 different foods at a meal, but eat a wide VARIETY of foods...fruits, vegetables, grains, nuts and legumes...throughout the week and month.

- Eat wholesome, unrefined foods . . . whole grain breads and cereal, and natural sweets. As far as possible, remove from the general diet foods that have been altered to any great extent in manufacturing, such as white sugar and its products, and white flour and its products.

- Limit your use of visible fats such as butter, margarine, oils, Crisco, and use few fried foods.

- Do not overeat as it is the worst of all offenses. Do not eat to the point of discomfort. Eat the quantity of food which will keep your weight within the desirable range for your height and body build.

- Include plenty of fresh fruits and vegetables in the diet every day .. both raw and steamed . . . 2 to 4 servings of fruit, and 3-5 servings of vegetables. Use dark green leafy or yellow vegetables 3-4 times per week. Include a Vitamin C-rich food daily.

- Limit desserts that are rich in sugar, fats and/or refined starches.

- Be careful in your use of salt. Americans use 8-15 grams daily, but ideally should use no more than 5 grams or 1 teaspoon. Avoid the use of pickles and spiced foods.

- Limit your use of eggs to 2 or 3 per week, including what you use in cooking—but no egg yolk at all if your blood cholesterol is above average. Eggs are the highest single source of cholesterol in the American diet.

- Limit your use of high cholesterol foods: whole eggs, whole milk products, cheddar and cream type cheeses, and meat products.

- If overtired, rest a while before eating in order for your food to be properly digested. If nervous, stressful or hurried, it is best not to eat at that time.

- Serve fruits at one meal, vegetables at another for better digestion.

BOOSTING NUTRITION IN RECIPES

What do you do when you find a recipe that sounds so enticing you just have to cook it, but it makes use of highly refined ingredients that you may want to replace with whole, unrefined counterparts? If you've been rejecting recipes that sound almost good enough to eat, here is your chance to learn a few simple ingredient exchanges to boost both nutrition and savings. See chart next page. →

INGREDIENT EXCHANGE

To Replace	Use	Benefits
1 c. white flour in baking (for every cup of flour used, with other liquid)	1 c. minus 2 tbsp. whole wheat flour. Exchange 1 tbsp. of the oil.	Increases protein quality, B. vitamins, and trace minerals; adds roughage.
1 c. sugar in baking	Count to 1/2 c. and increase flour by 1/3 c. or omit and try date sugar, ground-up dates or raisins, and use fruit juices for the liquid.	Reduces or avoids use of refined sugar. Sugar is not a whole food, supplies empty calories, and may contribute to disease.
1 c. butter, shortening, margarine, or oil in baking.	Cut in half or to 1/4 c. or omit, adding applesauce, water or juice plus 2 tbsp. per cup soy flour in its place.	Decreases saturated fats and cholesterol, reduces total calories.
1/2 c. whipping cream	1/2 c. nonfat dry milk powder whipped with 1/2 c. ice water.	Reduces fat and calories, saves money.
1 c. sour cream	1 c. yogurt OR 1 c. low-fat cottage cheese plus 4 tbsp. yogurt blenderized.	Reduces fat and calories, increases protein, saves money.
1 egg in baking to bind	1 tbsp. soy or garbanzo flour. 3 tbsp. potato flour or tapioca. 1/2 c. cooked oatmeal. For other egg replacers/ binders, see p. 260.	Decreases fat and cholesterol.
1 egg in baking to leaven	2 egg whites, stiffly beaten OR 1 tsp. baking yeast dissolved in 1/4 c. warm water with pinch sugar or honey and add 1 tbsp. soy flour to recipe.	Decreases fat and cholesterol.
1 tsp. baking powder	2 beaten egg whites folded in last thing OR 1-2 tsp. baking yeast dissolved in 1/4 c. warm water sweetened with 1/2 tsp. sugar or honey.	Baking powder and soda are B-vitamin destroyers and cause inflamation of the stomach. Baking yeast contains B vitamins.

I hope this ingredient exchange will inspire you to rewrite and rework your favorite but not-so-healthy recipes.

CHOLESTEROL IN FOODS

FOOD	mg CHOLESTEROL in 3 1/2 oz.(100mg)
HI	
Brains	2000
Egg Yolk, Fresh	1500
Kidney, Uncooked	375
Caviar or Fish Roe	300
Liver	300
Butter	250
Oysters	200
Lobster	200
Heart, uncooked	150
Crab Meat	125
Shrimp	125
Cheese, Cream	120
MED	
Cheese, Cheddar	100
Lard or Other Animal Fat	95
Veal	90
Whipping Cream	85
Cheese (25-30% fat)	85
Beef, Uncooked	70
Fish, Steak	70
Lamb, Uncooked	70
Pork	70
Cheese Spread	65
Margarine (2/3 animal, 1/3 vegetable)	65
Mutton, Flesh only uncooked'	60
Chicken, Flesh only	60
Ice Cream	45
Sour Cream	45
LOW	
Cottage Cheese, Creamed	15
Milk, Fluid Whole	33
Milk, Fluid Skim	3
Egg White	0
Fruits	0
Nuts	0
Grains	0
Vegetables	0

Compiled and calculated from USDA Handbook No. 8.

What About Meat?

Why is it that so many people, especially young people today, are going off meat? They don't want to kill animals. They don't think it is humane. But there are good scientific reasons for what they are doing.

CANCER POTENTIAL

Some scientists today believe that there is an increased risk of cancer with the use of meat.

Viruses — Viruses are known to cause cancers. What is the chance of getting cancer if one eats meat with a cancer in it? This is what we know. Viruses can be transmitted from one animal to another within the same species. This is the case with the Rous chicken sarcoma (done about 1911) and is such with Bittner's mammary tumor (1936). Mice with breast cancers that nursed their young transmitted the virus to the young and they developed breast cancers. Human leukemia virus when injected into small animals caused not only leukemia, but a whole host of cancers. Here it is being transmitted from one species to another species. What is the chance of it going from the animal to a human? It is unethical to try. But top virologists state that it is unthinkable for something not to be happening.

Chemical Carcinogens — There is in the smoke from 1 kg. (2.2 lbs) of charcoal-broiled steak as much benzopyrene (a carcinogen) as you have in the smoke from 600 cigarettes. Of course, the one is inhaled and the other is ingested. That would make a difference. But when benzopyrene was given to small animals to eat, it caused not only gastric tumors, but leukemia. But someone might say he doesn't eat that much of the benzopyrene. Let's look at methylcholanthrene, another carcinogen, which is produced by the overheating of the fat of meat. Anyone who eats meat routinely is bound to get some methylcholanthrene in his diet. This, when given in large quantities, does cause cancer. However, even if given in very small amounts so as not to cause cancer of itself, it makes small animals more susceptible to other carcinogenic agents also given in sub-carcinogenic doses.

Beef — Some preliminary reports suggest a relationship between beef and cancer. Further studies need to be done on this.

Lack of Fiber — Meat has very little fiber and this lack in the diet is now thought to increase the risk of colon cancer.

ATHEROSCLEROSIS

There is considerable evidence today relating saturated fat in the diet to Atherosclerosis, of which over half the U.S. population dies. Two out of three men die from this. Meat is the largest single source of saturated fat in the American diet. The P/S ratio is poor for meats. The amount of saturated fat is high in most meats.

ENDURANCE

It was shown in a study done in Sweden on nine athletes that a diet higher in carbohydrate and lower in fat and protein caused them to have almost three times the endurance as the diet low in carbohy-drate and high in fat and protein. Meat is a carbohydrate-deficient food. It has practically no carbohydrate.

POPULATION EXPLOSION AND ECONOMICS

With the ever-expanding population, we need to produce more food on the land which we now have. An acre of land may produce 8,000,000 calories from grains or vegetables, but only 200,000 if the vegetation is fed to cows and the milk used for people. The animals use the other 600,000 calories. Animals are poor converters of both protein and calories. Only 23 percent of the total protein consumed by the cow is returned for human consumption as milk, 12 percent by the pig, and only 10 percent is returned by beef cattle. Soybeans produce 7.1 times more available amino acids per acre, the soybean produces close to 17 pounds per acre, compared to about two for milk and less than one for beef. It is estimated that the recover of the calories fed to animals is only 15% from the production of milk, 7% from eggs, and 4% from beef. A wheat based diet can produce 14 times as many calories on the same acreage as a meat-milk based diet, and a rice and beans diet, as in Japan, 21 times as many calories.

KIDNEYS

Dogs on a high meat diet develop more kidney disease, This has been shown with rats also. A high protein diet of any kind, including soybeans will cause the kidneys of rats to enlarge by 25% and many of them become diseased.

Waste products of the animal body are contained in all meat juices. The fluids of the body not only carry food nutrients to the tissue, but they also carry such waste products as urea and uric acid to the kidneys for elimination. With the death of the animal, all body processes stop and the wastes contained in the body at the moment remain there. Meat owes most of its flavor to these waste products contained in the juices. If the animal is well bled and the tissues are thoroughly washed to remove these undesirable materials, the meat becomes quite tasteless.

LIFE EXPECTANCY

It has been shown the life expectancy of rats will be decreased by 25-50% on a high protein diet, such as one gets with meat.

OTHER PARASITES AND VIRUSES OF MEAT

Trichinosis — a round worm larva, is contained in some pork. The meat must be cooked internally at least 170 degrees.

Salmonella — poultry largest single carrier in the country, can invade the ovaries of a hen, causing her eggs to carry the infection. (Housewives are instructed to wear gloves when handling poultry.)

Leukemia — transmitted in dairies.

Even though many of the parasites and viruses are killed under extreme heat, there are some which are not killed even under high heat and pressure which can be given in a home.

THE MARKETING OF CANCEROUS MEAT

The same agency that has the responsibility of protecting the public from unwholesome meat also has the responsibility of promoting meat production.

It takes a physician and a clinical laboratory 24 hours or more to determine the causative organism of infection in a human body. In poultry, for example, as inspection is practiced in this country by the federal government, a lay-man is expected in as little as 2 seconds to determine the wholesomeness and freedom from infection of the meat of a chicken. The same goes for inspection of cattle, sheep, and pigs that the public eats.

Consider a typical poultry plant. Lay inspectors (with from 1-6 weeks' training), operating under an inspector in charge, must examine 48,000 birds daily. The birds pass by on a conveyor belt at the rate of 100 per minute, giving the inspectors about 3 1/2 seconds per bird. All he can do is look at it, feel it, and perhaps smell it.

Consider the living condition of the chickens. Today's bird never sees sunlight or breathes fresh air. It is cramped in a 12 by 12-inch cage with four other birds. Their lives are electronically controlled from timed spray baths that send them into a frenzy, to bright fluorescent lamps 16 hours at a time to increase feeding. Their feed has a variety of drugs and hormones to speed up growth.

Chemists have invented artificial dyes that are added to feed to transform the pasty whiteness of chicken flesh into a rich golden color.

Over 90% of chickens from most flocks in this country and abroad are infected with a viral cancer called leukosis. To help the industry over what it considered an "economic hardship," the USDA relaxed its ruling on condemned chickens infected with cancer viruses by permitting them on the market "if they do not look too repugnant," and stating that tumors should be simply cut off while the rest of the chicken could be sold as chicken parts.

The reason for this ruling is because of the failure of recent experiments to show that poultry cancer viruses present any danger to humans.

There is presently no requirement for inspection of pork and no grading standard; the consumer buys at his or her own risk.

KNOW YOUR CONDIMENTS

IRRITATING SUBSTANCES

Name	Chemical	Effect
Black pepper (& white)	Eugenol & peperidine	GI* and GU* irritation, ↑BP*
Chili peppers	Eugenol	↑Cancer, ↑BP*
Cayenne		Stomach irritation
Horseradish		GU* irritation
Cloves	Oil of cloves	↑Cravings, irritates nerves
Allspice	Eugenol	↑Cravings, irritates nerves
Cinnamon	Eugenol & cinnamic aldehyde	↑Cravings, irritates nerves
Mustard seed	Allyl oil	GI* and GU* irritation, ↑BP*
Ginger		GU* irritation, ↑BP*
Nutmeg	Myristicin	Breaks mucus barriers in stomach and bowel, hallucinations, may depress or irritate central nervous system
Vinegar	Acetic acid	Breaks mucus barriers, irritates nerves
Baking soda, powder	Sodium salts	↑BP*, ↑stomach irritation, hydrochloric acid flow in stomach
Salt	Sodium chloride	↑BP*, ↑Cravings

*GI: Gastrointestinal
*GU: Genitourinary
*BP: Blood pressure
↑: Increase

NON-IRRITATING HERBS

Basil	Garlic	Rosemary
Bay Leaf Caraway	Marjoram	Saffron
Caraway	Mint	Sage
Celery Seed	Onion	Sesame Seed
Coriander	Oregano	Spearmint
Cardamom	Paprika (Spanish type, bright red)	Tarragon
Chives	Parsley	Thyme
Dill Seed	Peppermint	Turmeric
Fennel Seed	Poppy Seed	Wintergreen

LEMON JUICE VS. VINEGAR

"Vitamin C losses were studied in individual cabbage salads containing vinegars. The losses in salads made with French Dressing were lower than those containing the same amount of plain vinegar." —*U.S. Department of Agriculture, Handbook No. 8.*

Bronson in *Nutrition and Food Chemistry* declares that vinegar lengthens the time that vegetables remain in the stomach. Vinegar's acidity hinders digestion.

"Vinegar is naturally or artificially-flavored acetic acid, commonly ranging between 4 and 6 percent . . . Mild gastritis or enteritis may be caused by it." — *Journal of the American Medical Association.*

"When salads are prepared with oil and vinegar, fermentation takes place in the stomach, and the food does not digest, but decays or putrefies; as a consequence, the blood is not nourished, but becomes filled with impurities, and liver and kidney difficulties appear." — E.G. White, *Counsels on Diet and Foods.*

By definition, vinegar is formed by the action of mycoderma aceti on an alcohol commonly obtained from fruit juices, wine, or other fermented liquids. Food and Drug regulations state that the word vinegar without an adjective means vinegar made from apple juice.

In addition to the 4 percent acetic acid which by law it must contain, vinegar has in it a variety of other substances such as lactic or maltic acids, alcohol, glycerin, sugars, esters such as ethyl acetate, pentosans, artificial coloring and inorganic salts.

As has been said by others, "Vinegar is great for washing windows. Keep it for that, but keep the lemons and limes for use in your wholesome recipe!"

KERNEL OF WHEAT

The kernel of wheat is a storehouse of nutrients needed and used by man since the dawn of civilization. This cross section shows the nutrients in each part of the kernel. They are considered essential in the human diet.

ENDOSPERM . . . about 83 percent of the kernel. Source of white flour. The Endosperm consists mostly of starch and protein with a small amount of B-complex vitamins but no fiber. Whole wheat flour naturally contains 16 minerals and 14 vitamins. While bread is made from the Endosperm part of the wheat. "Enriched" white flour has had three vitamins (thiamine, riboflavin, and niacin) added back and one mineral (iron).

BRAN . . . about 14 percent of the kernel included in whole wheat flour. The bran contains all the fiber of the kernel and large amounts of vitamins and minerals.

GERM . . . about 2-1/2 percent of the kernel. The embryo or sprouting section of the seed, usually separated because it contains fat which limits the keeping quality of flours. Available separately as human food. The germ is the life-giving part from which the wheat plant sprouts and is one of the richest known sources of B and E vitamins. It also contains valuable proteins and fat.

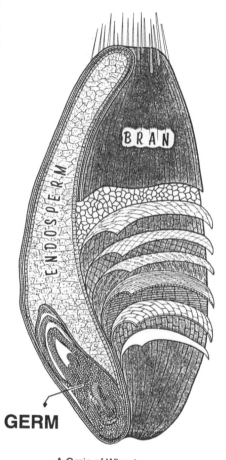

A Grain of Wheat
(enlarged approximately 18 times)

NUTRIENTS FOUND IN THE KERNEL OF WHEAT:

MINERALS

Calcium	Iodine	Boron
Iron	Fluorine	Copper
Phosphorus	Chlorine	Sulphur
Magnesium	Sodium	Silver
Potassium	Silicon	Barium
Manganese		

VITAMINS

Thiamine (B-1)	Biotin
Riboflavin (B-2 or G)	Folic Acid
Pantothenic Acid	Choline
Pyridoxine (B-6)	Vitamin E

(and other trace minerals and vitamin factors)

Applesauce
  Applesauce-Peanut Butter, Hot,
    Over Toast, 53
  Fresh, 204
  Layered, 216
Avocado
  Fruit Salad, 206
  Grapefruit/Avocado/Banana
    Salad, 194
  Guacamole, 200
  Salad Dressing, 195
Bagels, Whole Wheat, 79
Bananas
  Apricot and Banana Salad, 210
  Apple and Banana, 208
  Banana Salad, 210
  Banana and Nut Salad, 210
  Banana Milkshake, 219
  Blueberry Sauce over Banana
    Slices, 219
  Fresh Fruit Cup, 207
  Grapefruit/Avocado/Banana
    Salad, 194
  Piña Colada, 247
  South-of-the-Border
    Bananza, 216
  Strawberry-Banana
    Smoothie, 246
  Tropical Ice Cap, 245
Beans (See also Legumes,
  Patties)
  Baked Soybeans, 109
  Bean Casserole, 111
  Bean-Oat Patties, 117
  Black Beans on Rice, 111
  Boston Baked Beans, 113
  Chili Beans, 111
  Cooking Soybeans and
    Garbanzos, 108
  Delicious Blackeye Peas, 112
  Family Favorite Lima
    Beans, 110
  Frijoles Vaquero, 113
  How to Cook Dry Beans and
    Peas, 107

  Island Soybeans, 110
  Mashed Bean Sandwich, 59
  Preparing Dry Beans, Steps
    for, 106
  Pressure Cooker Method
    (Soybeans or
    Garbanzos), 109
  Reducing Gas-Forming
    Properties, 108
  Salad, 192
Bear Claws, No-Sugar, 90
Beverages (See also Shakes and
  Smoothies)
  Banana Milkshake, 219
  California Citrus Punch, 242
  Cranberry Hailstorm, 245
  Cranberry Orange Sparkle, 244
  Frosty Cooler, 243
  Fruit Cooler, 242
  Hurry-Up Breakfast Drink, 38
  Ideal Beverage, 240
  Milk Shake Refresher, 246
  Mix 'N' Match Fruit Drinks, 242
  Mock Hot Chocolate, 245
  Nature's Milk, 244
  Orange Frostie, 243
  Orange Julius, 247
  Peach Frosty, 247
  Piña Colada, 247
  Pink Punch, 243
  Root Beer Slush, 243
  Russian Mock Choc, 244
  Strawberry-Banana
    Smoothie, 246
  Strawberry Snowdrift, 246
  Tropical Cooler, 246
  Tropical Ice Cap, 245
Biscuits, Yeast, 98
Bread Crumbs and Cubes
  Plain, 262
  Seasoned, 147 and 262
Bread Sticks, Whole Wheat, 101
Breading
  Meal, 153 and 261
  Mix, for Tofu, 125

Breads
Auto Bakery Mix, 95
Bagels, Whole Wheat, 79
Basic By-Hand, 93
Basic Mixer, Marcella's, 77
Basic Sweet Dough, 91
Bear Claws, No-Sugar, 90
Boston Brown, 98
Bran Muffins, 99
Burger Buns, 81
Buttermilk Burger Buns, 88
Communion, 100
Corn Pones, Old-Fashioned, 96
Dark Mixed-Grain, 94
Date Muffins, 100
Do's and Don'ts of Dough, 68
Ezekiel's, 65
French, 87
French Onion, 83
Fruit-Nut Breakfast Rolls, 81
Garlic, 83
Herb, 94
Herbed Seed, 86
Hoecakes, Old-Fashioned, 96
Lecithin-Oil Mixture for Greasing
    Pans, 100
Linda's Wheat-Free, 92
Marcella's Basic Mixer, 77
Marcella's Orange-Raisin-
    Nut, 85
Millet, 86
No-Sugar Bear Claws, 90
Old-Fashioned Corn Pones, 96
Old-Fashioned Hoecakes, 96
Orange Raisin Nut, 94
Orange-Raisin-Nut,
    Marcella's, 85
Pizza Crust, Whole Wheat, 80
Pocket, 79
Poppy Seed Bubble Loaf, 94
Pumpernickel, 94
Quick Cornbread, 97
Raisin-Citron, 93
Raisin-Nut, 83
Rye, 83 and 94

Rye, (Electric Mixer Method), 84
Rye, Swedish Variation, 84
Seven Grain — Four Seed, 82
Seven Grain Flour, 82
Soy Graham, 94
Swedish Rye Variation, 84
Sweet Rolls, Fruit-Nut
    Breakfast, 81
Wayfarer's Bread, 95
Wheat-Free, Linda's, 92
Yeast Biscuits, 98
Yeast Cornbread, 97
Breakfast
Menus, 274
Suggestions, 39
Broth (See Sauces)
Burger Buns, 81
Buttermilk, 88
Burgers (See Patties)
Butter (See Jams and Jellies, and
    Spreads)
Cake, Apple, 225
Calories, Daily
    (recommended), 261
Candies
Almost Almond Roca, 232
Carob Super Fudge, 231
Carob-Coated Peanut Butter
    Kisses, 232
Date-Nut Clusters, 231
Martha's Candy Logs, 231
Old-Fashioned Fruit Candy, 233
Sesame Seed Drops, 233
Canning Fruits Without
    Sugar, 237
Cashews
Cashew Nut Casserole, 135
Cashew Nut Cheese
    Sauce, 147
Cashew Pimento Cheese
    Topping, 80
Cashew-Oat Waffles, 51
Cheese, 146
Cream Topping, 216
French Toast, 51

Gravy, 256
Mayonnaise, 195
Stuffing, 135
Casseroles
Baked Garbanzo, 114
Bean, 111
Cashew Nut, 135
Eggplant Crunch, 172
Holiday Stuffing, 151
Mock Chicken, 154
Savory Millet, 136
Sprouted Lentil, 252
Catsup
Lemon Juice (cooked), 263
Quick Catsup, 263
Cereals
Armenian Christmas
Porridge, 44
Blue-Ribbon Buckwheat
(Kasha), 43
Cooked Whole Kernel Wheat, 42
Cooking Guide, Whole Kernel
Grains, 40
Familia, 41
Four Grain Cereal, 42
Golden Grain Granola, 41
Hot Cereal Blend, 42
Microwave Hot Cereal, 43
Millet Breakfast Cereal, 42
Prairie "Fish" Hotcake, 44
Thermos-Cooked Whole Wheat
Cereal, 43
Cheese Replacers
Cashew Pimento Cheese, 80
Cashew Cheese, 146
Cashew Nut Cheese Sauce, 147
Soy Cheese Whiz, 264
Chili
Beans, 111
Powder Substitute, 260
Chocolate (Mock)
Mock Hot Chocolate, 245
Russian Mock Choc, 244
Cholesterol in Foods, 294

Cinnamon Substitute, 226
Condiments, Know Your, 300
Cookies
Carob Chip, 229
Fruit Crisps, 229
Granola Macaroons, 228
Haystacks, 230
Kitchen Sink, 226
Polynesian Bars, 227
Raisin-Nut Oat, 227
Simple Simon Fruit Crunch, 228
Tahini, (Sesame Seed
Butter), 228
Coolers
Frosty, 243
Fruit, 242
Tropical, 246
Corn
Chowder, 184
Double Corn Flapjacks, 49
Old-Fashioned Corn Pones, 96
Quick Cornbread, 97
Scalloped, 177
Tamale Pie, 139
Yeast Cornbread, 97
Cornbread
Quick Cornbread, 97
Yeast Cornbread, 97
Corn Pones, Old-Fashioned, 96
Cottage Cheese
Cottage Baked Potato, 162
Loaf, 142
Luncheon Plates I & II, 207
Patties, 142
Tofu (replacer), 125
Crackers
Communion Bread, 100
Sesame Soup Thins, 101
Whole Wheat Sticks, 101
Cream (See Sour Cream)
Crepes, Eggless Whole
Wheat, 53
Curry
Powder (non-irritating), 260
Vegetarian Indian, 150

Desserts (See also Cakes, Candies, Cookies, Desserts — Toppings, and Pies)
Apricot Whip, 219
Banana Milkshake, 219
Blueberry Sauce over Banana Slices, 219
Fruit Juice Tapioca, 215
Glorified Rice (pudding), 220
Hi "C" Fruit Delight, 218
January Fresh Fruit Whip, 217
Layered Applesauce, 216
Millet-Date Pudding, 220
Persimmon Dessert, 217
Persimmon Parfaits, 217
Persimmon Parfaits, Quick, 217
South-of-the-Border Bananza, 216
Sweet Rolls, Fruit-Nut Breakfast Rolls, 81
Tutti-Fruiti Ice Cream, 218
Yogurt Popsicles, 219
Desserts—Toppings
Cashew Cream Topping, 216
Connie's Tofu Pie, Topping, 224
Crumb Topping (for pies and cobblers), 221
Crunchy Oat Topping, 216
Glaze for Fresh Fruit Pie, 222
Glaze for Sweet Rolls, 82
Lemon Sauce, 226
Low Fat Whipped Topping, 222
Pineapple Whipped Topping, 222
Poly Whipped Topping, 224
Soy Whipped Topping, 223
Dinner Menus, 278
Dips (see also Salads— Dressings)
Fresh Tartar Sauce, 153 and 200
Guacamole, 200
Pimiento Dip Spread, 200
Spinach, 200
Sunflower-Yogurt, 199

Dressing (See Salads—Dressings or Vegetables—Dressings)
Eating Habits, Check up on Your, 29
Eating Right Pyramid, 269
Eating, Principles of Healthful, 291
Egg Replacement, 260
Entrees (See Casseroles, Gluten, Legumes, Pasta Dishes, Patties, Grains and Nuts, Pilafs, Pizza, Potato Dishes, Rice Dishes, and Tofu)
Fettuccine, Vegetable Sauté, 147
Food Pyramid, Vegetarian, 269
French Fries, Oven, 163
French Toast
Cashew, 51
Garbanzo, 51
Tahini, (Sesame Seed Butter), 51
Fruit Canning Without Sugar, 237
Fruit Dishes (See also Desserts and Salads—Fruit)
Apple and Banana, 208
Apples, Stuffed Baked, 205
Applesauce, Fresh, 204
Apricot and Banana Salad, 210
Apricots, Orange, 209
Apricots, Stewed Dried, 209
Avocado Fruit Salad, 206
Banana and Nut Salad, 210
Banana Salad, 210
Blueberries with Cream, 204
Cottage Cheese Luncheon Plates I and II, 207
Date Fruit Cup, 208
Dates and Apricots, 210
Fresh Applesauce, 204
Fresh Fruit Cup, 207
Fresh Fruit Plate, 204
Fruit Toast, 53
Grape, Pineapple, And Fig, 209
Hawaiian Sunset, 204

Hot Peanut Butter-Applesauce
Over Toast, 53
Individual Fruit Plate, 206
Pear and Cherry Salad, 208
Pineapple-Orange Salad, 208
Prune Tapioca, 209
Garbanzos
Baked Garbanzo Casserole, 114
Cooking, 108
Cooking, Pressure Cooker
Method, 109
Easy Garbanzo Noodle
Dish, 115
Foo Young, 117
French Toast, 51
Garbanzo-Rice Patties, 116
Garbanzo-Soy-Oat Patties, 115
Garbanzo-Wheat Pilaf, 114
Loaf, 115
Quick Pot Pie, 116
Savory Filling (Falafal), 63
Savory Zucchini Garbanzos, 114
Spread Special, 59
Sprouted, 254
Glaze
For Sweet Rolls, 82
Fruit, for Fresh Fruit Pies, 222
Glossary of Unusual
Ingredients, 14
Gluten (Meat Analog)
Broccoli and Gluten Over
Rice, 152
Creamy Chicken Surprise, 155
Holiday Stuffing Casserole, 151
Mock Chicken Casserole, 154
One Dish Meal, 152
Prepare and Serve, How to, 148
Stroganoff, 155
Stuffed Bell Peppers, 151
Sukiyaki, 153
Swiss Style "Steaks", 150
Tacos, 154
Tasty Steaks, 150
Vegetable Skallops, 153

Vegetarian Indian Curry, 150
Grains (See also Cereals and
Grains and Nuts)
Cooking Guide, Whole Kernel
Grains, 40
Get Acquainted with Whole
Grains, 33
Grain Glossary, 16
Kernel of Wheat Chart, 302
Seven Grain Flour, 82
Grains and Nuts (See also Pasta
Dishes and Pizza)
Basic Roast, 137
Brown Rice Pilaf, 132
Brown Rice-Wheat Pilaf, 134
Buckwheat Kasha, 135
Bulgur Vegetable Pilaf, 133
Cashew Stuffing, 135
Cashew Nut Casserole, 135
Cottage Cheese Loaf, 142
Cottage Cheese Patties, 142
Corn Tamale Pie, 139
Curried Quinoa, 141
Four-Grain Pilaf, 132
Garbanzo-Wheat Pilaf, 114
Meatless Loaf, 140
Millet 'N' Vegetables, 136
Millet Patties, 137
Nut and Rice Loaf, 138
Oatmeal Patties Deluxe, 140
Oatmeal Potato Patties, 139
Savory Millet Casserole, 136
Savory Pecan Loaf, 138
Sesame Seed Pilaf, 134
Seven Grain Loaf, 133
Stuffed Pumpkin, 135 and 141
Sprouted Wheat Burgers, 253
Sunflower Seed Roast, 139
Thanksgiving Lentil-Nut
Ring, 118
Vegetarian Meat Balls, 145
Granola
Golden Grain, 41
Granola Macaroons, 228
Granola Pie Crust, 221

Gravies (See also Sauces,
  Syrups, and Sour Cream)
  Brown, 257
  Cashew, 256
  Chicken, 256
  Mom's White, 256
  Mushroom, 142
  Quick Tomato, 258
  Tomato, 258
Guacamole, 200
Hash
  Hurry-Up Hearty, 54
  Browns, Griddle, 54
Healthful Eating Principles, 291
Hoecakes, Old-Fashioned, 96
Ice Cream, Tutti-Frutti, 218
Ideal Weight Chart, 289
Ingredient Exchange, 293
Jams and Jellies (See also
  Spreads and Syrups)
  Apple Butter, 235
  Apple-Date Spread, 234
  Baked Fig Jam, 234
  Baked Fruit Jam, 235
  Date Butter, 236
  Date Jam, 235
  Dried Fruit Jam, 234
  Frozen Fruit Jam, 234
  Instant Gel Jam, 236
  Marmalade Ambrosia, 235
  Marmalade Deluxe, 236
  Natural Fruit-Juice Jelly, 236
Ketchup (see Catsup)
Kitchen Organizing, Natural
  Food, 20
Know Your Condiments, 300
Lasagna, Tofu, 146
Legumes
  Baked Garbanzo
    Casserole, 114
  Baked Soybeans, 109
  Bean Casserole, 111
  Bean-Oat Patties, 117
  Black Beans on Rice, 111
  Boston Baked Beans, 113
  Chili Beans, 111
  Cooking Soybeans and
    Garbanzos, 108
  Delicious Blackeye Peas, 112
  Easy Garbanzo Noodle Dish,
    115
  Esau's Pottage, 119
  Family Favorite Lima
    Beans, 110
  Frijoles Vaquero, 113
  Garbanzo Foo Young, 117
  Garbanzo Loaf, 115
  Garbanzo-Rice Patties, 116
  Garbanzo-Soy-Oat Patties, 115
  Garbanzo-Wheat Pilaf, 114
  How to Cook Dry Beans and
    Peas, 107
  Island Soybeans, 110
  Italian Lentils, 120
  Lentil Loaf, 118
  Lentil Patties, 119
  Lentil Pot Pie, 120
  Lentil Tostados, 121
  Pot O' Lentils, 119
  Preparing Dry Beans, Steps
    for, 106
  Pressure Cooker Method
    (Soybeans or
    Garbanzos), 109
  Quick Garbanzo Pot Pie, 116
  Reducing Gas Forming
    Properties in Beans, 108
  Savory Garbanzo Filling
    (Falafal), 63
  Savory Soy Patties, 109
  Savory Zucchini
    Garbanzos, 114
  Sprouted Garbanzos, 254
  Sprouted Lentil Casserole, 252
  Tacos, 154
  Thanksgiving Lentil-Nut
    Ring, 118
  Yummy Soybean Loaf, 110
Lemon Juice vs. Vinegar, 301
Lemon Sauce, 226

Lentils
  Basic Soup, 182
  Cream of Lentil Soup, 182
  Esau's Pottage, 119
  Italian, 120
  Loaf, 118
  Patties, 119
  Pot Pie, 120
  Pot O' Lentils, 119
  Sprouted Lentil Casserole, 252
  Sprouted Lentil Cream
    Soup, 253
  Stew, 181
  Thanksgiving Lentil-Nut
    Ring, 118
  Tostados, 121
Lunch
  Pack-It Lunch Menus, 276
  Suggestions, 57
Macaroons, Granola, 228
Mayonnaise (See also Salads—
  Dressings and Spreads)
  Cashew, 195
  Instant, 194
  Olive Branch, 194
  Tofu, 196
Meal Planning
  Breakfast Menus, 274
  Breakfast Suggestions, 39
  Daily Menu Planner, 272
  Dinner Menus, 278
  Fast Meatless Menus, 280
  Food Pyramid, Vegetarian, 269
  Kitchen Organizing, 20
  Lunch Suggestions, 57
  Pack-It Lunch Menus, 276
  Staples List, 26
  Supper Menus, 279
  Weekly Menu Planner, 273
Meat, What About, 295
Meat Balls
  Tofu Spaghetti Balls, 128
  Vegetarian Meat Balls, 145
Menu (See Meal Planning)

Milk Drinks
  Mock Hot Chocolate, 245
  Nature's Milk, 244
  Russian Mock Choc, 244
Millet
  Millet Bread, 86
  Millet Breakfast Cereal, 42
  Millet-Date Pudding, 220
  Millet 'N' Vegetables, 136
  Millet Patties, 137
  Millet Spread, 102
  Savory Millet Casserole, 136
Muffins
  Bran, 99
  Date, 100
  Make-Ahead Pancake Mix, 48
Nutrition Information (See also
  Meal Planning)
  Calories, Daily
    (recommended), 261
  Cholesterol in Foods, 294
  Condiments, Know Your, 300
  Eating Habits, Check up on
    Your, 29
  Eating, Principles of
    Healthful, 291
  Egg Replacement, 260
  Food Pyramid, Vegetarian, 269
  Fruit Canning Without
    Sugar, 237
  Ideal Weight Chart, 289
  Ingredient Exchange, 293
  Lemon Juice vs. Vinegar, 301
  Meat, What About, 295
  Organizing The Natural Food
    Kitchen, 20
  Staples List, 26
  Sugar Intake, Suggestions for
    Controlling, 213
Nuts (See Grains and Nuts)
Oats
  Bean-Oat Patties, 117
  Cashew-Oat Waffles, 51
  Crunchy Oat Topping, 216

Garbanzo-Soy-Oat Patties, 115
Oatmeal Patties Deluxe, 140
Oatmeal Potato Patties, 139
Raisin-Nut Oat Cookies, 227
Sunflower Seed-Oat Waffles, 50
Tofu Oatmeal Patties, 124
Orange Julius, 247
Organizing the Natural Food
Kitchen, 20
Oriental Dishes
Almond Vegetables
Mandarin, 171
Bean Sprouts and Pea
Pods, 174
Browned Tofu, 125
Broccoli with Almond
Sauce, 171
Chinese Cabbage Salad, 191
Chinese Wok Delight, 126
Garbanzo Foo Young, 117
Oriental Rice, 160
Oriental Salad, 193
Savory Fried Rice, 160
Scrambled Tofu, 54 and 123
Sukiyaki, 153
Sweet and Sour Tofu, 126
Tofu-Green Bean Sauté, 125
Tofu and Rice Bake, 124
Wok Cooked Vegetables, 170
Wok Vegetables and Tofu, 127
Pancakes
Basic Oatmeal Waffles, 50
Breakfast Wheat Cakes, 49
Cashew-Oat Waffles, 51
Double Corn Flapjacks, 49
Hoecakes, Old-Fashioned, 96
Make-Ahead Pancake Mix, 48
Old Fashioned Steam Leavened
Waffles, 49
Prairie "Fish" Hotcake, 44
Sunflower Seed-Oat Waffles, 50
Tofu, 124
Parfaits, Persimmon, 217
Pasta Dishes
Basic Homemade Pasta, 143

Creamed Vegetable Pasta, 145
Easy Garbanzo Noodle
Dish, 115
Macaroni and Cashew Nut
Cheese, 147
Mama Glenda's Ravioli's in
Sauce, 144
Spaghetti Sauce, Italian, 258
Spaghetti Sauce, Quickie, 144
Stroganoff, 155
Tofu Lasagna, 146
Tofu Spaghetti Balls, 128
Vegetable Sauté
Fettuccine, 147
Vegetarian Meat Balls (for
Pasta), 145
Wok Vegetables and Tofu, 127
Patties
Barley Burgers, 253
Bean-Oat Patties, 117
Cottage Cheese Patties, 142
Fundamental Burger, The, 62
Garbanzo Foo Young, 117
Garbanzo-Rice Patties, 116
Garbanzo-Soy-Oat Patties, 115
Lentil Patties, 119
Meatless Rice Burgers, 63
Millet Patties, 137
Oatmeal Patties Deluxe, 140
Oatmeal Potato Patties, 139
Savory Soy Patties, 109
Sprouted Wheat Burgers, 253
Tofu Burgers, 61 and 128
Tofu Oatmeal Patties, 124
Vegetarian Burger, The, 61
Peanut Butter
Hot Applesauce-Peanut Butter
Over Toast, 53
Sandwiches, 59
Pies (See Pies—Crust and Pies—
Toppings)
Carob Cream, 222
Connie's Tofu, 224
No-Sugar Apple, 220
No-Sugar Lemon Filling, 223

312 · INDEX

Pies—Crust
Coconut, 225
Connie's Tofu (Wheat-Oat), 224
Easy Whole Wheat, 221
Granola, 221
Pies—Topping
Cashew Cream Topping, 216
Connie's Tofu Pie, Topping
  for, 224
Crumb Topping, 221
Crunchy Oat Topping, 216
Fruit Glaze (for Fresh Fruit
  Pie), 222
Low Fat Whipped Topping, 222
Pineapple Whipped
  Topping, 222
Poly Whipped Topping, 224
Soy Whipped Topping, 223
Pilafs
Brown Rice Pilaf, 132
Brown Rice-Wheat Pilaf, 134
Bulgur Vegetable Pilaf, 133
Four-Grain Pilaf, 132
Garbanzo-Wheat Pilaf, 114
Sesame Seed Pilaf, 134
Piña Colada (Beverage), 247
Pizza
Whole Wheat Pizza (Crust), 80
Pizza Sauce, Cashew Pimento
  Cheese, 80
Pizza Sauce, Homemade, 80
Pizza Sauce, Quick, 262
Popsicles, Yogurt, 219
Potato Dishes
Baked (conventional), 161
Baked (microwave), 161
Boston Style Potato Soup, 183
Cottage Baked, 162
Dutch Oven Meal, 162
Griddle Hash Browns, 54
Hurry-Up Hearty Hash, 54
Marcella's Favorite Potato
  Soup, 183
Oatmeal-Potato Patties, 139
Oven French Fries, 163

Oven-Roasted Potato
  Chunks, 163
Quick Meatless Meals Over
  Potatoes, 161
Salad, 192
Sauteed Mushrooms in Olive
  Oil, 162
Tofu Pancakes, 124
**Principles of Healthful
  Eating**, 291
Pudding (See Desserts)
Pumpkin, Stuffed, 135 and 141
Quinoa, Curried, 141
Ravioli's, Mama Glenda's, 144
Relish
Home-Style Mustard, 262
Lemon Juice Tomato, 263
Zesty Tomato, 264
Rice Dishes
Basic Roast, 137
Black Beans on Rice, 111
Broccoli and Gluten Over
  Rice, 152
Brown Rice Pilaf, 132
Brown Rice-Wheat Pilaf, 134
Cooking, 159
Four-Grain Cereal, 42
Four-Grain Pilaf, 132
Garbanzo-Rice Patties, 116
Glorified Rice, (Pudding), 220
Holiday Rice Ring, 159
Hurry-Up Hearty Hash, 54
Meatless Rice Burgers, 63
Nut and Rice Loaf, 138
One Dish Meal, 152
Oriental Rice, 160
Savory Fried Rice, 160
Sesame Seed Pilaf, 134
Stroganoff, 155
Stuffed Bell Peppers, 151
Tofu and Rice Bake, 124
Wok Vegetables and Tofu, 127
Rolls
Basic Sweet Dough, 91
Fruit-Nut Breakfast, 81

Root Beer Slush, 243
Salads (See also Salads—
  Dressings and Salads—Fruit)
  Asparagus, 189
  Avocado Alfalfa, 190
  Bean, 192
  Chinese Cabbage, 191
  Greek Tomato, 190
  Marinated Cauliflower, 191
  Oriental, 193
  Potato, 192
  Sally's Salad Bowl, 189
  Spinach, 191
  Sprout, 190
  Stuffed Tomatoes, 190
  Tabouli, 192
  Zesty Zucchini, 189
Salads—Dressings (See also
  Dips, Mayonnaise, and Sour
  Cream)
  Avocado, 195
  Celery, 195
  Creamy Cabbage Slaw, 199
  Fruit Salad, 196
  Guacamole, 200
  Hidden Valley Ranch, 198
  House, 196
  Italian, 198
  Riviera French, 197
  Sesame Seed, 195
  Sunflower, 199
  Sunflower-Yogurt, 199
  Yogurt Herb, 197
  Yogurt Lemon, 197
  Zero (Low Calorie), 198
Salads—Fruit (See also Desserts
  and Fruit Dishes)
  Apple and Banana, 208
  Apricot and Banana Salad, 210
  Avocado Fruit Salad, 206
  Banana and Nut Salad, 210
  Banana Salad, 210
  Cottage Cheese Luncheon
    Plates I and II, 207
  Fresh Fruit Plate, 204

  Grapefruit/Avocado/
    Banana, 194
  Hawaiian Sunset, 204
  Individual Fruit Plate, 206
  Pear and Cherry, 208
  Pineapple-Orange, 208
  Waldorf, 193
Salt, Do-It-Yourself
  Seasoned, 261
Sandwiches (See also Patties)
  Garbanzo Spread Special, 59
  Mashed Avocado Sandwich, 59
  Mashed Bean Sandwich, 59
  Nuteena-Olive Filling, 60
  Peanut Butter-Apple, 59
  Peanut Butter-Banana-
    Raisin, 59
  Peanut Butter-Cucumber, 59
  Savory Garbanzo Filling
    (Falafal), 63
  Soybean Filling, 59
  Sweet Sandwich Filling, 60
  Tofu Sandwich Slices, 59
  Tomato Nuttose, 60
Sauces (See also Gravies, Relish,
  Syrup, Salads—Dressings, and
  Spreads)
  Almond, Broccoli with, 171
  Berry, 52
  Blueberry, over Banana
    Slices, 219
  Cashew Cheese, 146
  Cashew Nut Cheese, 147
  Cashew Pimento Cheese, 80
  Chicken Style Broth, 261
  Dill, 120 and 257
  Green, for Noodles, 144
  Lemon, 226
  Low Fat Cream, 145
  Mama Glenda's Ravioli's in
    Sauce, 144
  Natural Fruit-Juice, 236
  Olive Oil-Lemon Juice Dressing
    for Vegetables, 177
  Pizza, Homemade, 80

Pizza, Quick, 262
Savory Broth I (Dark), 149
Savory Broth II (Light), 149
Sesame, 172
Spaghetti, Italian, 258
Spaghetti, Quickie, 144
Strawberry Orange, 52
Tarragon Lemon Butter, 177
Tartar, Fresh, 153 and 200
Tomato, 146
White, 257
Seasonings
Breading Meal, 153 and 261
Breading Mix for Tofu, 125
Chicken Style Seasoning, 261
Chili Powder Substitute, 260
Cinnamon Substitute, 226
Curry Powder
  (non-irritating), 260
Do-It-Yourself Seasoned
  Salt, 261
Herbs for Seasoning
  Vegetables, 166
Home-Style Mustard Relish, 262
Savory Broth I (Dark), 149
Savory Broth II (Light), 149
Seasoned Bread Crumbs, 262
Shakes and Smoothies
Banana Milkshake, 219
Cranberry Hailstorm, 245
Milk Shake Refresher, 246
Orange Julius, 247
Peach Frosty, 247
Piña Colada, 247
Strawberry Banana
  Smoothie, 246
Strawberry Snowdrift, 246
Tropical Cooler, 246
Tropical Ice Cap, 245
Skallops, Vegetable, 153
Soups
Basic Lentil, 182
Boston Style Potato, 183
Corn Chowder, 184
Cream of Broccoli, 185

Cream of Lentil, 182
Cream of Mushroom, 181
Cream of Tomato, 182
Cream of Vegetable, 184
Favorite Split Pea, 181
Hearty Vegetable, 185
Lentil Stew, 181
Marcella's Favorite Potato, 183
Pot O' Lentils, 119
Sprouted Lentil Cream, 253
Sour Cream
Sunflower, 199
Creamless, 199
Soy (See also Tofu)
Baked Soybeans, 109
Cheese Whiz, 264
Cooking Soybeans, 108
Cooking Soybeans, Pressure
  Cooker Method, 109
Garbanzo-Soy-Oat Patties, 115
Instant Mayonnaise, 194
Island Soybeans, 110
Savory Soy Patties, 109
Soy Graham Bread, 94
Soybean Sandwich Filling, 59
Sprouting Soybeans, 249
Whipped Topping, 223
Yummy Soybean Loaf, 110
Spaghetti Sauce
Italian, 258
Quickie, 144
Spreads (See also Dips, Gravies,
  Jams and Jellies, Mayonnaise,
  Relish, Salads—Dressings,
  Sauces, and Sour Cream)
Almond-Date, 103
Better Butter, 102
Cashew Pimento Cheese, 80
Filbert, 103
Garbanzo Spread Special, 59
Millet, 102
Nut or Seed Butters, 103
Olive-Nut, 103
Orange Honey Butter, 44
Pimiento Dip Spread, 200

Sesame Seed, 102
Soy Cheese Whiz, 264
Sweetened Nut, 103
Sprouts
Alfalfa, 254
Barley Burgers, 253
Garbanzos, 254
Growing, Methods of, 250
Salad, 190
Seeds That Will Sprout, 249
Serve Sprouts, Ways to, 251
Sprouted Lentil Casserole, 252
Sprouted Lentil Cream
  Soup, 253
Sprouted Wheat Burgers, 253
What Seeds Will Sprout, 251
Why Sprout Seeds, 251
Squash (See Pumpkin and
Vegetables)
Staples List, 27
Steaks, Swiss Style, 150
Stroganoff, 155
Stuffing
Cashew, 135
Holiday Stuffing Casserole, 151
Savory Garbanzo Filling
  (Falafal), 63
Stuffed Pumpkin, 135 and 141
Sukiyaki, 153
Supper Menus, 279
Sweet Rolls
Basic Sweet Dough, 91
Fruit-Nut Breakfast Rolls, 81
Syrup (See also Jams and Jellies,
Sauces, and Spreads)
Apple Syrup, 52
Orange Syrup, 52
Tacos, 154
Tartar Sauce, Fresh, 153 and 200
Tofu (See also Soy)
Breading Mix for Tofu, 125
Broccoli and Gluten Over
  Rice, 152
Browned, 125
Burgers, 61 and 128

Chinese Wok Delight, 126
Connie's Tofu Pie, 224
Cottage Cheese, 125
Cottage Cheese Patties, 142
Lasagna, 146
Loaf, 123 and 128
Mayonnaise, 196
Pancakes, 124
Sandwich Slices, 59
Scrambled Tofu, 54 and 123
Spaghetti Balls, 128
Sweet and Sour Tofu, 126
Tofu and Rice Bake, 124
Tofu-Green Bean Sauté, 125
Tofu Oatmeal Patties, 124
Wok Vegetables and Tofu, 127
Toppings (See Desserts—
Toppings, Dips, Glaze, Gravies,
Jams and Jellies, Mayonnaise,
Pies—Toppings, Relish,
Salads—Dressings, Sauces,
Sour Cream, Spreads, and
Syrup)
Vegetables (See also Potatoes,
Salads, and Soups)
Almond Vegetables
  Mandarin, 171
Baked Potatoes, 161 and 162
Bean Sprouts and Pea
  Pods, 174
Beets, Company, 172
Bell Peppers, Stuffed, 151
Broccoli and Gluten Over
  Rice, 152
Broccoli with Almond
  Sauce, 171
Bulgur Vegetable Pilaf, 133
Carrots, Company, 172
Cauliflower with Almonds, 175
Chinese Wok Delight, 126
Company Beets or Carrots, 172
Cooking Tips, 167
Corn, Scalloped, 177
Creamed Vegetable Pasta, 145
Dutch Oven Meal, 162

Eggplant Crunch Casserole, 172
Eggplant, Sesame, 172
French Fries, Oven, 163
Green Beans, Greek Style, 171
Green Beans Supreme, 174
Greens, Leafy, 169 and 173
Greens, Mustard with
   Turnips, 174
Greens, Spring, 173
Herbs for Seasoning, 166
Millet 'N' Vegetables, 136
Mushrooms, Sauteed in Olive
   Oil, 162
Peas Amandine, 175
Peas and Mushrooms, 175
Potato Chunks, Oven
   Roasted, 163
Seasoning, Herbs for, 166
Spinach Roman Style, 173
Squash, Nutty Baked, 175
Squash, Stuffed Yellow, 176
Squash, Stuffed Zucchini, 176
Squash, Summer Duo, 176
Sukiyaki, 153

Tofu-Green Bean Sauté, 125
Turnips with Mustard
   Greens, 174
Vegetable Sauté Fettuccine,
   147
Vegetarian Indian Curry, 150
Wok Cooked Vegetables, 170
Wok Vegetables and Tofu, 127
Yams, Orange-Pineapple, 177
Zucchini Continental, 176
Zucchini Garbanzos,
   Savory, 114
Zucchini, Stuffed, 176
Vegetables—Dressings
Olive Oil Lemon Juice, 177
Sesame Sauce, 177
Tarragon Lemon Butter, 177
Vegetarian Food Pyramid, 269
Vinegar, vs. Lemon Juice, 301
Waffles (See Pancakes)
Weight Control (See Nutrition
Information)
Weight, Ideal, Chart, 289
Wheat Sticks, Whole Wheat, 101

COOKING BY THE BOOK

1325 Isabelle Avenue • Mountain View, CA 94040

Quantity	Item	Price	Total
_____	<u>Cooking By the Book</u> Cookbook	$19.95	_____
_____	*Video Set I (13 30-minute lessons)	$89.95	_____
_____	with Cookbook	$99.95	_____
_____	†Video Set II (12 30-minute lessons)	$79.95	_____
_____	with Cookbook	$89.95	_____

Order Total $ _____

California residents add 8.25% sales tax _____

Shipping (add $4.00 per cookbook, $8.00 per video set) _____

Enclosed is my check or money order for $ _____

Name _____

Address _____

City _____ State _____ Zip _____

*Video Set I Titles (set follows cookbook chapters):
1. Organizing the Natural Food Kitchen
2. Better Breakfasts I
3. Better Breakfasts II
4. Pack a Lively Lunch
5. Bread with that Something Extra
6. Meatless Dinner Meals I
7. Meatless Dinner Meals II
8. Meatless Dinner Meals III
9. Vegetables All Around
10. Supper Time
11. Favorite Salads and Salad Dressings
12. The Blessing of Fresh Fruit
13. Sugar-Less Desserts

†Video Set II Titles:
1. Eating God's Way
2. Menu Planning for a Day God's Way
3. Sabbath Dinner
4. Why I am a Vegetarian (Gluten Making)
5. Picnic in the Park
6. Cooking Without Cheese
7. Cooking With Tofu
8. Cooking Without Eggs
9. Healthful Desserts
10. Healthy Party Snacks
11. Vegetarian Holiday Menu
12. Bread Making